Object-Role Modeling Fundamentals

A Practical Guide to Data Modeling with ORM

Object-Role Modeling Fundamentals

A Practical Guide to Data Modeling with ORM

Terry Halpin

INTI International University

Technics Publications

New Jersey

Published by:

2 Lindsley Road

Basking Ridge, NJ 07920 USA

http://www.TechnicsPub.com

Cover design by Mark Brye

ISBN, print ed. 9781634620741

ISBN, Kindle ed. 9781634620758

ISBN, ePub ed. 9781634620765

First Printing 2015

Library of Congress Control Number: 2015935403

Contents

Foreword

Serge Valera
Senior Software Engineer, System, Software and In-Orbit Demonstration Department
European Space Agency

Developing and operating space systems entails complex activities involving many partners, distributed in location and time. This requires efficient and effective exchanges of information between all partners involved. Years of work developing *centralized* information systems revealed the complexity of such development, often resulting in inadequate and inefficient products that fail to satisfy all the needs. Years of work building *distributed* information systems by reusing (and adapting) "proprietary" systems also revealed that such approaches often suffer from loss of semantics in the resulting data exchange.

These deficiencies always have the same source: the difficulty for the customers to fully and adequately specify their needs and to validate the resulting system requirements specifications prior to contracting the development of the required products.

Most information modelling approaches used in industry today are technology driven rather than adequately addressing the customer's needs. By focusing on the structuring of the information in terms of data items according to the required storage and access performances, such approaches provide little emphasis on the *semantics*.

The Object-Role Modelling (ORM) methodology introduced in this book addresses information modelling from the customers' viewpoint, the WHAT. This approach focuses on capturing all stakeholders' information requirements in a conceptual model that can be expressed as system requirements specifications, i.e. the contractual language, for the purpose of being validated by these stakeholders prior to any contract agreement.

ORM is a Fact Based Modelling (FBM) methodology in which all facts are modelled as relationships (unary, binary, ternary, etc.). How facts are grouped into structures is an implementation issue that is out of scope for the customer. This results in greater semantic stability for any contractual business. By capturing information in terms of atomic facts, ORM expresses the information requirements in the simplest possible way.

At ESA since the late 1980s, I searched for a means to fully and formally specify the WHAT, i.e. applying the Conceptualization and 100% Principle of ISO TR9007. I discovered fact based modelling in the early 90's and successfully used ORM to develop in-house information systems, and to conceptualize situations for the purpose of verifying and validating the adequacy of related industrial developments.

In 2006, I met with Terry and others in the FBM research community, and have been collaborating with them ever since. Today, at the European Space Agency we have the technology to develop any information system as a stand-alone product. The use of FBM and ORM in the specification of these systems reduces the risk of expensive developments due to lack of understanding the stakeholders' needs.

What is missing in the European Space Business and more generally in all large products development involving many industrial and agencies partners is the adequate means to address the interoperability, i.e. the means to address interoperability at a semantic level.

Thanks to Terry's constant willingness to share his knowledge, to transfer his many years of research and knowhow to ESA, we are now facing a new evolution in the Software business that is "from Product Modelling to Enterprise Modelling", "from semantic modelling to semantic interoperability".

Enabling semantic interoperability requires semantic modelling of the products involved, using a modelling approach such as FBM/ORM to fully and precisely capture the relevant semantics. This raises the question of how to best train industrial practitioners in ORM.

Previously published books on ORM have provided an in-depth and broad coverage of multiple information systems modelling approaches, including formal discussion of the logical foundations of ORM, or instead have focused on use of a specific ORM modelling tool. In contrast, Terry's new book is mainly aimed at practitioners, providing a simple and short introduction to the key aspects of ORM and explaining how it can be used in practice to develop information systems.

Transferring academic knowledge to industry has always been a difficult task. Industry needs to estimate the maturity of the research technology, the industrial work needed to develop operational solutions, and the value of the resulting solutions to positively impact the business. This technology readiness level assessment is on-going in the European space business. Terry's new book will play an important role in this assessment. Together with the NORMA freeware tool discussed in the book, it offers newcomers a way to discover the benefit of conceptual modelling with ORM by applying that methodology for example to the development of new information systems or to facilitate the process of validating the adequacy of existing or under-development systems, resulting in a reduction of the overall maintenance costs.

Terry's book is well written and sufficiently detailed to allow newcomers to understand how to conceptualize information requirements with ORM. The availability of the NORMA tool, the ORM graphical notation and automated verbalization in FORML provides the means to easily learn and quickly exploit ORM as a way to capture the semantics of business domains.

For those who work with relational databases, NORMA's automatic mapping from ORM to relational models helps one realize the benefits of first modelling the semantics in a natural way before dropping to the level of implementation.

I highly recommend this book to any customer who desires clarity in the way their information modeler documents their needs. I also strongly recommend the book to any conceptual modeler who wishes a formal, logic-based means to capture the needs of their stakeholders, and validate the specification of the business domain before even considering the prototyping of some of the specified features.

Preface

This book provides a practical introduction to data modeling using the Object-Role Modeling (ORM) approach. ORM is a fact-based modeling method that expresses the information requirements of any business domain simply in terms of objects that play roles in relationships. All facts of interest are treated as instances of attribute-free structures known as fact types, where the relationship may be unary (e.g. Person smokes), binary (e.g. Person was born on Date), ternary (e.g. Customer bought Product on Date), or longer.

Fact types facilitate natural expression, are easy to populate with examples for validation purposes, and have greater semantic stability than attribute-based structures such as those used in Entity Relationship Modeling (ER) or the Unified Modeling Language (UML).

All relevant facts, constraints and derivation rules are expressed in controlled natural language sentences that are intelligible to users in the business domain being modeled. This allows ORM data models to be validated by business domain experts who are unfamiliar with ORM's graphical notation. For the data modeler, ORM's graphical notation covers a much wider range of constraints than can be expressed in industrial ER or UML class diagrams, and thus allows rich visualization of the underlying semantics.

I've written this book mainly for data modeling practitioners, whether novice or experienced. Although ORM has strong formal foundations in logic, I've avoided any symbolic logic notation, instead trying to cover the fundamentals of the ORM approach in easy-to-understand language. The bulk of the book describes in detail how to design an ORM model, illustrating each step of the design process with simple examples.

Each chapter ends with a practical lab that discusses how to use the freeware NORMA tool to enter ORM models and use it to automatically generate verbalizations of the model and map it to a relational database.

Chapter 1 provides an overview of information modeling in general and ORM in particular. It discusses the various levels at which information may be represented, and highlights the distinguishing features of the ORM approach, using a simple example is used to illustrate these ideas. ORM's conceptual schema design procedure (CSDP) is then overviewed, and a brief history of fact-based modeling tools is presented.

Chapter 2 focuses on the first five steps of the CSDP. Of these steps, the first is the most important, as it is here that we verbalize examples of the required information in natural language, and rephrase them where needed so that each fact is atomic. The picture on the book's front cover is symbolic of this approach, where we analyze the information required about the world being modeled in terms of atomic facts. In Step 2 of the CSDP we draw the fact types and apply checks by populating them with sample data. Step 3 of the CSDP includes checks for entity types that should be combined as well as facts that can be derived from others by arithmetic derivation rules. In CSDP Steps 4 and 5 we add uniqueness and mandatory role constraints and perform checks on the length of fact types and whether some can be derived by logical derivation rules.

Chapter 3 focuses on step 6 of the CSDP. Here we add any relevant value constraints, set-comparison (subset, equality, or exclusion) constraints, and subtyping.

Chapter 4 covers step 7 of the CSDP. Here we add any relevant frequency constraint, ring constraints, value-comparison constraints, cardinality constraints, deontic constraints, and textual constraints, and conclude with some final checks.

Appendix A briefly sketches some aspects of the procedure for mapping ORM schemas to relational database schemas, and then shows how to use the NORMA tool to generate code from ORM models, focusing on generation of SQL in particular.

Appendix B provides a summary of the ORM graphical notation discussed in the book.

Appendix C concludes with some recommendations for further resources that may be of interest, including some books, journal papers, software, and websites.

While US spelling is used throughout, I've adopted Australian punctuation style for quoted expressions and a few other cases. For example, commas or periods appear after, rather than just before, closing quotes, and a comma appears before rather than after contractions such as "e.g." or "i.e.". Moreover, no period is appended to abbreviations whose end letters agree with the full word (e.g. "Mr" is used instead of "Mr.").

Acknowledgements

My sincere thanks go to Serge Valera, who was kind enough to write the foreword as well as proof-read and make suggestions on some of the chapters. I also appreciate the many thousands of hours of programming by Matt Curland who together with me is continuing the evolution of the NORMA tool. I also wish to acknowledge the pioneering work on fact-based modeling conducted by Sjir Nijssen and Eckhard Falkenberg, who first introduced me to the NIAM variant of the approach. Finally, I thank Steve Hoberman for inviting me to write a short introduction to ORM for practitioners, and for overseeing the publication process.

1 Overview of Object-Role Modeling

1.1 Information Modeling

This book discusses how to model the *information requirements* for any business domain in a way that can be easily understood by the business users, and automatically generate a database structure to store that information. Although information models are commonly called *data* models, information adds *semantics* or meaning to the data, which may be just a bunch of numbers or character strings. For example, consider the data in the table extract shown in Figure 1.1(a). As un-interpreted syntax, this could be assigned infinitely many possible meanings. For instance, *x* and *y* might denote boxes of 10 and 100 pencils, or line segments of length 10 cm and 100 cm, or robots of mass 10 and 100 kg, etc.

Figure 1.1(b) is a bit more informative. Most of us would assume this conveys the fact that the number 100 is the square of 10, although in principle it might mean something else (e.g. the building numbered 10 is located on square 100). Even saying that the number 100 is the square of 10 is ambiguous unless we agree on the numeration scheme being used. By default, this is typically assumed to be the Hindu-Arabic decimal notation, but the sample data are also consistent with binary notation (the binary numerals "10" and "100" denote the numbers denoted by the decimal numerals "2" and "4"). Of course, if we added the pair (5, 25) as a second row of data this would rule out the binary interpretation.

Now consider Figure 1.1(c). How would you verbalize the fact conveyed by this example? Most humans would say something like "The patient with patient number 10 has a temperature of 100 degrees". This draws upon background knowledge of the relevant business domain (e.g. knowing that patients are identified by patient numbers, and that the temperature is of the patient).

(a)

x	*y*
10	100

(b)

Number	*Square*
10	100

(c)

PatientNumber	*Temperature*
10	100

(d)

PatientNumber	*Temperature* (°F)
10	100

Figure 1.1 What information is intended to be conveyed by these examples?

Of course, this is still ambiguous unless we know the temperature scale being used, presumably Fahrenheit, since 100 degrees Celsius and 100 degrees Kelvin are far too extreme for living humans. To avoid possible misinterpretation with measurement quantities, the relevant unit should always be made explicit, as in Figure 1.1(d). So the intended fact may be verbalized as "The Patient who has PatientNumber 10 has a Temperature of 100 degrees Fahrenheit". In short, humans familiar with the business domain are needed to add semantics to data, thereby transforming data into information.

The key to successful information modeling is to express the intended semantics in terms of concepts readily understood by the business users. An information model that satisfies this requirement is a *conceptual model*[1]. The term *universe of discourse* (*UoD*) is used for those aspects of the business domain that we wish to discourse about. So a conceptual model is a model of the relevant UoD expressed in terms of natural, human concepts. When complete, the model includes all the structural details of interest. The structure of any model (conceptual or otherwise) is called a *schema*, so the structure of a conceptual model is a *conceptual schema*. A set of object and fact instances that conform to the schema is a *population* of the schema. As shown in Figure 1.2(a), a *model* is the combination of a schema with its population, where the population may be empty[2].

In developing an information system, information may be treated at different levels, as shown in Figure 1.2(b). The *conceptual level* is where models and queries are formulated in terms of concepts naturally understood by humans (e.g. entities, attributes, relationships). At the *logical level*, information models and queries are formulated in terms of abstract structures for data and operations supported by a logical data model (e.g. relational, object-oriented, hierarchic, deductive). For instance, relational models cluster facts into tables, and constrain them using primary key and foreign key declarations etc.

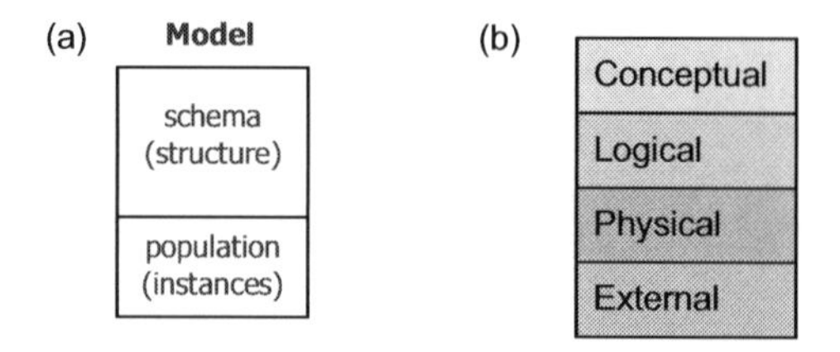

Figure 1.2 Models and levels involved in information systems development

---

[1] Some authors use the term "conceptual model" in a weaker sense, covering only the main aspects of the business domain.

[2] Some authors treat the term "model" as a synonym for "schema", but we allow models to also include populations.

At the *physical level*, a specific database management system (DBMS) and/or coding language is chosen to implement the logical level structures and add performance tuning. For example, a relational model might be implemented as a database model in SQL Server, DB2 or Oracle. The physical level structures might also be divided into transient (in-memory) structures and persistent (database) structures, along with mapping between them.

The *external level* is where humans interact directly with the system, often via a forms-based or graphical user interface. Different user groups may be assigned different access rights to the underlying data, and queries may be entered by the user with results generated on-screen or in printed reports.

In practice, not all information systems are developed using all four levels, and some structures may span multiple levels (e.g. class models in UML arguably combine aspects from conceptual, logical and physical levels). Moreover, technical users might interact directly with a system at the physical level. Ideally however, the modeling should first be done at the conceptual level, validated there with business domain experts, and then *forward engineered* by transforming the conceptual structures automatically or at least semi-automatically to the other levels. This overall process is referred to as *model-driven engineering*.

Object-Role Modeling (ORM), the focus of this book, is a model-driven engineering approach that starts with typical examples of required information or queries presented in any external formulation familiar to users, and then *verbalizes* these examples at the conceptual level in terms of simple *facts* expressed in a *controlled natural language*—a restricted version of natural language that is unambiguous, so the semantics are readily grasped by humans, and is also formal, so it can be used to automatically map the structures to lower levels for implementation, as shown in Figure 1.3. As part of this overall process, this book discusses how to create ORM models and map them to relational database models. ORM models may also be mapped to other kinds of models (object-oriented, deductive etc.).

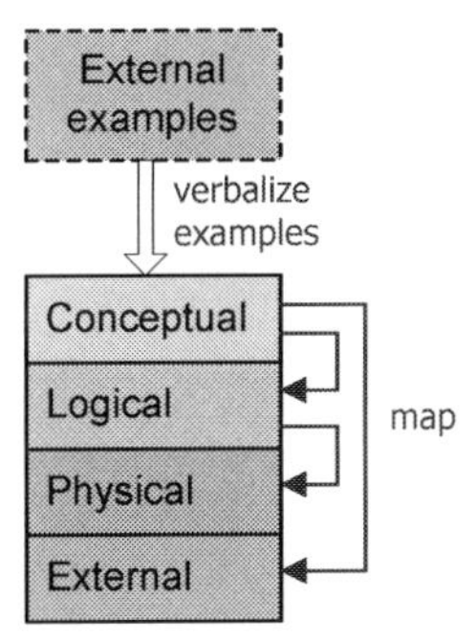

Figure 1.3 Model-driven engineering based on verbalization of examples

1.2 Fact-Based Modeling

Object-Role Modeling is a prime example of *fact-based modeling*, also known as *fact-oriented modeling*, which is a general approach for modeling, querying and transforming information in conformance to the following principles:

- All facts of interest are conceptually represented in terms of *attribute-free* structures known as *fact types.*
- Conceptual models are developed from *concrete examples* of the required information.
- Conceptual models are verbalized in a *controlled natural language*.

Fact-based modeling originated in Europe in the 1970s, and has since evolved into a family of related approaches including Object-Role Modeling (ORM), Cognition enhanced Natural Language Information Analysis Method (CogNIAM), Fully Communication Oriented Information Modeling (FCO-IM), and the Developing Ontology-Grounded Methods and Applications (DOGMA) approach. While all of these approaches include textual and graphical languages as well as modeling and transformation procedures, they differ in the details. Some restrict fact types to infix binary relationships, some support a richer range of constraints than others, and different approaches may use a different syntax for the same semantics. This book focuses on Object-Role Modeling (ORM), covering the main aspects of its modeling procedure and graphical language and using its textual Formal ORM Language (*FORML*) as a controlled natural language for verbalization.

In ORM, an *object* is simply any individual thing of interest (excluding nulls, which may be used in physical models to denote absence of data). An object is either a domain object or a data value. A *domain object* is part of the specific business domain and carries more semantics than a generic *data value* such as an integer or character string. A domain object is either an entity or a domain value. A *domain value* is a semantically typed constant. For example, the country code ‘CH’ is a domain value represented by the data value ‘CH’ (a plain character string) but its type (CountryCode) carries additional semantics relevant to the business domain. For example, the country code ’CH’ is based on Latin (*confoederatio helvetica*, meaning Swiss confederation) but the character string ‘CH’ is not.

An *entity* is a concrete or abstract object that is identified by relating it to one or more domain objects. For example: the entity Switzerland may be identified by a definite description such as “the Country that has the CountryCode ‘CH’”, or “the Country that has the CountryName ‘Switzerland’”. People, cars and countries are typical example of concrete or tangible entities. The university course identified as “the Course that has CourseCode ‘CS100’” is an example of an abstract or intangible entity.

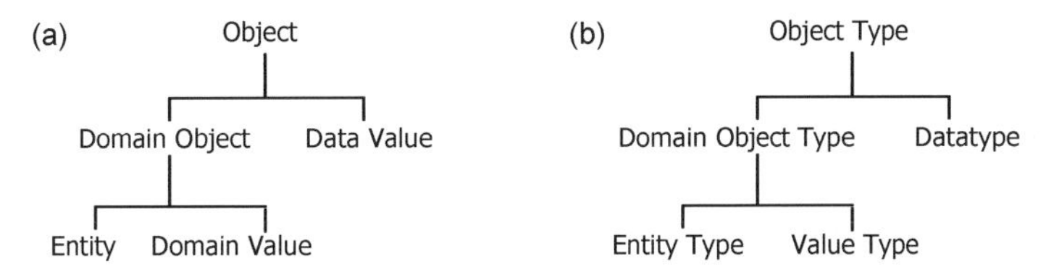

Figure 1.4 Object Instances and Object Types in ORM

The set of all possible objects of a given kind is called an *object type*. As shown in Figure 1.4, domain value types are simply called *value types*, while types for data values are called *datatypes*. When there is no danger of confusion, we often abbreviate "domain value" simply to "value".

In ORM, a *fact* (or fact instance) is an atomic or conjunctive proposition taken to be true by the relevant business community. An *atomic fact* can't be split into two or more facts involving the same object types without information loss, and is either an elementary fact or an existential fact. An *elementary fact* applies a logical predicate to one or more objects. For example, each of the following sentences expresses an elementary fact: the President named 'Barack Obama' is male; the President named 'Barack Obama' was born in the Country that has CountryCode 'US'.

Logical predicates are denoted by predicate readings (e.g. "... is male", "... was born in ..."), with placeholders (shown here as an ellipsis "...") for their objects. Elementary fact sentences place object terms in the predicate placeholders. In the above examples, the identifying object terms are definite descriptions.

An *existential fact* simply asserts the existence of a single object. For example, the following sentence expresses an existential fact: There exists a Country that has CountryCode 'US'. A *conjunctive fact* is a logical conjunction of two or more atomic facts. For example, the following sentence expresses a conjunctive fact: the President named 'Barack Obama' is male *and* was born in the Country that has CountryCode 'US'. The set of all possible facts of a given kind is called a *fact type*. The overall classification of facts and fact types is summarized in Figure 1.5.

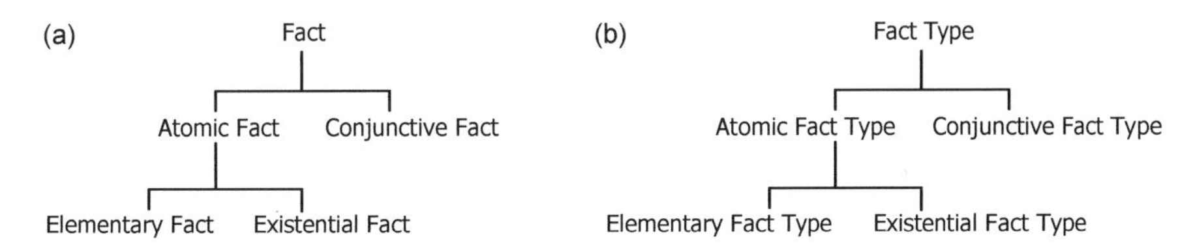

Figure 1.5 Fact Instances and Fact Types in ORM

In ORM, an atomic fact type corresponds to a non-empty set of one or more typed predicates that enable the same kind of fact to be expressed. For example, each of the following sentences expresses the same fact:

(1) The President named 'Barack Obama' was born in the Country that has CountryCode 'US'.

(2) The Country that has CountryCode 'US' is the birth country of the President named 'Barack Obama'.

Sentence (1) uses the *fact type reading* "President was born in Country". Here the object types are President and Country and the predicate reading is "was born in". Sentence (2) uses the fact type reading "Country is the birth country of President", and the predicate reading "is the birth country of". ORM allows you to provide as many readings as you like for the same fact type.

Although conjunctive facts are allowed at the external level, *ORM conceptual models require all facts to be atomic.* This ensures that all facts are modeled as simply as possible, which helps to clarify the intended semantics as well as avoiding use of nulls. Various mapping procedures are used later to group facts into various structures used at the logical, physical and external levels.

At the conceptual level, various *constraints* are applied to restrict the possible or permitted populations of the atomic fact types. For example, the following constraint (expressed in FORML) should be added to the above birth fact type: **Each** President was born in **at most one** Country.

If a fact type can be derived from others, it should be marked as derived and a *derivation rule* provided. For example, if the model includes the fact type President died on Date, instances of the fact type President is dead may be derived using this derivation rule: **For each** President, **that** President is dead **if that** President died on **some** Date.

As shown in Figure 1.6, an ORM conceptual schema includes atomic fact types, constraints and derivation rules. A conceptual model also includes a population (set of atomic facts). Different populations may be used for different purposes.

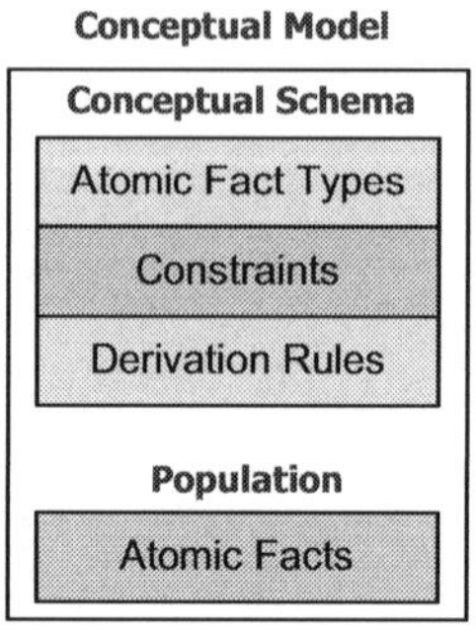

Conceptual Model
Conceptual Schema
Atomic Fact Types
Constraints
Derivation Rules
Population
Atomic Facts

Figure 1.6 Conceptual model components in ORM

Atomic facts inform us about roles played by objects. In the above birth fact example, the president plays the role of being born in the country, and the country plays the role of being the birth country of the president. So a *role* (or fact role) is a part played by an object in some fact. If desired, *role names* may be given to roles (e.g. "native", "birthCountry"). Object-Role Modeling is so-called because it views the world in terms of objects playing roles.

The number of roles in a fact type is called its *arity*. ORM allows fact types of any arity above zero. A *unary fact type* has exactly one role (e.g. Person smokes; Person is dead). This enables unary facts to be verbalized much more naturally than assigning true to a Boolean attribute (e.g. Person.isSmoker). A *binary fact type* has two roles (e.g. Person was born in Country; Person likes Person). A *ternary fact type* has three roles (e.g. Person played Sport for Country). A *quaternary* fact type has four roles (e.g. Store in Month sold Product in Quantity), and so on.

Attribute-free models have the following advantages over attribute-based models such as those used in Entity-Relationship (ER) modeling, the Unified Modeling Language (UML) and Relational Database (RDB) models.

- They promote *semantic stability*
- They facilitate *validation by sample populations*
- They facilitate *validation by natural verbalization*

Semantically stable models adapt more easily to change. For example, suppose an ORM model includes the fact types Person has PersonTitle and Person has Gender, and we now decide to record which person titles are restricted to which genders (e.g. the person title "Mrs" is restricted to the female gender). To do this, we add the fact type PersonTitle is restricted to Gender, leaving the rest of the model unchanged[3].

An attribute-based model would instead typically model the title and gender facts as attributes of Person (e.g. Person.title and Person.gender). Since attributes may not themselves have attributes or participate in other relationships, there is now no way to model title-gender restrictions without remodelling the existing structure (e.g. by replacing the title attribute with a relationship to a PersonTitle entity type or class). If the model had previously been populated with instances, and queries had been formulated on them, these would also need to be changed.

This greater semantic stability of attribute-free models is enjoyed not only by fact-based modeling but by other approaches that model all facts as relationships, such as the Semantics of Business Vocabulary and Business Rules (SBVR) approach, semantic web languages such as the Web Ontology Language (OWL), and the Object-oriented Systems Model (OSM).

---

[3] ORM also allows you to add a join-subset constraint to ensure that if a person has a title that is restricted to some gender then that person must be of that gender.

Attribute-free models with a controlled natural language facilitate *model validation by verbalization and population.* Model validation should be a collaborative process between the modeler and the business domain expert who best understands the business domain. All facts, fact types, constraints and derivation rules may be verbalized naturally in unambiguous language that is easily understood by domain experts who might not be experts in the software systems ultimately used for the physical implementation.

As a simple example, suppose an information system is to record our solar system planets and their moons. Table 1.1 shows an extract from a report that the system is required to output. To save typing, I omitted details for the three known planets beyond Jupiter. At the time of writing Jupiter has 50 confirmed moons as listed, Saturn has 53 confirmed moons, Uranus has 27 confirmed moons, and Neptune has 13 confirmed moons. Most of the outer planets have many other suspected but not yet confirmed moons, so these numbers will likely grow over time. You can check out the latest details online at https://solarsystem.nasa.gov/planets/. Table 1.1 uses the Latin name "Luna" for our moon. It is also called "Earth's moon" or somewhat misleadingly "the moon".

Since this report is at the external level, the data may be displayed in any desired format. To develop an ORM model for this report, we first *verbalize at least one example of each kind of required information as an atomic fact.* For example, we may verbalize the entry "Mercury" in the Planet column as the following existential fact: There exists a Planet named 'Mercury'. As discussed in chapter 2, constraints are applied to existential relationships to ensure identification, in this case allowing definite descriptions such as "**the** Planet named 'Mercury'" as identifying terms for entities. Similarly, we may verbalize the entry "Luna" in the Moons column as the existential fact There exists a Moon named 'Luna'.

Table 1.1 A sample report extract about our solar system planets and their moons

Planet	*Moons*
Mercury Venus Earth Mars Jupiter	 Luna Phobos, Deimos Io, Europa, Ganymede, Callisto, Amalthea, Himalia, Elara, Pasiphae, Sinope, Lysithea, Carme, Ananke, Leda, Thebe, Adrastea, Metis, Callirrhoe, Themisto, Megaclite, Taygete, Chaldene, Harpalyke, Kalyke, Iocaste, Erinome, Isonome, Praxidike, Autonoe, Thyone, Hermippe, Aitne, Eurodome, Euanthe, Euporie, Orthosie, Sponde, Kale, Pasithee, Hegemone, Mneme, Aoede, Theixinoe, Arche, Kallichore, Helike, Carpo, Eukelade, Cyllene, Kore, Herse ...

We may verbalize the placing of "Earth" and "Luna" in their columns on the same row of the table as the elementary fact The Planet named 'Earth' is orbited by the Moon named 'Luna', or equivalently, The Moon named 'Luna' orbits the Planet named 'Earth'. All of the data in the table verbalize as instances of one of these three kinds of fact.

Using *ORM's graphical notation*, we may display a *conceptual schema diagram* for the three atomic fact types, including relevant constraints, as shown in Figure 1.7. The *entity types* Moon and Planet *are depicted as named, soft rectangles* (rounded corners). A moon or planet is identified by its relationship to a single value (in this case its name). Each such relationship is an example of a *simple reference scheme,* involving a single existential fact type. The mode (manner) in which a single value refers to a single entity is called a *reference mode*. For compactness, simple reference schemes may be displayed in abbreviated form by listing the reference mode in parentheses below the entity type name, as in Figure 1.7(a). For example, Moon(.Name) uses the reference mode .Name to abbreviate an explicit existential fact type (also called a *reference type*) with forward reading "Moon has MoonName" and inverse reading "MoonName is of Moon" that is constrained to be identifying (see later), as shown in Figure 1.7(b). The *value types* MoonName and PlanetName are depicted as named, soft rectangles with *dashed line borders.*

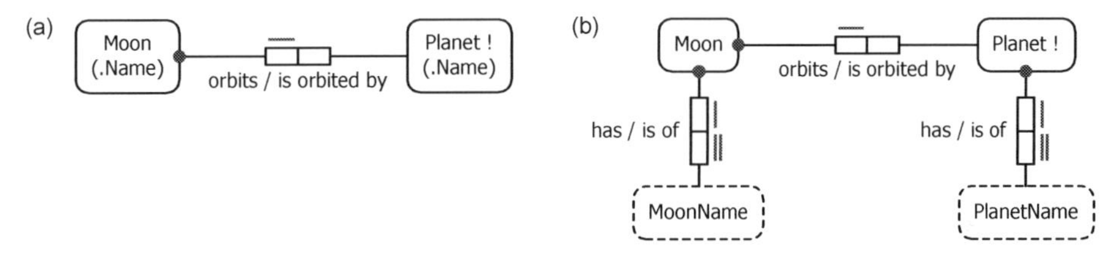

Figure 1.7 An ORM schema diagram in (a) compact form, and (b) expanded form

Fact type *roles* are depicted as *role boxes,* connected by a line segment to the object type that hosts the role. A *predicate* is depicted as an *ordered set of role boxes,* with a *predicate reading* beside it. The binary fact type displayed explicitly in Figure 1.7(a) has forward and inverse predicate readings, "orbits" and "is orbited by", separated by a slash "/". Read from left to right, we obtain the fact type reading "Moon orbits Planet". Read from right to left, we have the fact type reading "Planet is orbited by Moon".

The large violet dot in Figure 1.7(a) on the role connector to Moon depicts a *mandatory role constraint,* indicating that the role must be played by each instance in the population of Moon. In FORML, this constraint verbalizes as follows: **Each** Moon orbits **some** Planet.[4]

[4] Our UoD excludes moons that orbit dwarf planets (e.g. Pluto) or asteroids (also called minor planets). If we were to include these objects, the constraint would not apply.

Similarly, the mandatory role constraints on the existential fact types shown explicitly in Figure 1.7(b) verbalize as: **Each** Moon has **some** MoonName and **Each** Planet has **some** PlanetName. In this book, we adopt the convention of *starting object type names with an uppercase letter*, and displaying logical words such as "**Each**" and "**some**" in bold when included as part of the verbalization.

For validation purposes, a *sample population* is provided for the fact types. In Figure 1.8, a sample population is displayed in *fact tables* shown below the schema diagram, with one column for each object type or fact type role. For example, the entries in the first rows of the three fact tables assert the following facts: there exists a Moon named 'Luna'; the Moon named 'Luna' orbits the Planet named 'Earth'; there exists a Planet named 'Mercury'. You can see that the sample population satisfies the mandatory role constraint on the orbiting fact type.

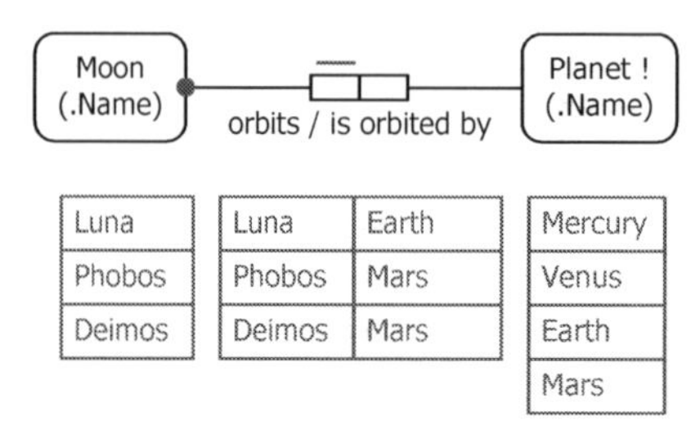

Figure 1.8 An ORM model with a satisfying population

An atomic fact asserting that a given moon orbits a given planet actually implies the existence of that moon and planet. Since each moon orbits some planet, there is no need to explicitly assert existential facts for the moons, as these will be implied by their orbit facts. However some planets (Mercury and Venus) have no moons, so separate existential facts are required to assert their existence.

Since some planets don't have to be orbited by moons, Planet's role in the fact type Moon orbits Planet must not be marked as mandatory, so there is no mandatory role dot on its role connector in Figure 1.8. A role in an elementary fact type is called an *elementary role*. If the model included another elementary role for Planet that is mandatory (e.g. if the mass of each moon must also be recorded), the lack of a mandatory role mark on its orbiting role would be enough to indicate that its orbiting role is optional. However, in the Figure 1.8 model, Planet hosts no other elementary role.

ORM assumes that each instance in the population of each object type plays at least one elementary role unless that object type is declared *independent*. This assumption simplifies many modeling tasks as well as ORM's underlying formal theory. For example, it avoids the need to explicitly update the mandatory/optional status of many roles as the model grows. In

ORM's graphical notation, *appending an exclamation mark "!" to the name of an object type indicates that the object type is independent* (i.e. it may include instances that exist independently of playing any elementary role), as shown for Planet in Figure 1.8.

The violet bar over the role hosted by Moon depicts a simple *uniqueness constraint* which verbalizes in FORML as follows: **Each** Moon orbits **at most one** Planet. Hence each entry in the fact column for the uniquely constrained role must appear there at most once. The lack of a uniqueness constraint on Planet's role in this fact type verbalizes in FORML as follows: **It is possible that some** Planet is orbited by **more than one** Moon. If you look at the sample population, you can see that it satisfies this constraint pattern.

For explanation purposes, Figure 1.9 populates the expanded form of the schema diagram with one instance of each fact type, this time depicting the moon and planet directly by their images. Conceptually, the elementary fact instance declares that that a specific, actual moon orbits a specific, actual planet. The existential fact instances relate these entities to their names ('Luna' and "Earth'). The uniqueness constraints on the top roles of the existential fact types verbalize as: **Each** Moon has **at most one** MoonName and **Each** Planet has **at most one** PlanetName.).

The uniqueness constraints on the bottom roles of the existential fact types verbalize as: **Each** MoonName is of **at most one** Moon and **Each** PlanetName is of **at most one** Planet. The *double uniqueness bar* on the roles hosted by MoonName and PlanetName indicate that these uniqueness constraints underpin the *preferred reference scheme* for Moon and Planet. The combination of mandatory and uniqueness constraints on the Moon has MoonName relationship ensures that each moon has exactly one moon name, and that name refers to at most one moon. Such a *mandatory, one-to-one relationship* is called an *injection*, and provides the simplest kind of reference scheme for an entity type. Similarly, the injective relationship from Planet to PlanetName provides its preferred reference scheme.

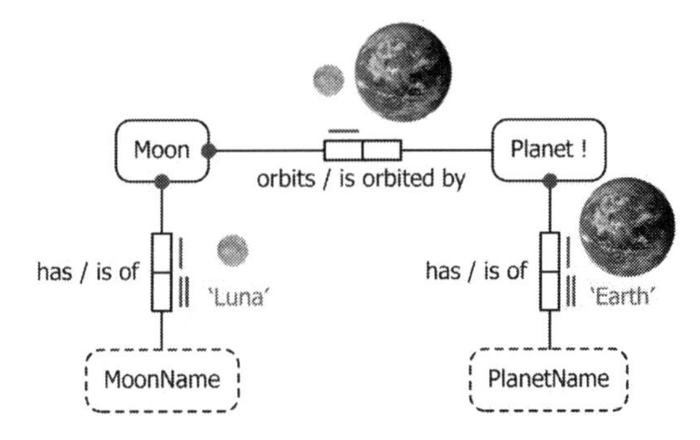

Figure 1.9 Conceptualizing elementary and existential facts

Verbalizing constraints in a controlled natural language and illustrating them with sample populations makes it much easier for domain experts to validate the model. If ever a constraint is still doubtful, a good way to double-check it is to provide a *counterexample* (an example that violates the constraint) and ask whether this kind of situation is possible.

Figure 1.10 shows a population with a moon orbiting two planets, thus providing a counterexample to the uniqueness constraint that each moon orbits at most one planet. If the domain expert says that this kind of situation can't happen, then the constraint is confirmed. Of course, if the domain expert were to confirm that this kind of situation can happen, then the constraint would be incorrect and should be removed (e.g. suppose the UoD is widened to include extra-solar planets, and a moon is found that does orbit more than one planet).

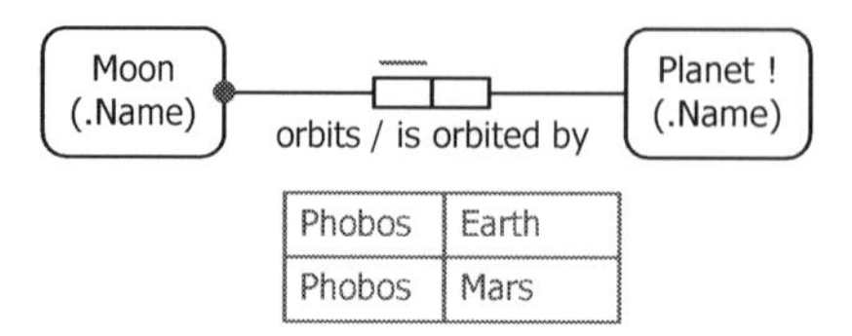

Phobos	Earth
Phobos	Mars

Figure 1.10 An ORM model with a counterexample to the uniqueness constraint

Modeling all facts as instances of fact types enables satisfying examples and counterexamples to be provided in a simple, uniform way by populating fact tables. It is much more awkward to do this with attribute-based structures. Verbalization is also much more natural, especially with ORM, because ORM supports *mixfix predicates* of any arity. Mixfix predicate readings allow their object placeholders to be mixed in at any position. For example, the ternary fact type Country exports Product to Country uses the mixfix predicate reading "... exports ... to ...".

As well as allowing more natural expression, and supporting unary and *n*-ary facts, mixfix predicates cater for sentences in *any natural language*. In English, binary facts are often expressed using infix predicates, conforming to a Subject-Verb-Object structure (e.g. the sentence "Luna orbits Earth" uses the infix predicate reading "... orbits ..."). However, Japanese sentences are typically expressed using a Subject-Object-Verb structure. For example, the fact that our moon orbits Earth is rendered in Japanese as "*Tsuki wa chikyū o shūkai suru*", which uses the mixfix predicate reading "*... wa ... o shūkai suru*". Here, *Tsuki* (the Moon[5]) is the subject and *chikyū* (the Earth) is the object, and *shūkai suru*" (goes around, does) is the verb, and *wa* and *o* are particles appended to the sentence's topic (here, the subject) and grammatical object.

---

[5] If we instead wish to refer in Japanese to Earth's moon by its Latin name "Luna", this would be rendered as "Runa".

ORM's *richly expressive graphical notation* enables the modeler to easily visualize complex constraints (e.g. pair-exclusion constraints, external frequency constraints, ring constraints) that can't be captured in the graphical notation of industrial versions of ER or in UML class diagrams. Its attribute-free nature also better exposes semantic connections, by explicitly displaying how object types host roles.

1.3 The Conceptual Schema Design Procedure

ORM's procedure for designing a conceptual schema small enough to manage conveniently as a single unit is called the *Conceptual Schema Design Procedure* (*CSDP*). For larger information systems, the business domain is first divided into smaller subareas (possibly overlapping) of convenient size. These subareas are then prioritized to determine the order in which they will be designed, and the CSDP is applied to each. The subschemas are then merged or integrated to produce the global conceptual schema that covers the whole business domain—in practice this integration is often performed iteratively. In this book, all our examples are small enough to design directly, without needing to apply the initial top-down division and final integration stages.

The CSDP itself comprises seven main steps, as shown in Table 1.2. The first main step (Step 1) is by far the most critical, and is divided into two sub-steps (Step 1a and Step 1b). In practice, all seven steps are usually performed for each component of the model as it is discussed with the domain expert, rather than performing the same step on all components before moving on to the next step.

Table 1.2 ORM's Conceptual Schema Design Procedure (CSDP)

Step Nr	*Description*
1	1a: Verbalize familiar examples in natural language (domain expert's task)
	1b: Re-verbalize the examples as atomic facts (modeler's task)
2	Draw the fact types and apply a population check
3	Check for entity types that should be combined and note any arithmetic derivations
4	Add uniqueness constraints and check the arity of the fact types
5	Add mandatory role constraints and check for logical derivations
6	Add value constraints, set-comparison constraints, and subtyping
7	Add frequency, ring, value-comparison, cardinality and deontic constraints, then add any textual constraints and perform final checks

When developing a *process* model, it can help to start with typical use cases of required processes. However, when developing a *data* model we ought to begin with a clear understanding of the data requirements. As Sherlock Holmes rightly emphasized, "Data! Data! Data! I can't make bricks without clay"[6]. Hence ORM's CSDP seeds the data modeling procedure with *data use cases* (cases of required data being used). These may take the form of sample output reports, sample input forms, or sample queries that the information system is required to support. Sometimes, such data use cases are readily available (e.g. when automating a paper-based information system or re-engineering an automated information system). Otherwise, we as modelers should work with the domain experts to produce such examples as input to CSDP Step 1.

Since data use cases exist at the external level, they may come in many shapes. Tables provide a common kind of output report. The planet-moon table considered earlier is a simple example, and we'll now use the shorter extract shown in Table 1.3 to better illustrate how Step1 of the CSDP works in practice.

Table 1.3 A sample report extract about our solar system planets and their moons

Planet	*Moons*
Mercury	
Venus	Luna
Earth	Phobos, Deimos
Mars	...
....	

If we are already familiar with the data, we can function as both domain expert and modeler. However, if we (as the modeler) are not familiar with the business domain we will need a separate domain expert to clarify the meaning of the data. In short, modeling is typically a collaborative process between modeler and domain expert.

In CSDP *Step 1a*, we ask the domain expert to verbalize the sample information in natural language. For example, for Step 1a let's say that the domain expert verbalizes the information as the following three sentences:

S1 Mercury, Venus, Earth and Mars are planets.

S2 Earth has the moon Luna.

S3 Phobos and Deimos are the moons of Mars.

[6] Arthur Conan Doyle, *The Adventure of the Copper Beeches.*

In CSDP *Step 1b*, we refine the domain expert's verbalizations where needed to ensure that all facts are atomic (elementary or existential) with all objects properly identified. Sentence S1 is conjunctive, not atomic, because we can rephrase it as the following four facts without losing information: Mercury is a planet; Venus is a planet; Earth is a planet; Mars is a planet. So we now focus on just one of these smaller fact sentences, e.g. "Mercury is a planet". This makes sense if we treat "Mercury" as an individual constant that can be used only to identify a planet. However, when developing computerized information systems, individual constants are typically unsuitable for identifying entities. For example, suppose we extend our model to include the chemical composition of planets and moons, and now add the fact "Mercury is an element". This won't work because the individual object Mercury can't be both a planet and an element.

In everyday discourse, we commonly identify objects by contextual, individual constants, but this typically relies on the audience using their background knowledge of the context to determine the intended object. In different contexts the sentence "Venus is pretty" might refer to a planet, a goddess, or a specific woman. Unlike humans, computers typically can't be relied on to determine the relevant context so we need a more precise way to let computers know what we are referring to.

For such reasons, entities are best identified by means of definite descriptions that indicate the type of entity, as well as how it relates to one or more other objects used to reference it. For example, the definite description "the Planet named 'Mercury'" indicates the entity type (Planet) and a naming relationship to relate the entity to a domain value (the planet name "Mercury"). The definite description "the Element named 'Mercury'" clearly involves a different entity type (Element).

If we ask the domain expert what kind of label (e.g. a name or a code) "Mercury" is for the planet, he or she will reply that this is the planet's name. So now we rephrase the information conveyed by the first entry in the Planet column as the existential fact F1: "There exists a Planet named 'Mercury'". If we include the constraints on the existential relationship (see earlier) we can verbalize the constrained existential fact as "The Planet named 'Mercury' exists".

The domain expert verbalized the information on the third row of the table as sentence S2 ("Earth has the moon Luna"). Although this is atomic, it needs some refinement. To begin with, we rephrase the entity terms as follows using definite descriptions to include the entity types and the nature of the referring relationship: "The Planet named 'Earth'"; "the Moon named 'Luna'". Finally, we rephrase the verb "has" using the more informative predicate reading "is orbited by", as shown below. Although the verb "has" is usually reasonable for existential facts, it's typically better to provide a more informative reading for elementary facts.

F2 The Planet named 'Earth' is orbited by the Moon named 'Luna'.

For binary facts like F2, it's often useful to supply readings in both directions, as this can lead to more elegant verbalizations of associated constraints (or lack of constraints). Fact F2 can be verbalized in the opposite direction as follows:

F2 The Moon named 'Luna' orbits the Planet named 'Earth'.

As discussed earlier, an elementary fact implies the existence of its objects, so there is now no need to explicitly verbalize the existential fact that there exists a moon named 'Luna'.

The domain expert verbalized the fourth row of the table as sentence S3 ("Phobos and Deimos are the moons of Mars."). This may be rephrased as the conjunction of two atomic facts: The Moon named 'Phobos' orbits the Planet named 'Mars'; The Moon named 'Deimos' orbits the Planet named 'Mars'.

All the data in the sample report shown in Table 1.3 can be verbalized in terms of the atomic facts discussed. Abstracting from these fact instances to their fact types, we obtain the two existential fact types and one elementary fact type discussed in the previous section. Both readings for the elementary fact type may be set out compactly using a slash between the forward and inverse predicate readings, as follows: Moon orbits / is orbited by Planet.

In CSDP Step 2 we draw the fact types and check that they can be populated with the sample data, as shown in Figure 1.11(a). As discussed in the previous section, we typically abbreviate the reference schemes for the entity types by listing their reference modes in parenthesis.

CSDP Step 3 is not relevant to this example, so is not discussed here. In CSDP Steps 4 and 5 we add uniqueness and mandatory role constraints, and mark Planet as independent, as discussed previously, thus arriving at Figure 1.11(b).

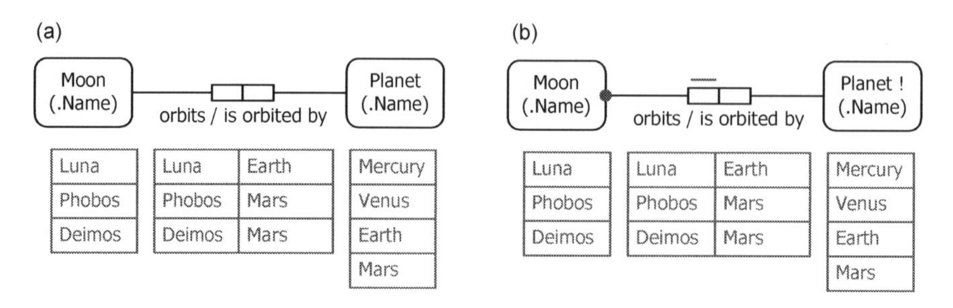

Figure 1.11 (a) Drawing, populating and (b) constraining an ORM model

As discussed in the previous section, the constraints are validated with the domain expert by verbalization and population. CSDP Steps 6 and 7 are not relevant to this example, so we now have the final version of the ORM model. CSDP steps not discussed here are covered in later chapters.

1.4 Fact-Based Modeling Tools

The fact-based modeling approach originated in Europe in the 1970s, with pioneering work by Eckhard Falkenberg, Sjir Nijssen, Robert Meersman and others. In the late 1980s, while teaching at The University of Queensland with Eckhard and Sjir, I completed a PhD that formalized and extended their Natural Information Analysis Method (NIAM), and in later years I revised and extended the approach evolving it to Object-Role Modeling (ORM). More recently, others joined me in extending ORM further to second generation ORM (ORM2), which is the version of ORM discussed in this book.

Over the years, many people have contributed to developing the fact-based modeling approach, and there is no space here to mention all their individual contributions. For further historical details on the development of the fact-based modeling approach, see Halpin & Morgan (2008, pp. 106-108). Bibliographic details for references cited in this book are included in the Further Resources section at the back of this book.

Over the years, many software tools have been developed to support different flavors of the fact-based modeling approach. An early pioneer was the RIDL* tool developed at a Control Data laboratory at the Free University of Brussels. This tool enabled NIAM models to be both designed and queried using the Reference and IDea Language (RIDL), but is now discontinued. Sjir Nijssen later extended NIAM to Cognition enhanced NIAM (CogNIAM) which is currently supported by DocTool. Current binary relationship modeling tools specifically designed for ontological modeling include Dogma Studio and Collibra. Tools supporting the FCO-IM approach include CaseTalk and Infagon.

Early ORM tools include InfoDesigner, InfoModeler, ActiveQuery (an ORM query tool), VisioModeler, and Microsoft Visio for Enterprise Architects, but these tools are no longer supported. Current ORM tools include Natural ORM Architect (NORMA), ORM-Lite, and ActiveFacts. For drawing purposes only, a free ORM2 stencil is available for use with Microsoft Visio—the ORM diagrams shown earlier in this book were drawn using this stencil.

Further details on currently available fact-based modeling tools are provided in the Further Resources section. In this book, our software tool discussion focuses on the public domain, open source version of the *NORMA tool*. This is a free plug-in to Microsoft Visual Studio, and may be downloaded from SourceForge at http://sourceforge.net/projects/orm/. It works with any version of Visual Studio from 2005 onwards, including the free Community Edition of Visual Studio 2013 (http://www.visualstudio.com/products/visual-studio-community-vs).

Each chapter of this book concludes with a NORMA Lab to provide hands-on experience with applying the concepts and techniques discussed in the chapter.

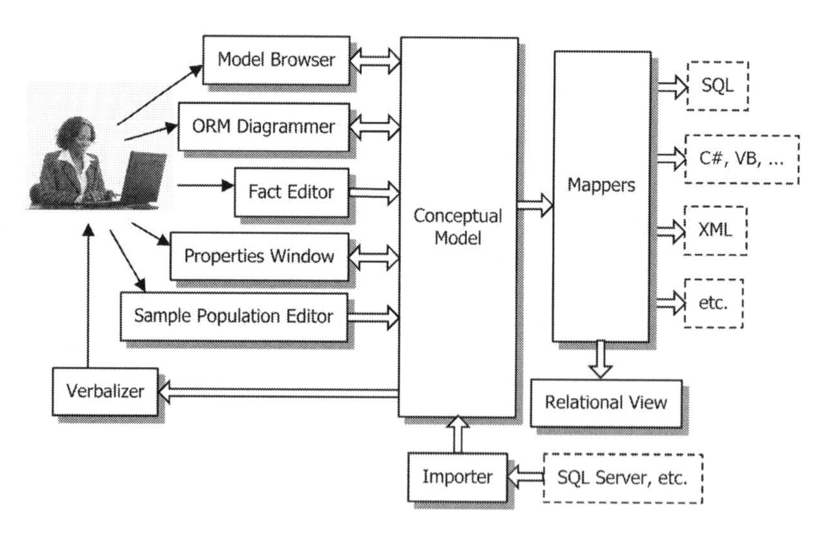

Figure 1.12 Main components of the NORMA tool

An overview of the main components of the NORMA tool is shown in Figure 1.12. Fact types may be entered textually using the Fact Editor, and NORMA will automatically display them in graphical format. You can also enter fact types directly in graphical format by dragging shapes from the toolbox in the ORM diagrammer. Constraints and rules are typically entered using the diagrammer, model browser, or properties window. Sample populations are entered using the Sample Population Editor.

NORMA automatically verbalizes whatever part of the ORM model is selected, and can automatically map the ORM model to various targets for implementation. NORMA's relational view facility maps ORM schemas to relational database schemas and displays them in graphical format. These logical level relational schemas can then be mapped to the physical level by generating SQL code in a supported SQL database system (e.g. SQL Server, DB2 or Oracle). The NORMA Labs in this book provide details on how to enter ORM models, and generate relational schema diagrams and SQL code.

Though not covered in this book, NORMA can also map ORM models to other targets such as the eXtensible Markup Language (XML) and programming languages such as C# and Visual Basic, and can be used to reverse engineer existing SQL database schemas to ORM schemas.

At the time of writing, a more powerful, professional version of NORMA is under development that supports formal entry of derivation rules, multi-page relational views, and other advanced features. As this version is not currently available, we confine our attention to the free public domain version of NORMA.

1.5 NORMA Lab 1

NORMA works only as a plug-in to Microsoft Visual Studio (2005 or later edition). If you do not already have Visual Studio installed, please install it now. If you wish to use the free Community Edition of Visual Studio 2013, please access http://www.visualstudio.com/products/visual-studio-community-vs.

For the NORMA screenshots shown in this book, I've used Visual Studio 2008, but all versions work similarly. After you have Visual Studio installed, download the latest public build of NORMA for your version of Visual Studio (e.g. Visual Studio 2005, 2008, 2010, 2012, or 2013). You can download this as a zip file from SourceForge at http://sourceforge.net/projects/orm/. To download NORMA for an earlier version of Visual Studio (e.g. 2008), click the "NORMA for VisualStudio" folder to show its subfolders, then click the top subfolder (e.g. 2015-01-CTP) to show its subfolders, and then select the relevant zip file. Alternatively, you can download the relevant NORMA zip file from the ORM Foundation website at http://www.ormfoundation.org/[7]

Now right-click the NORMA zip file in File Explorer to open its context menu, choose Extract All ... and then press the Extract button to extract the files to a folder. Now open that folder. If you wish, double-click the file Readme.htm in the extracted folder to view the Readme file in your web browser. This file includes many useful tips.

If you are using Windows Vista or a later version of Windows (Windows 7, Windows 8, etc.) double-click the file SetupVistaOrLater.bat to execute it, and answer Yes when prompted to allow changes to your computer. Otherwise, right-click the file Setup.bat and choose Run as administrator from its context menu.

If you already had a previous version of NORMA installed, this will now be removed (without removing any of your previous ORM model files). The Setup wizard will now guide you through the new installation of NORMA. Accept all the defaults (e.g. press Next on its opening screen, then Install on the following screen). After some minutes, you should be presented with a screen inviting you to press Finish to complete the installation.

Once both Visual Studio and NORMA installed, you can add ORM models to NORMA and have NORMA automatically verbalize the models and map them to relational database models for implementation. In this lab, we'll see how to do this for the planet-moons model discussed earlier in the chapter. I'll include some screenshots along the way to help explain the procedure.

---

[7] To access files from the ORM Foundation, you need to register as a member by clicking the Join button at the top of the opening page and filling out the form provided there.

To start, launch Visual Studio and choose the menu options File > New . File... (i.e. select File from the top menu, then New from its submenu, then File...) as shown opposite. The New File dialog box now appears. Select the General category, the Object-Role Modeling File template, and press the Open button as shown below. Depending on your settings, NORMA now displays various components such as those shown in the screenshot at the bottom of this page.

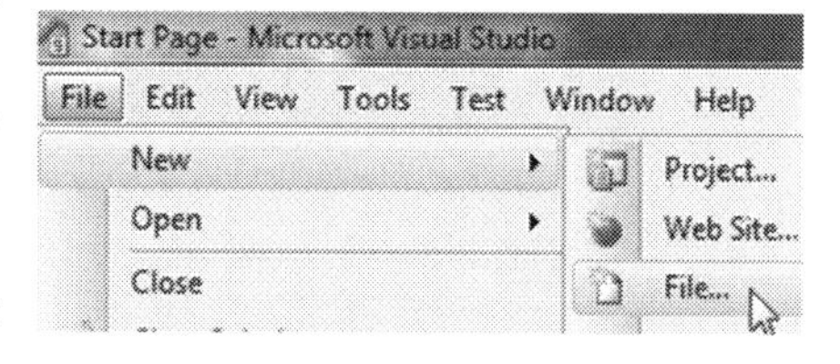

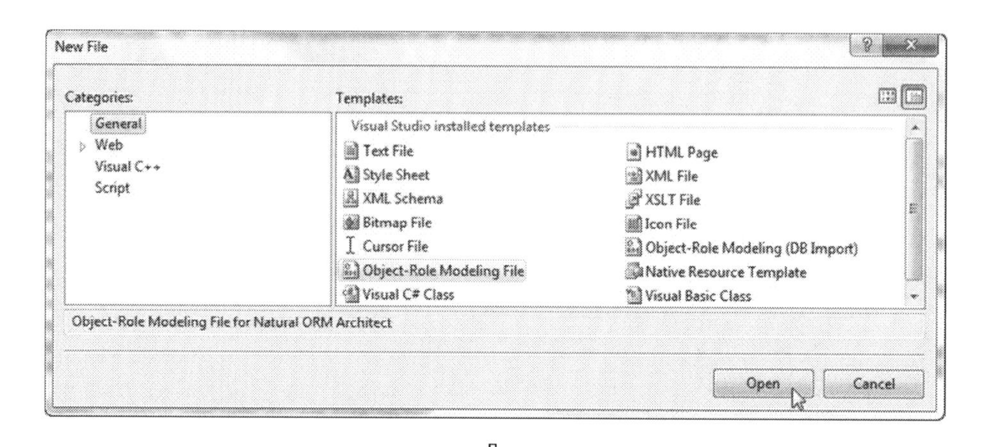

⇩

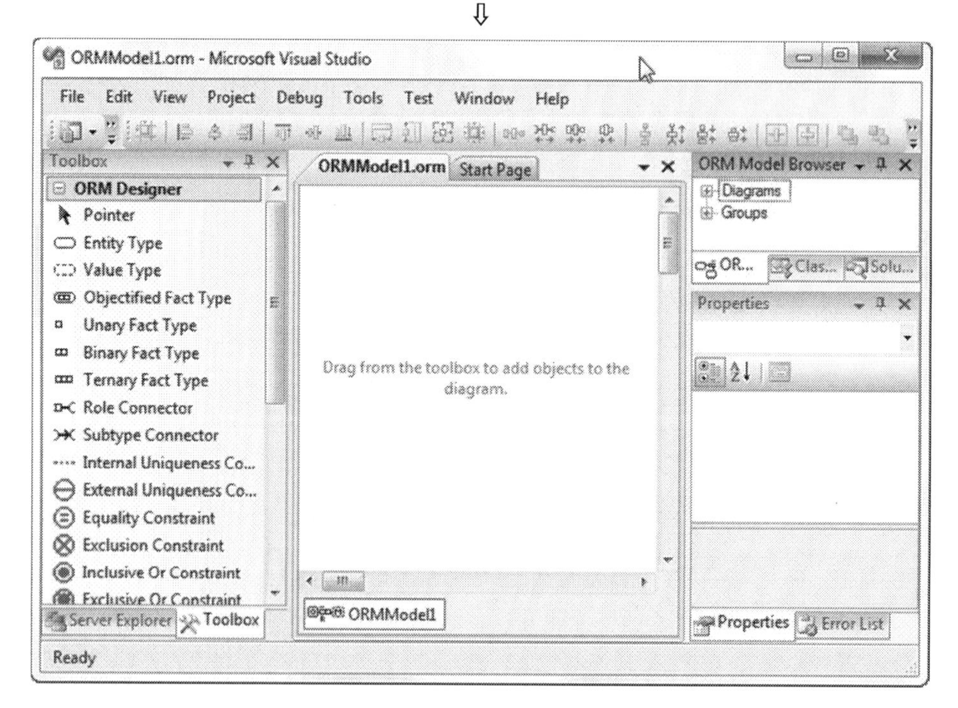

The area in the middle is called the *Document Window* and is used for displaying ORM diagrams. By default, the ORM model is initially assigned the name "ORMModel1". You can change this later when you save the model. The *Toolbox* on the left of the screen is used for dragging graphical shapes onto the document window. The *ORM Model Browser* shown on the top right of the previous screenshot provides an explorer interface for listing the various components of the model (currently empty). The *Properties Window* shown on the bottom right of the previous screenshot is used for editing the properties of the currently selected model elements. If the Model Browser and/or Properties Window don't yet display on your screen, you can display them as discussed in the next paragraph.

Right-click the empty space in the Document Window to show its context menu, and select ORM Tool Windows to display all available windows, as shown below. If needed, select ORM Model Browser and Properties Window to display them.

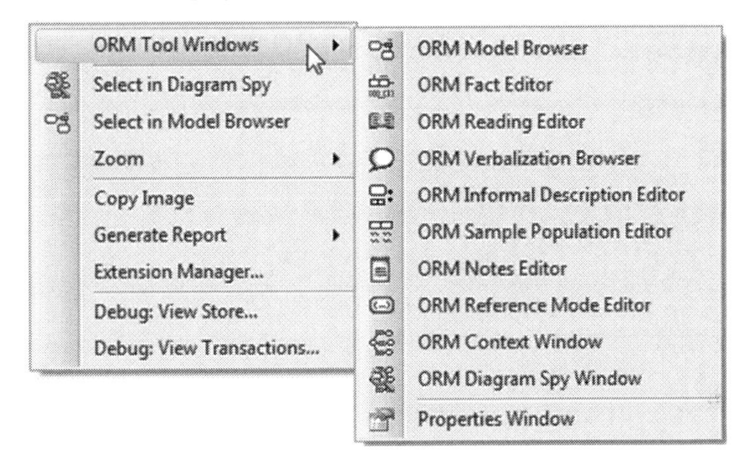

The *Fact Editor* is used to enter fact types in textual form. To open this editor, move the cursor to the ORM Fact Editor option and click the mouse (see below). The Fact Editor window should now be displayed.

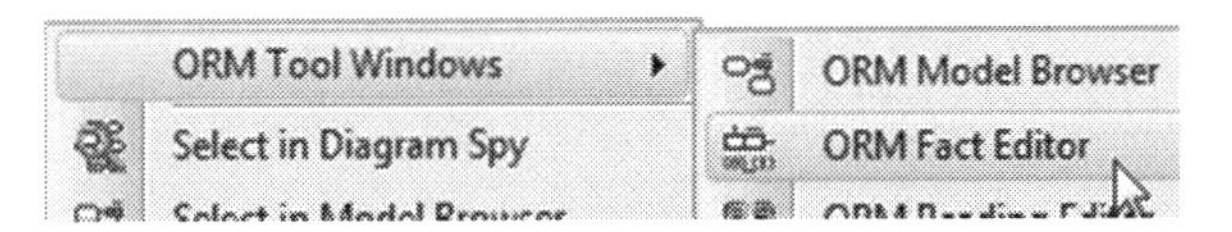

Our planet-moons model includes the entity types Moon and Planet, each identified by their name, as well as the elementary fact type with forward and inverse readings Moon orbits Planet, and Planet is orbited by Moon. We will now enter this information textually in the Fact Editor and have the NORMA tool automatically draw the ORM diagram for us, by carrying out the following steps.

1. In the Fact Editor, type "Moon(" (i.e. "Moon" with first letter in capitals, followed by a left parenthesis). A drop-down list of predefined reference modes now appears.
2. Click the .Name entry on this list. Then type the closing parenthesis ")". The fact editor should now display the Moon entity type with its reference mode in parenthesis, i.e. Moon(.Name).
3. Type " orbits/is orbited by Planet(". Include a space before "orbits", start "Planet" with a capital letter, and end with a left parenthesis.
4. Select .Name from the drop-down list of reference modes for Planet, and then type the closing parenthesis ")". The complete fact type entry "Moon(.Name) orbits/is orbited by Planet(.Name)" should now appear, as shown below.

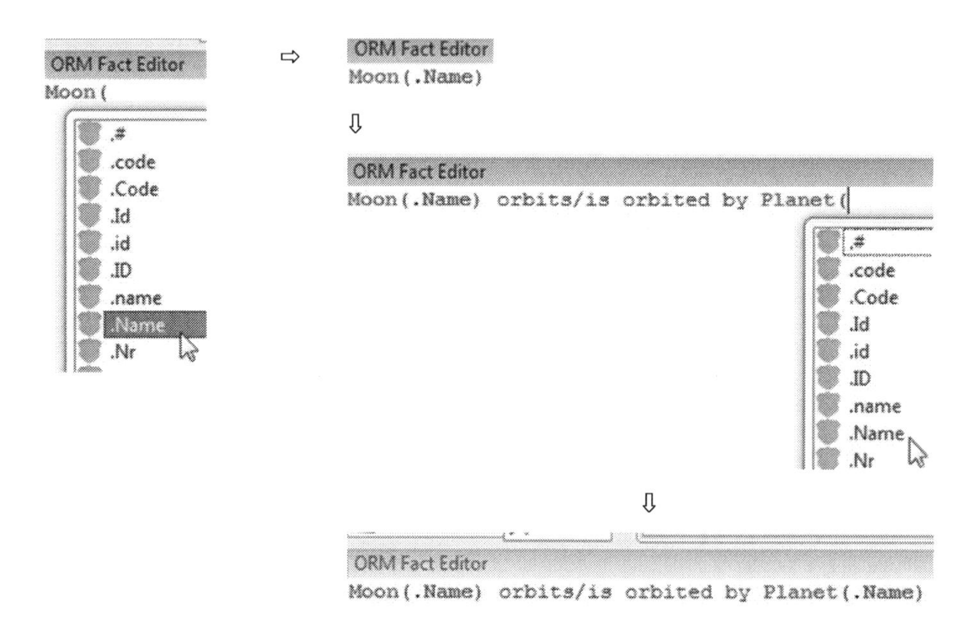

5. To add this fact type to the model, press Ctrl-Enter (i.e. hold the Control key down as you press the Enter key). The ORM diagram now appears in the Document Window, as shown below. Notice that the predicate shape is not aligned with the object type shapes. Although this makes no semantic difference to the model, let's see now how to align them to make the diagram look better.

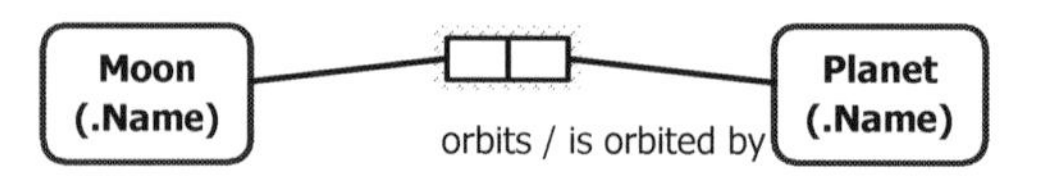

Display the *Layout Toolbar* by selecting the View option from the main menu, then select Toolbars and then Layout, as shown below.

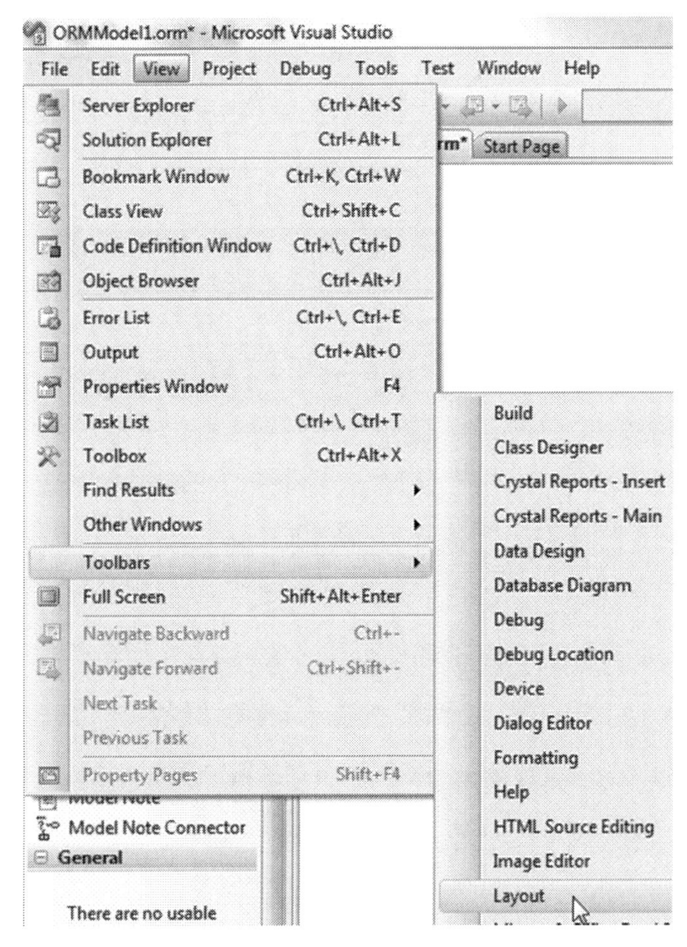

Drag the mouse over the diagram to select the object type and predicate shapes, then align these shapes horizontally by choosing the Align Middles icon in the Layout Toolbar, as shown[8]. Tooltips appear over the icons when you hover the mouse over them.

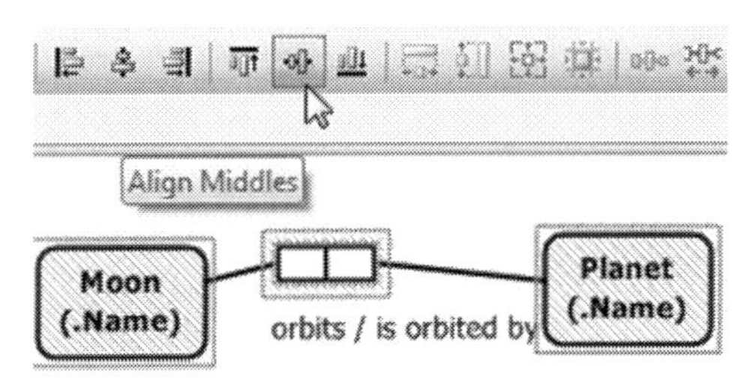

---

[8] Instead of using the Layout toolbar, you may use the menu options Format > Align > Middles.

Alignment is based on the last shape selected. For finer layout, *nudge* the "orbits / is orbited by" predicate readings by selecting the text and pressing the left-arrow key on your keyboard to move the text to the left. Similarly, nudge the Moon shape and Planet shapes to the left or right by selecting them individually and pressing the left-arrow or right-arrow key on your keyboard, until you are happy with the layout (see below).

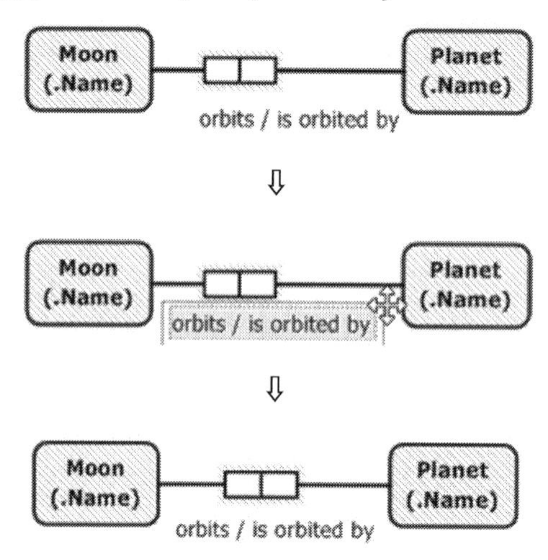

Unless you have configured a default datatype, the Moon and Planet shapes will be displayed with red fill, indicating an error state. To view errors on an element, right-click its shape to show its context menu, then select Validation Errors. A relevant error message for that element will then be displayed[9]. As shown below, the error message for Moon indicates that we need to assign a datatype to its value type (in this case MoonName).

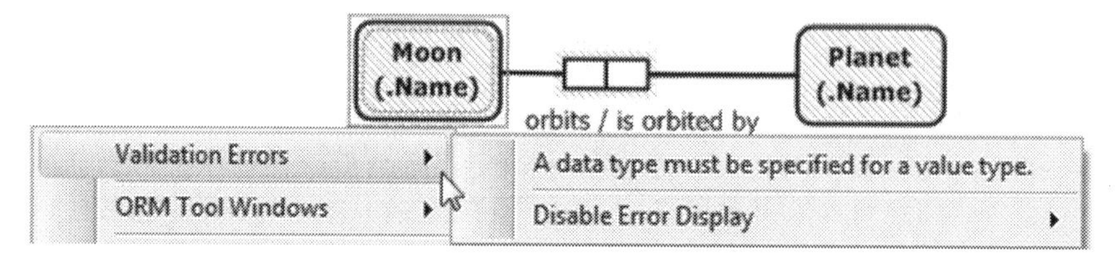

To assign a datatype to Moon's value type, select Moon and then go to its DataType property in the *Properties Window*. Currently, this has the entry <Data Type Not Set>. Move the cursor to the right of this entry, and select the down-arrow icon to open its drop-down list. Now use the scroll-bar at the right to scroll down to the datatype Text:Variable Length, and select this option to ensure that moon names will be stored as character strings of possibly different lengths.

[9] You can also display all error messages for part of all of the model by selecting it and viewing the messages in the Verbalizer (see later).

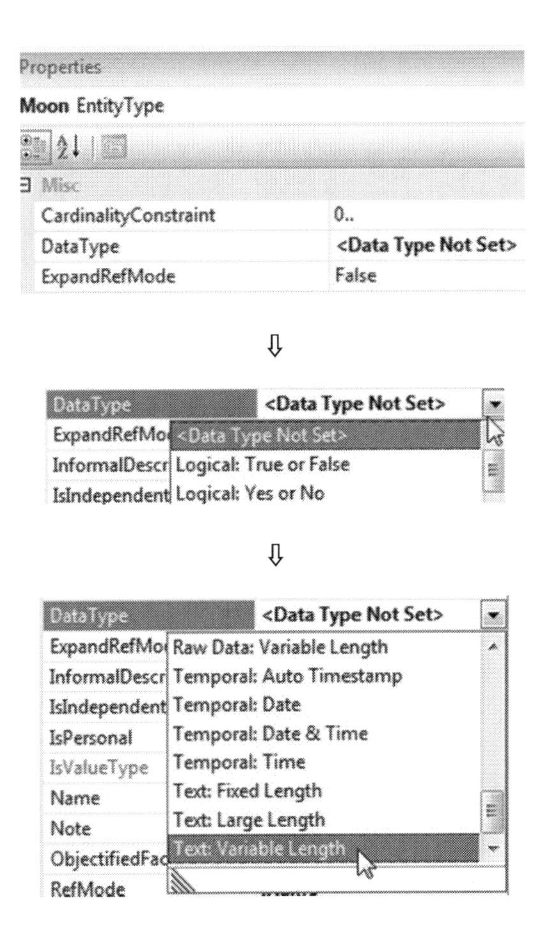

We now need to set the maximum number of characters allowed for a moon name. Currently the DataTypeLength property for Moon has the entry 0. If you look back at the sample data in Table 1.1, the longest moon name there was 10 characters long, but that list didn't include all the moons. You should check with the domain expert to see what size moon names should be allowed, but for now let's assume that a length of 20 characters should be sufficient. Move the cursor to the DataTypeLength property and change its value by typing in 20 (see below) and pressing Enter. That completes the entry of the datatype for moon names.

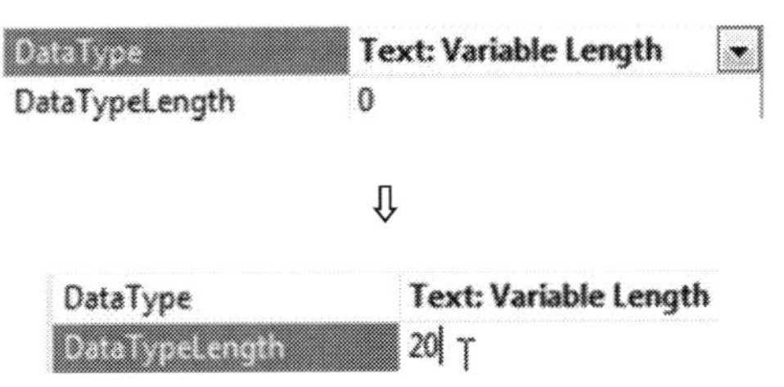

The Moon shape is now displayed with no error fill, indicating that the datatype error has been fixed.

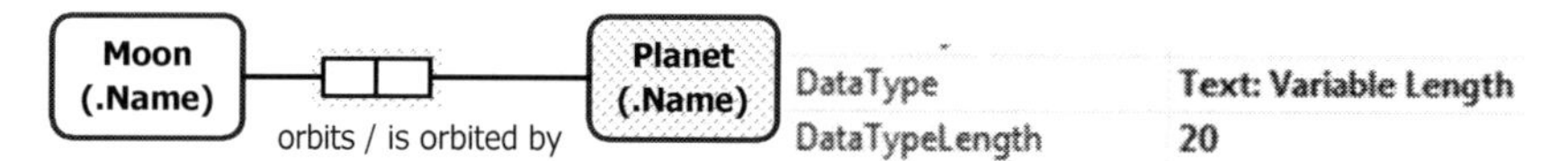

Similarly, select Planet and remove its error by assigning its value type's data type to be a variable length string of at most 20 characters. The diagram should now appear with no errors for Moon and Planet, as shown below.

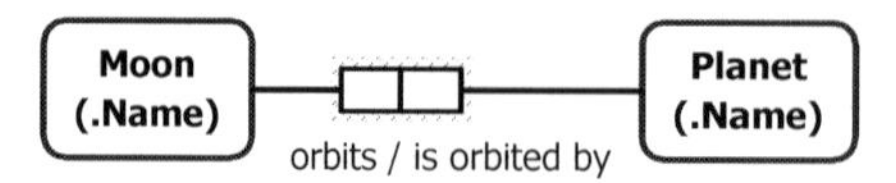

In typical models, most value types tend to have variable length string datatypes. To avoid having to set this property for those value types in future, configure NORMA to assume that data types are variable length string by default. To do this, choose Tools > Options from the main menu, then scroll down to select ORM Designer, to display the options specific to NORMA.

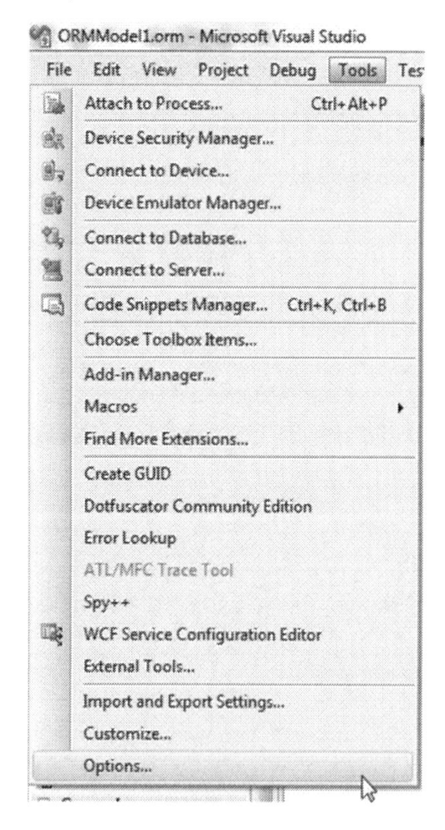

⇨

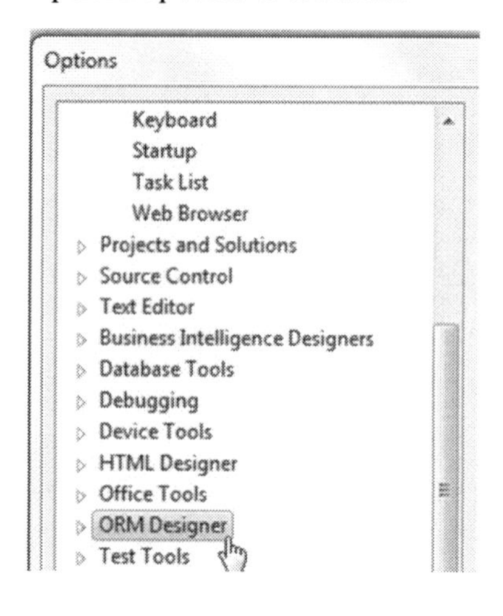

Now scroll up to the Data Types section, click its down-arrow icon to show the drop-down list of available data types, and select TextVariableLength. This changes the default data type from Unspecified to Te/xtVariableLength. Now press OK to commit the change (see below).

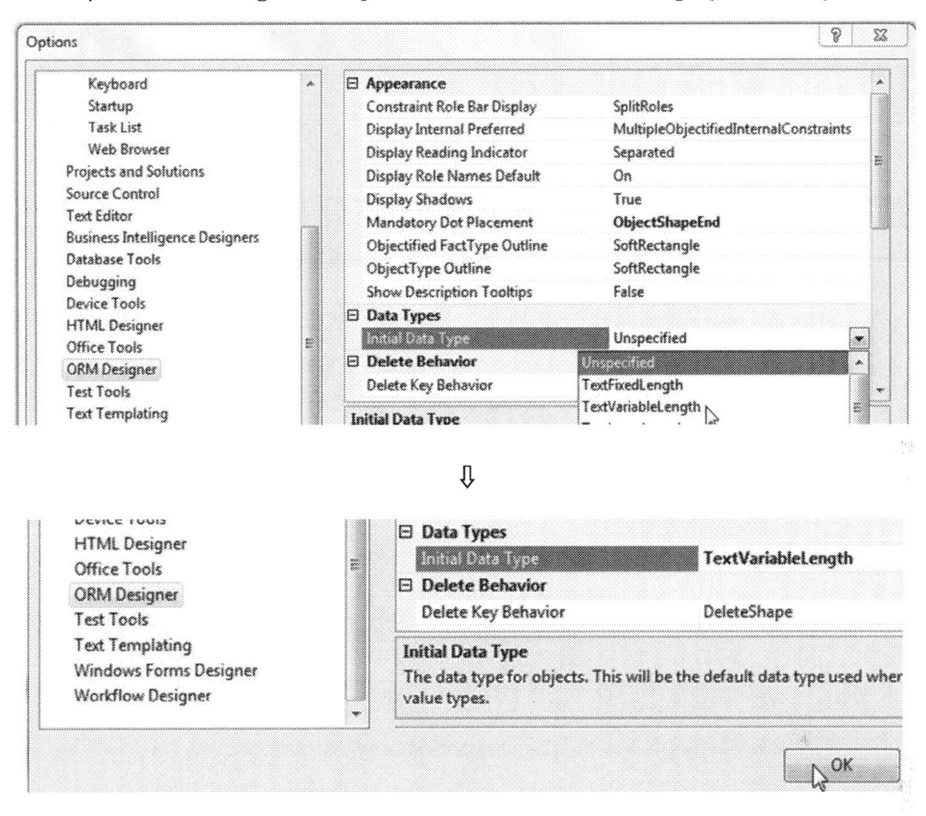

NORMA retains your configuration options for this and later models unless you change the options settings, so from now on you will not need to set data types explicitly to variable length text. However, you will still need to set their maximum length on an individual basis.

Returning to the ORM diagram, right-click the orbits predicate and select Validation Errors from its context menu. Note that the fact type needs an internal uniqueness constraint of alethic modality[10].

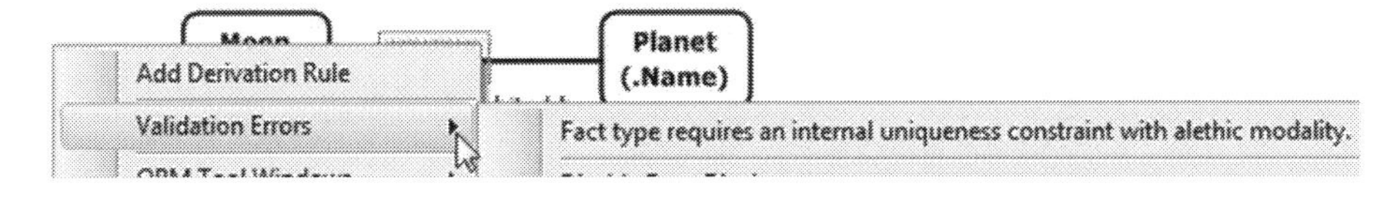

---

[10] *Alethic* constraints must be obeyed, so cannot be violated. NORMA also lets you declare *deontic* constraints, which ought to be obeyed but may be violated.

As discussed earlier, we should add a simple uniqueness constraint to Moon's role in this fact type. To do this, select the role, right-click it to open its context menu, then select Add Uniqueness Constraint. The uniqueness constraint bar is now displayed next to the role, and the error is removed.

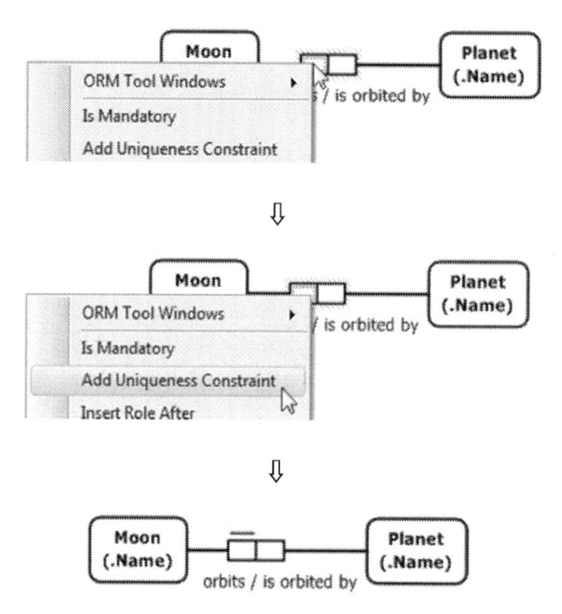

If the *Verbalizer* is not already displayed, open it by right-clicking an empty space in the Document Window and selecting ORM Verbalization Browser from the context menu.

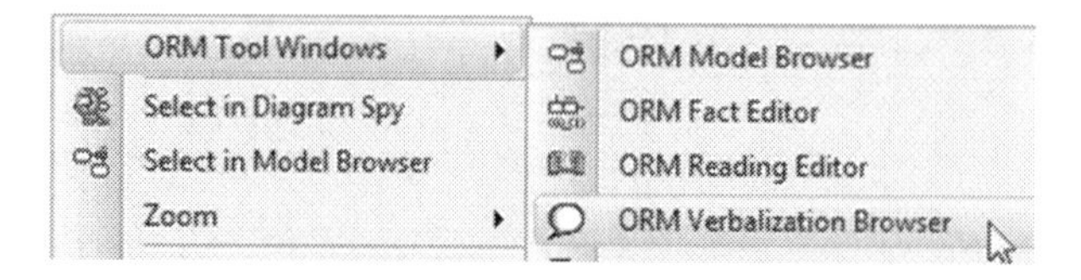

Select the constraint to display its *positive verbalization* in the Verbalizer. If you wish, you can also select the minus sign icon in the Verbalizer to see the constraint's *negative verbalization* (see below).

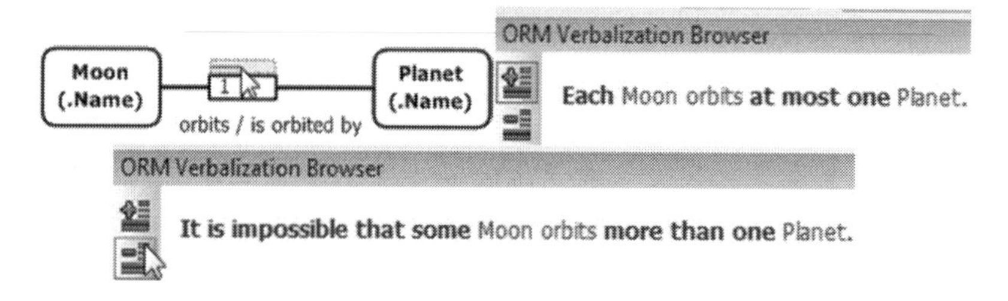

Now select the whole predicate shape by clicking just above the top right corner of the predicate shape. The Verbalizer now verbalizes the fact type, the uniqueness constraint on Moon's role, and the lack of a uniqueness constraint on Planet's role. The screenshot below shows the positive verbalization. If desired, you can also display the negative verbalization. For verbalization text, NORMA colors object type names in violet, predicate readings in green, and logical terms in blue.

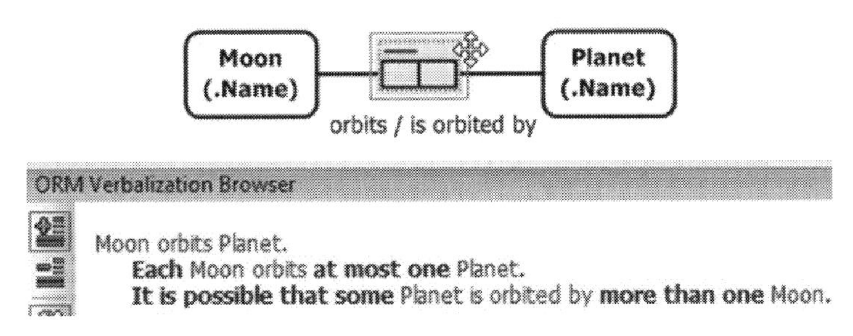

As discussed earlier, we need to add a *mandatory role constraint* to Moon's role in the orbiting fact type to constrain each moon to orbit at least one planet. To do this, right-click Moon's role in the fact type and select Is Mandatory from its context menu. The mandatory role constraint is now displayed (see below).

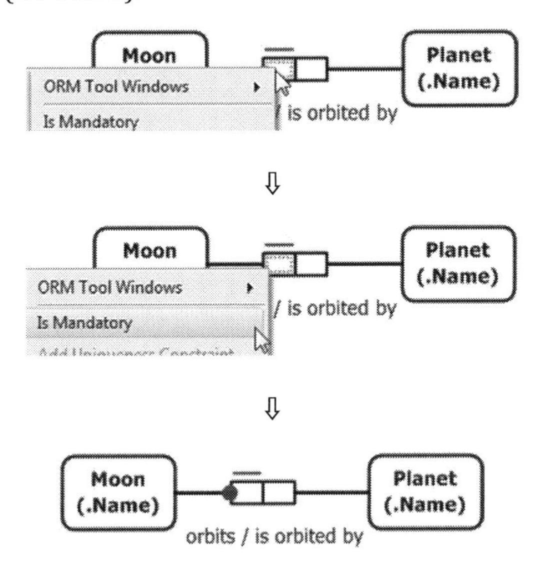

By default NORMA displays the mandatory role dot at the role end of the line segment that connects the role box to the object type shape. This helps to disambiguate the meaning of the constraint dot in rare cases when multiple role attachments are very close together. In typical cases however, my personal preference is to display the mandatory role dot at the object type end of the connector, as this indicates more clearly that the constraint applies to each population instance of the object type (unlike uniqueness constraints).

To change the default placement of mandatory role dots, choose Tools > Options from the main menu, scroll down to select ORM Designer, to display the options specific to NORMA, then go to Mandatory Dot Placement and press its down-arrow icon to open its drop-down list. Now select ObjectShapeEnd, and press OK. The mandatory role dot now appears at the object types shape end (see below).

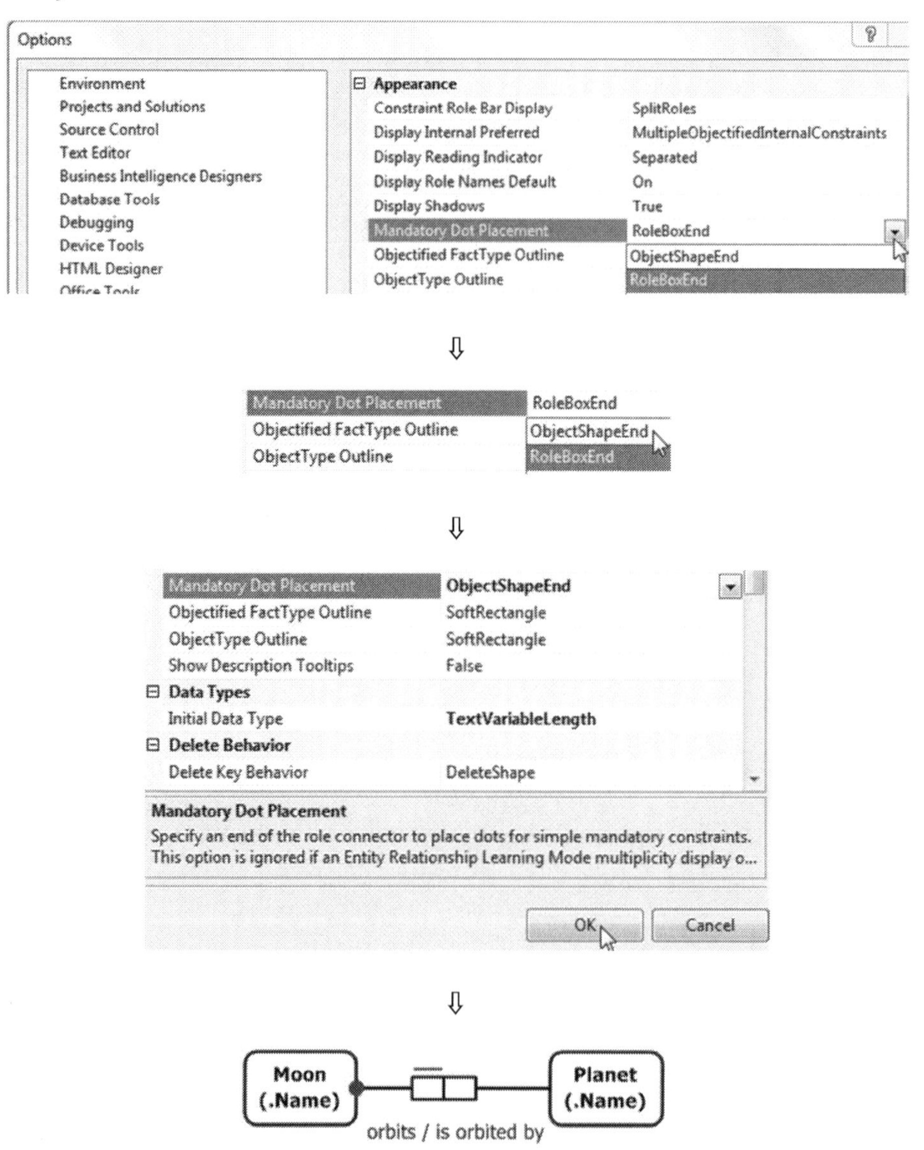

For the remainder of this book, all ORM diagrams will use this choice for the placement for mandatory role dots.

As discussed earlier, to complete the model we need to declare that Planet is an *independent object type* (i.e. instances of it may exist independently of playing any elementary role). To do this, select the Planet object type shape then in the Properties Window toggle its IsIndependent setting from False to True. The fastest way to toggle the setting is to double-click it. Alternatively, press the property's down-arrow icon and select the desired value (in this case, True) from the drop-down list (as shown below). An exclamation mark "!" now appears in the Planet object type shape to indicate its independent status.

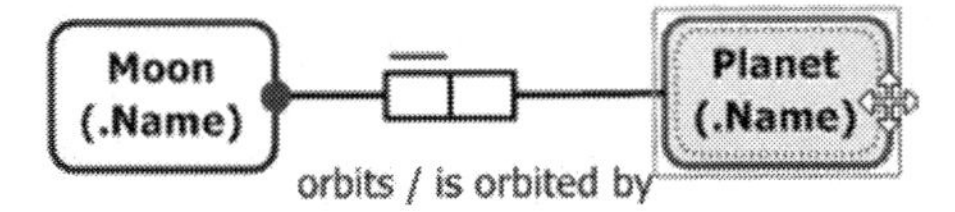

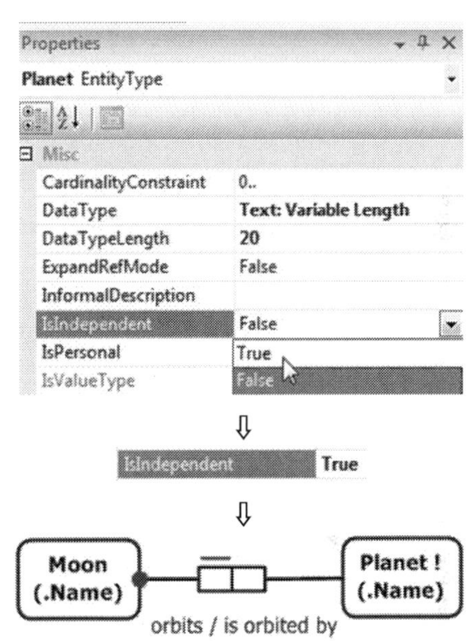

In previous sections, I used a Visio diagram to display the ORM schema for our moon-planets example, as well as a sample population, as shown in Figure 1.13. Although Visio is excellent for drawing ORM models, unlike NORMA it cannot automatically verbalize ORM models or generate implementations (e.g. relational databases) from them.

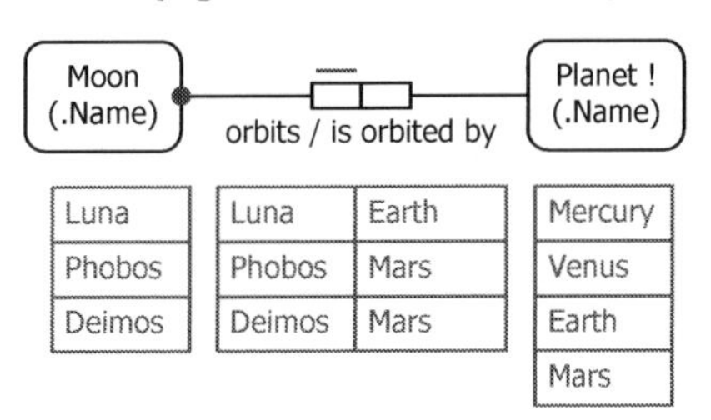

Figure 1.13 Visio diagram of an ORM model with sample population

Let's see now how to populate our NORMA schema with the sample data shown in Figure 1.13. Open the *Sample Population Editor* by right-clicking an empty space in the Document Window and selecting ORM Sample Population Editor from the context menu.

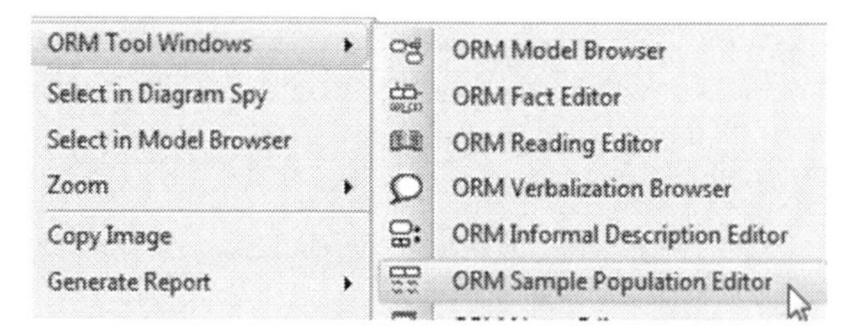

Now select just the predicate shape, and you'll see Moon and Planet columns appear in the Sample Population Editor. To resize the width of these columns, drag the vertical diver between the columns to the left, as shown below.

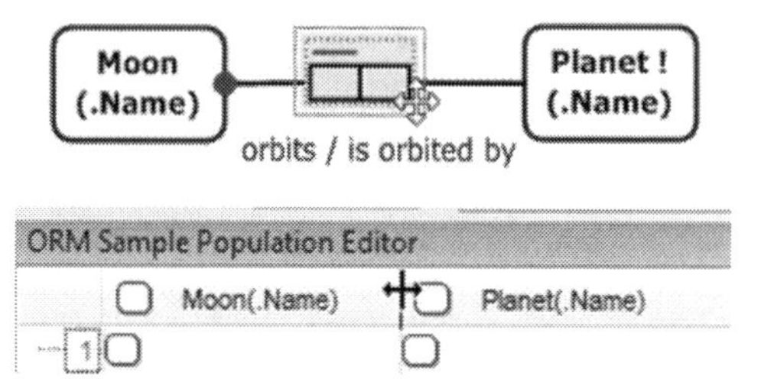

Now type in the three rows of data as shown below. Each time you add one row of data, NORMA adds a blank extra row.

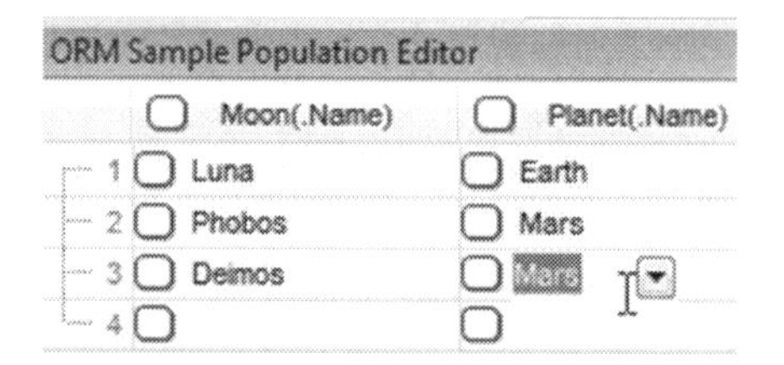

NORMA automatically populates the Moon and Planet object types with your entries for them. Select Moon and Planet individually to see their populations (see below).

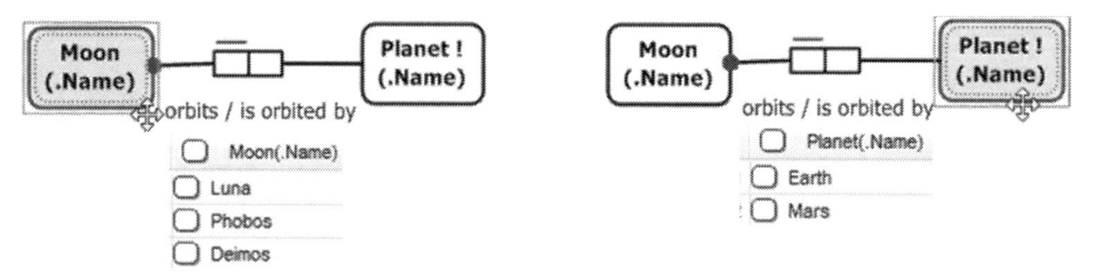

Not all planets have moons, so we need to add Mercury and Venus as planets to complete our sample data. To do this, select Planet and add the further two rows of data to its table in the sample Population Editor, as shown below.

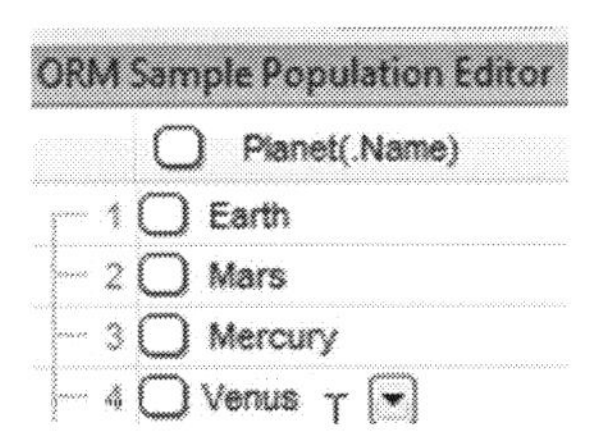

NORMA will verbalize whatever part of the model is selected. To verbalize all of our current model, drag the mouse to select all of it, as shown below. The Verbalization Browser now verbalizes the reference schemes and datatypes for the Moon and Planet entity types, as well as all the fact types (two existential and one elementary) and their constraints, and the sample populations, as shown. For documentation purposes, NORMA also allows you to save model verbalizations in reports.

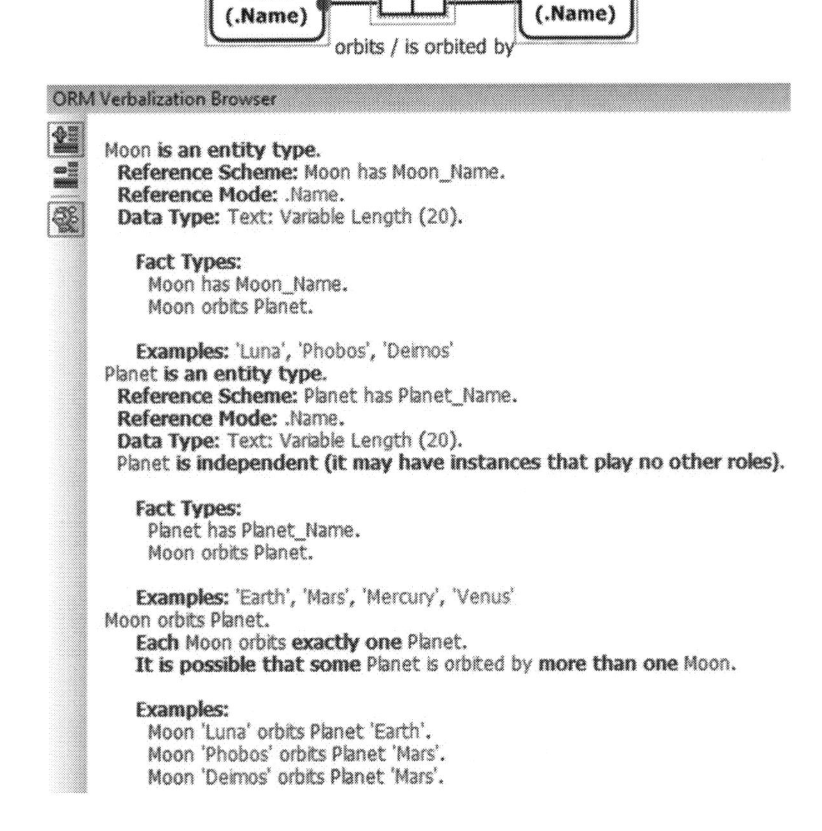

You can also use the Verbalizer to check that the sample data is consistent with the constraints. For example, if you now add Jupiter's moon Io to the sample population of Moon without adding the fact that it orbits a planet, this will violate the mandatory role constraint, as shown below.

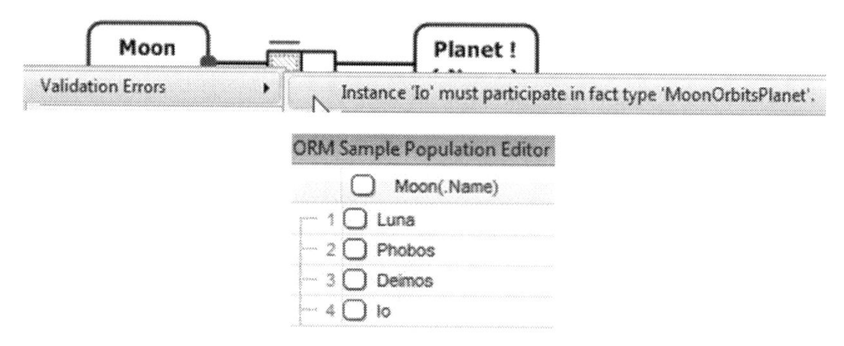

You can fix this error either by adding an (Io, Jupiter) row to the orbits fact table, or by deleting Io from Moon's sample data (by selecting the entry and pressing the Delete key). I chose the latter. We have now completed entry of the example ORM schema to NORMA, along with some sample data.

NORMA allows you to *move the diagram around the screen*. The Document Window has two scroll bars. Use the bottom scroll bar to scroll horizontally, and the side scroll bar to scroll vertically. To reposition any part of the diagram, select it then either drag it or use the arrow keys to nudge it. To select all of the diagram, press Ctrl+A (i.e. hold the Control key down as you press the A key).

To *zoom in* (magnify), press Ctrl+WheelUp (if you have a wheel mouse, hold the Control key down as you move the wheel upwards), or press Ctrl+Shift+LeftClick. To *zoom out*, press Ctrl+WheelDown, or press Ctrl+Shift+RightClick.

NORMA supports *unlimited Undo*, so you can remove any individual changes you've made since the start of the sessions. To undo the previous action, press Ctrl+Z (hold the Control key down as you press the Z key), or select Edit > Undo from the main menu.

Let's now use NORMA to *automatically generate a relational database schema* from the ORM schema. In this lab, we'll simply generate a *relational view* so we can see the relational schema diagram. Later in the book, we'll see how to generate actual SQL code for various DBMSs.

To create a relational view, right-click an empty space in the Document Window and select Extension Manager. This opens the Extension Manager dialog box. Now check the Relational View check box. NORMA automatically turns on two other extensions (Map to Abstraction Model and Map to Relational Model) needed to support the relational View extension, as shown on the next page.

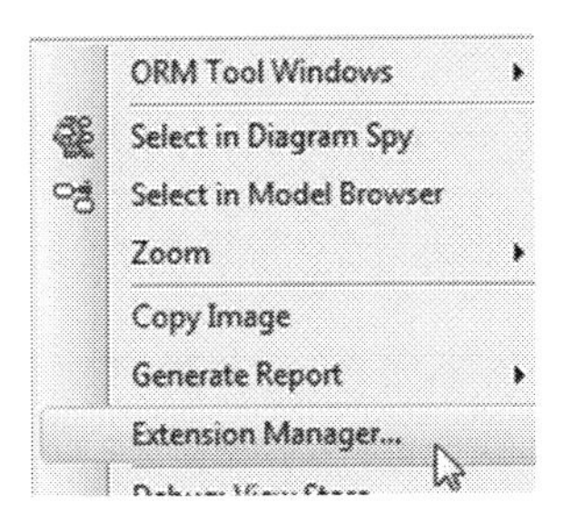

⇩

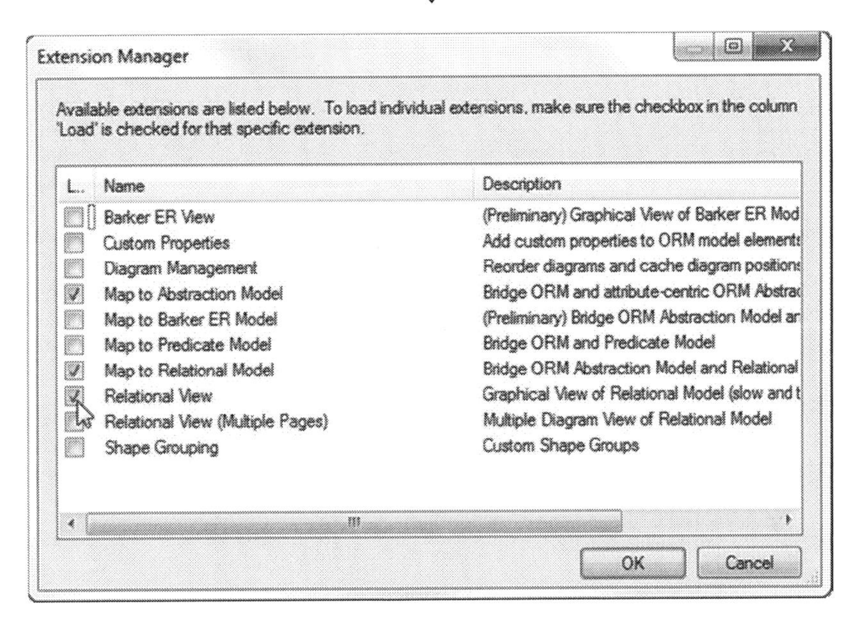

Now press OK. A Relational View tab now appears next to the ORM model tab at the bottom of the Properties Window. Select this tab to view the relational schema diagram. The *primary keys* of the two tables are marked "PK", and the *foreign key reference* from Moon.planetName to Planet.planetName is displayed as an *arrow*, with the foreign key itself prepended by "FK1", as shown.

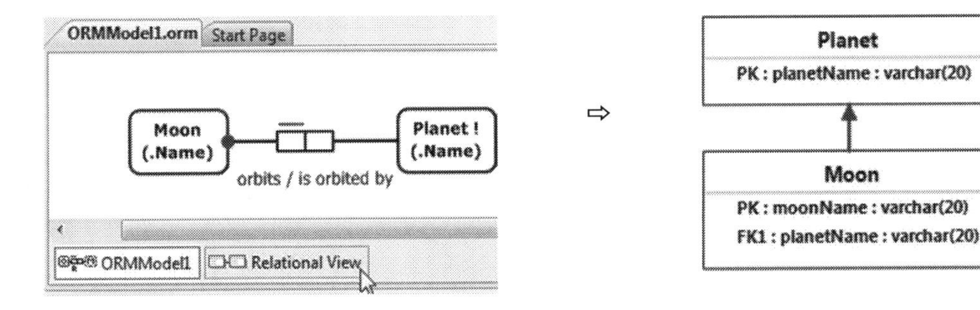

All the column entries are displayed in bold, indicating that they are not nullable. The ORM verbalization is also accessible directly from the relational model. This is handy for discussing the semantics of relational models with clients who are not familiar with the ORM diagram notation. For example, if you select the Moon table in the relational view, the following verbalization appears.

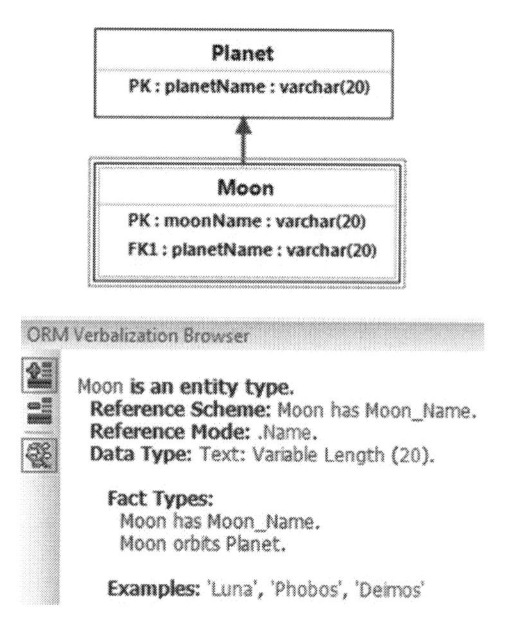

Now *save your work.* If you click the Save icon in the main menu (as shown on the left below), the model is saved under its current name (ORMModel1.orm). To save it under a different name, choose File > SaveModel1.orm As... from the main menu (as shown on the right below), enter your preferred filename (e.g. Lab1) in the Save File As dialog, and press Save. Then press the Close (X) button or select File > Close from the main menu to exit Visual Studio.

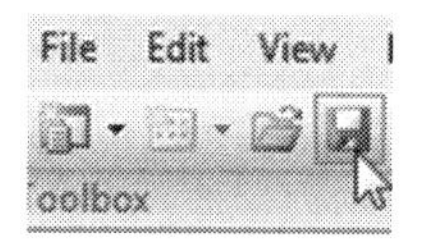

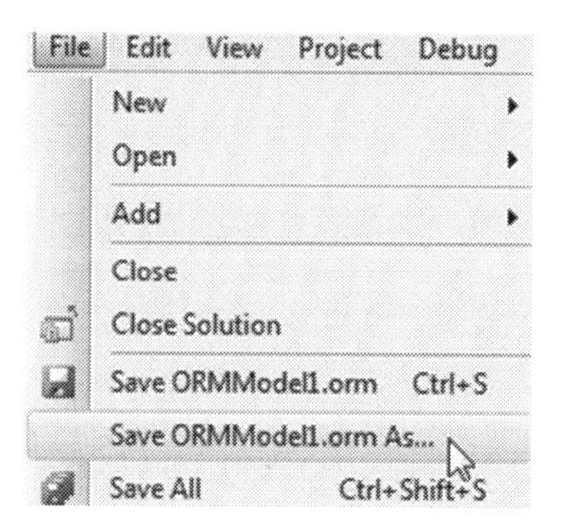

To open your saved model in future, launch Visual Studio, choose File > Recent Files from its main menu, and select your saved file (e.g. Lab1.orm).

2 CSDP Steps 1–5

As discussed in the previous chapter, ORM's Conceptual Schema Procedure (CSDP) comprises seven main steps. In this chapter we cover the first five steps, as summarized in Table 2.1. The design of the moon-planets model in the previous chapter involved a very simple application of CSDP Steps 1, 2, 4 and 5. In that model all the fact types were asserted, binary fact types, the entity types all had a simple reference scheme, and the only constraints were simple uniqueness constraints and simple mandatory role constraints. This chapter extends our coverage of ORM to include unary and *n*-ary fact types, derived fact types, external uniqueness constraints, disjunctive mandatory role constraints (also known as inclusive-or constraints), compositely identified entity types, and objectification.

Table 2.1 Steps 1–5 of ORM's Conceptual Schema Design Procedure

Step Nr	*Description*
1	1a: Verbalize familiar examples in natural language (domain expert's task)
	1b: Re-verbalize the examples as atomic facts (modeler's task)
2	Draw the fact types and apply a population check
3	Check for entity types that should be combined and note any arithmetic derivations
4	Add uniqueness constraints and check the arity of the fact types
5	Add mandatory role constraints and check for logical derivations

2.1 CSDP Steps 1–3

In CSDP Step 1, we verbalize examples of the required information in terms of atomic facts. To ensure that the correct semantics underlying the sample data is uncovered, a person who understands the data (a domain expert), should perform the initial verbalization, at least informally (CSDP Step 1a). As modelers, we then refine the verbalization where needed to ensure that the information is captured as atomic (either elementary or existential) facts, with entities properly identified by a reference scheme (CSDP Step 1b).

Information samples can be presented in many ways. For the moon-planet model discussed in the previous chapter, the example data was presented as a tabular report. Other common ways in which data is presented include forms, graphs and diagrams. Figure 2.1 shows three simplified examples of a university's employee record forms. For practice with CSDP Step 1, see if you can verbalize the information conveyed by these forms for yourself before reading on.

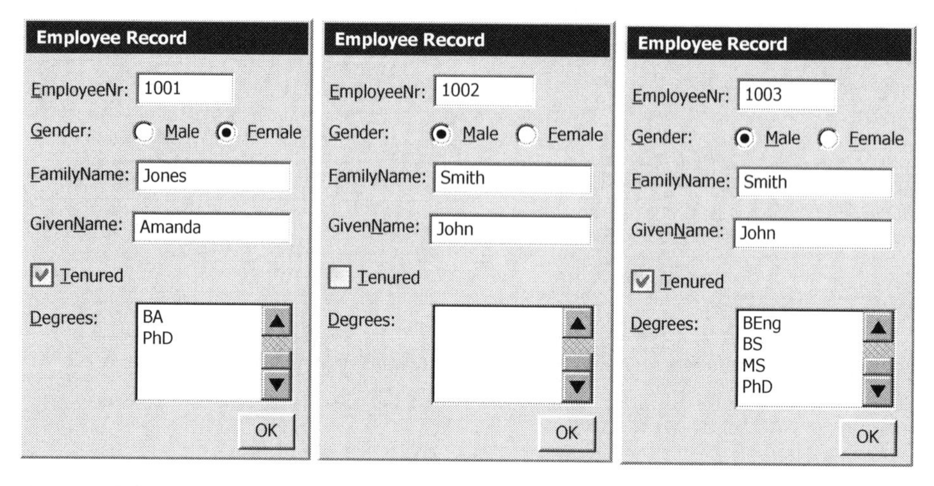

Figure 2.1 Simplified examples of three employee record forms

The first entry in the left-hand form may be verbalized as the unconstrained, existential fact: **There exists an** Employee **who** has **the** EmployeeNr 1001. In practice, "Number" is often shortened in labels to "Nr" or "No" or "#". The form itself does not tell us the employee numbers refer to employees, but our familiarity with such forms allows us to use our background knowledge to extract these semantics. That verbalization does not state that employee numbers are identifying, but we can check on that by asking the domain expert whether each employee has an employee number and whether each employee number refers to only one employee. Assuming the domain expert answers Yes to both those questions, we can now assert the constrained, existential fact: **The** Employee **who** has **the** EmployeeNr 1001 **exists**, and we can use the definite description "**The** Employee **who** has **the** EmployeeNr 1001" (or more briefly as "**The** Employee **with** EmployeeNr 1001") to identify that employee, and similarly for the other employees.

Moving down to the selected radio button on the left-hand form, we may verbalize that selection as the unary fact: **The** Employee with EmployeeNr 1001 is female. Again, the form itself does not tell us these semantics. Instead, we use our background knowledge to make the appropriate connection between the 1001 entry and the radio button selection. Similarly, we may verbalize the radio button selection on the middle form as: **The** Employee **with** EmployeeNr 1002 is male.

Although these unary fact verbalizations are correct, we may rephrase the information as the following binary facts: **The** Employee with EmployeeNr 1001 has **the** Gender **with** GenderName 'female'; **The** Employee **with** EmployeeNr 1002 has **the** Gender **with** GenderName 'male'. As discussed in Halpin & Morgan (2008), ORM includes conceptual schema optimization heuristics for choosing between various equivalent modeling alternatives. One such heuristic suggests remodeling a set of mutually exclusive unary fact types (e.g. Employee is female; Employee is male) as a single binary fact type (e.g. Employee has Gender). In practice, it is also often more efficient to use short codes (e.g. 'M', 'F') rather than names (e.g. 'Male', 'Female') as preferred identifiers for entities such as genders. So let's agree to verbalize the two radio button selections discussed as follows: **The** Employee with EmployeeNr 1001 has **the** Gender **with** GenderCode 'F'; **The** Employee **with** EmployeeNr 1002 has **the** Gender **with** GenderCode 'M'.

Using reference modes, the elementary facts conveyed by the radio button selections on the three forms may be set out more compactly in FORML as follows:

Employee(.Nr) 1001 has Gender(.Code) 'F'.

Employee(.Nr) 1002 has Gender(.Code) 'M'.

Employee(.Nr) 1003 has Gender(.Code) 'M'.

These facts are all instances of the following fact type.

Employee(.Nr) has Gender(.Code).

Notice the *dot* "." in ".Nr" and ".Code". This flags the reference modes as *popular reference modes*, enabling the underlying reference fact types (e.g. Employee has/is of EmployeeNr, Gender has/is of Gender) to be determined by appending the reference mode name to the entity type name to give the name of the relevant value type.

In CSDP Step 2, we draw and populate the fact type. A Visio rendering of this is shown in Figure 2.2. If you enter the above fact type verbalization in NORMA's fact editor, the schema diagram will be drawn for you automatically, and you can add the example data in the Sample Population Editor.

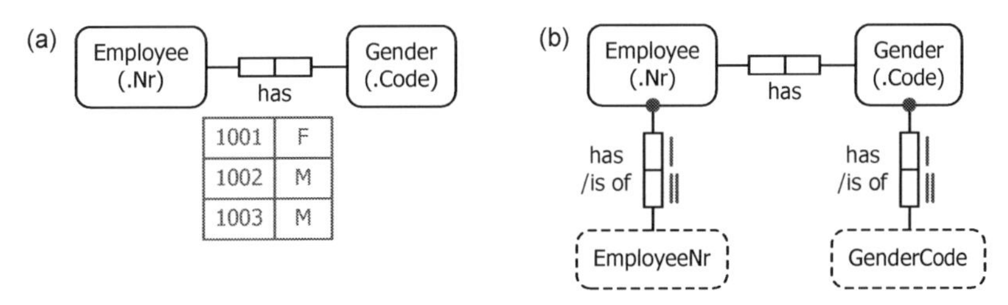

Figure 2.2 ORM diagram in (a) compact, populated form, and (b) expanded form

At this stage, we have not added mandatory role and uniqueness constraints to the Employee has Gender fact type. Nor have we added a value constraint on GenderCode to restrict its possible values to 'M' and 'F'. That's done in CSDP Steps 4–6, which we discuss later; but in practice it's normal to apply those steps as well before moving on to the next fact type. If desired, you can also include gender names ('female', 'male') in the model by adding the injective fact type Gender has GenderName, but we'll ignore that in our solution.

The next two fields on the Employee form in Figure 2.1 are used to record the family name and a given name of each employee. For example, the connections between the employee number and name entries on the left-hand form may be verbalized as follows: **The** Employee **with** EmployeeNr 1001 has FamilyName 'Jones'; **The** Employee **with** EmployeeNr 1001 has GivenName 'Amanda'. The fact types for these instances may be set out compactly in FORML as shown below:

Employee(.Nr) has FamilyName().

Employee(.Nr) has GivenName().

Appending *empty parentheses* "()" to an object type name indicates that the object type is a domain *value type*. Unlike entities, domain values (e.g. the FamilyName 'Jones') are self-identifying, so they can be referenced directly without relating them to another domain object for identification. FORML uses empty parentheses when declaring value types to indicate that they need no additional reference scheme.

If you have previously entered the Employee(.Nr) has Gender(.Code) fact type, the reference schemes for Employee and Gender are already declared, so when entering the family name and given name fact types in NORMA's Fact Editor, you may omit the reference mode for Employee. So these fact types may now be entered simply as follows: Employee has FamilyName(); Employee has GivenName().

Sometimes, an entity type might have more than one candidate reference scheme. For example, in some business domains people can be identified by the combination of family name and given name, e.g. "Amanda Jones", "John Smith". If you look back to Figure 2.1 it will be clear that this is not the case for our current business domain, because two different employees (identified by employee numbers 1001 and 1003) have the same combination of family name and given name.

The check box entries on the left-hand and right-hand forms in Figure 2.1 may be verbalized as the following unary facts: **The** Employee **with** EmployeeNr 1001 is tenured; **The** Employee **with** EmployeeNr 1003 is tenured.

The underlying fact type for these instances may be declared as follows:

Employee is tenured.

The lack of an entry in the middle form's check box indicates the *absence* of a fact to declare that the Employee with employee number 1003 is tenured. If we adopt the *closed world assumption* (assuming all relevant facts are known) for this fact type, we may infer that Employee 1003 is *not* tenured. If we adopt an *open world assumption*, we take it to be *unknown* whether this employee is tenured. We should check with the domain expert to see which meaning is intended.

The entries in the Degrees field of the left-hand form in Figure 2.1 may be informally verbalized in CSDP Step 1a as the following compound fact: Employee 1001 has a BA and a PhD. For CSDP Step 1b, we may formally verbalize this as the two atomic facts: **The** Employee **with** EmployeeNr 1001 holds **the** Degree **with** DegreeCode 'BA'; **The** Employee **with** EmployeeNr 1001 holds **the** Degree **with** DegreeCode 'PhD'. These are instances of the following fact type:

Employee holds Degree(.Code).

To complete CSDP Step 2, a populated ORM diagram is drawn, as shown in Figure 2.3. By default, fact types with a single predicate reading are read from left to right (or top to bottom if the predicates are displayed vertically). To *reverse the reading direction*, an *arrow tip* is added to show the reading direction, as shown for the family name and given name fact types. If you are using the NORMA tool, these directional arrows are added automatically.

The populations for the object types Employee, Gender and Degree may be omitted here, as they can be inferred from the fact type populations. Constraints will be added in later steps (you may wish to try adding the uniqueness and mandatory role constraints yourself, and checking that they are consistent with the sample data)

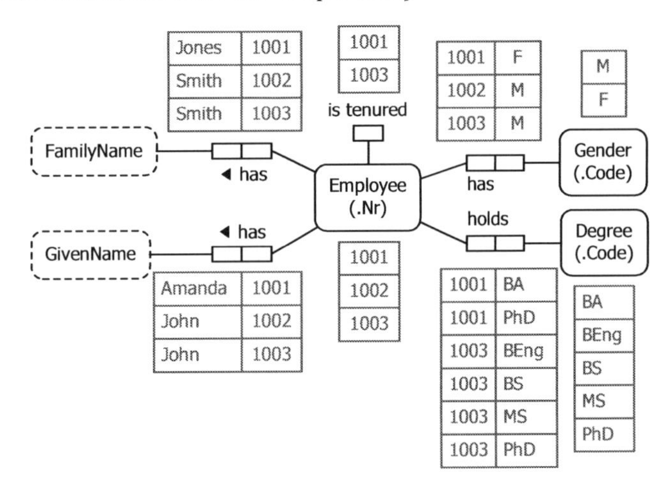

Figure 2.3 ORM model for the forms in Figure 2.1, with constraints yet to be added

Now consider the graphical report extract about flight routes shown in Figure 2.4. How would you verbalize the information conveyed by the arrow labelled "UA508"? Informally, we might express this as a ternary fact, e.g. "Flight UA508 goes from SEA to LAX". But this is not an atomic fact, because we can split it into the following two atomic facts without information loss: Flight UA508 starts at SEA; Flight UA508 ends at LAX. Formally, we can perform this split because each flight has only one start and only one end[11].

(a)

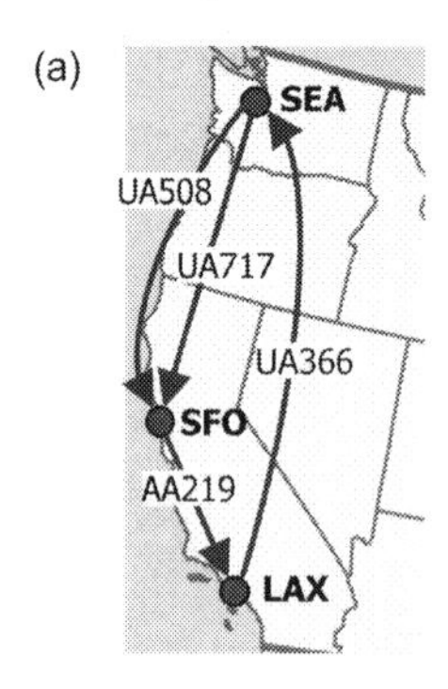

(b)

Flight	*Origin*	*Destination*
UA508	SEA	SFO
UA717	SEA	SFO
AA219	SFO	LAX
UA366	LAX	SEA

Figure 2.4 Sample extract of flight routes for Western USA

If the data were presented instead in tabular format, as shown in Figure 2.4(b), it's easier to see that two atomic fact types are involved. Suppose that we verbalized the first row of data as follows: Flight UA508 has Origin 'SEA'; Flight US508 has Destination 'SFO'. Treating the actual entries as numbers or codes for the entities involved, we might then draw the ORM diagram as shown in Figure 2.5, but this would be wrong. Why is that?

As the data shows, the origin of a flight might also be the destination of some flight (e.g. SEA). So the Origin and Destination types *overlap* (i.e. they have an instance in common). However, in Figure 2.5 Origin and Destination are shown as *top level entity types* (i.e. object types that are not subtypes). In ORM, top level types *are assumed to be mutually exclusive* (i.e. have no instances in common).

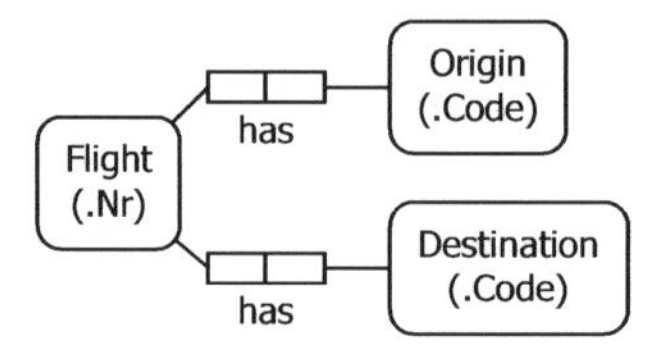

Figure 2.5 A faulty ORM schema

[11] As discussed later in CSDP Step 4, if we added the uniqueness constraint to the Flight role in the ternary fact type, this would violate the n–1 rule for arity checking. The NORMA tool can detect such violations, and would tell us to split the fact type in two.

To fix this error, we need to combine Origin and Destination into a single entity type. In general, *if entity types overlap, they must be combined*. This task is part of *CSDP Step 3*, which requires us to *check for entity types that should be combined*. In this particular case, we determine that flight origins and flight destinations are airports, so we may remodel the schema as shown in Figure 2.6.

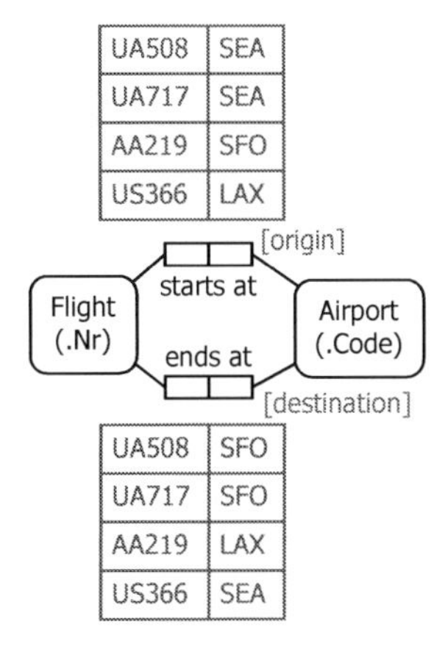

Figure 2.6 The former Origin and Destination types are combined as Airport

As well as a sample population, this diagram includes *role names* ('airport' and 'destination') for the roles hosted by Airport. On an ORM diagram, role names are displayed in blue color, inside square brackets placed beside the relevant role box. Role names are optional in ORM, but are useful for controlling the names generated for columns when the ORM schema is mapped to a relational schema. Role names can also be useful for specifying rules in attribute-style (see later).

Even if entity types do not overlap, it is sometimes useful to combine them if their instances may be meaningfully compared (e.g. measurements with the same or compatible units).

The final stage of CSDP 3 is to *note any arithmetic derivations*. If a fact type can be derived from others by applying an arithmetic rule, then this *derivation rule should be noted* and *the fact type should be marked as derived*. For example, consider the report extract shown in Table 2.2. Can some of the data be derived?

Table 2.2 A report extract about planets and their moons

Planet	*Moons*	*Nr Moons*
Mercury		0
Venus	Luna	0
Earth	Phobos, Deimos	1
Mars	...	2
...		...

You likely realized that the number of moons for a planet can be derived by counting the moons that orbit that planet. The ORM schema for this example (with constraints yet to be added) may be set out as shown in Figure 2.7. The fact type Planet has NrMoons is a *derived fact type*, as indicated graphically by *appending an asterisk "*" to its predicate reading.* The derivation rule for this fact type is set out below the diagram, prepended by an asterisk.

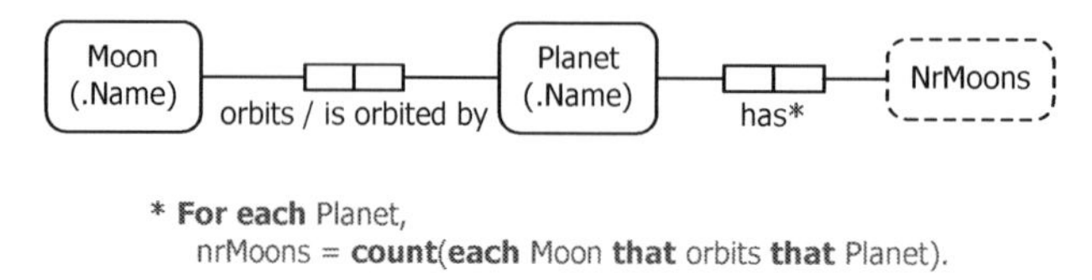

* **For each** Planet,
nrMoons = **count**(**each** Moon **that** orbits **that** Planet).

Figure 2.7 Planet has NrMoons is a derived fact type

By default, the populations of derived fact types are not stored, but are instead computed on demand (e.g. when querying for the number of moons). This "*derive on query*" approach is known as *lazy evaluation.*

ORM also allows you to declare that the population of a derived fact type is stored, so that it is always immediately available. This "*derive on update*" approach is known as *eager evaluation*. In this case, the fact type is both *derived and stored*, and a *double-asterisk* "**" is appended to its predicate reading, as shown in Figure 2.8.

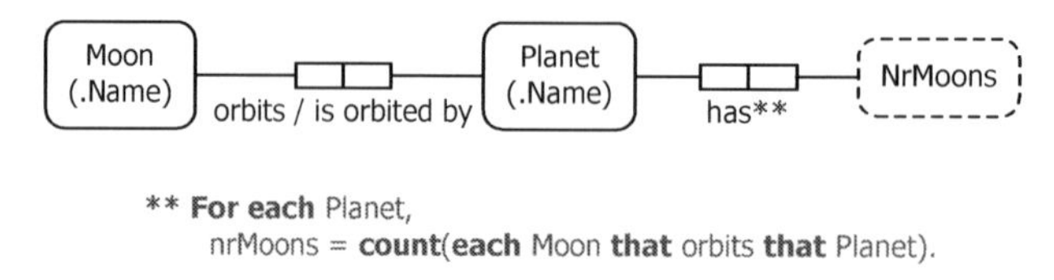

** **For each** Planet,
nrMoons = **count**(**each** Moon **that** orbits **that** Planet).

Figure 2.8 Planet has NrMoons is a derived fact type that is also stored

A fact type whose instances are all simply asserted is an *asserted fact type*. For example, Moon orbits Planet is an asserted fact type. In typical ORM models, most fact types are asserted. In addition to asserted and derived fact types, ORM also lets you declare a fact type as *semiderived*, so that some of its instances may be simply asserted while other instances may be derived. For example, if the population of the fact type of Person is a parent of Person is incomplete, some instances of Person is a grandparent of Person might be simply asserted rather than being derived from parenthood facts. Semiderived fact types are depicted by appending a plus superscript "$^{+}$" (intuitively, half an asterisk) to the predicate reading. Semiderived fact types that are also stored have a double-plus-superscript "$^{++}$" appended.

2.2 CSDP Step 4

In CSDP Step 4 we add uniqueness constraints to the fact types, and then use them as a check on the arity (number of roles) of the fact types. The previous chapter considered simple uniqueness constraints on binary fact types. As an example that includes a unary(one role) and a ternary (3 roles) fact type, consider the report extract shown in Table 2.3. This shows a tiny fragment of data from an information system that records details about the games of the Summer Olympics of the modern era. As an exercise, you might like to try to model this example in ORM before reading on.

Table 2.3 A sample report extract about the Summer Olympics Games

Olympiad	*Year*	*Held?*	*Country*	*Sports competed in*
I	1896	Yes	AU	athletics, tennis, ...
VI	1916	No	GR	athletics, swimming, tennis, ...
XXIX	2008	Yes	US	athletics, swimming, tennis,...
XXXII	2020	No	...	...
			US	baseball, swimming, ...
			...	...

Each Summer Olympics is primarily identified by its Olympiad number, traditionally shown in Roman numerals, as in the first column. For each Summer Olympics, the second column indicates the year assigned to it, whether or not that games is held (as indicated in the third column). For example, the games for Olympiad VI were cancelled because of World War I, and at the time of writing the games for Olympiad XXXII are scheduled for a future year. For each Summer Olympics, the last two columns indicate which countries competed in which sports for that games. Using FORML notation, the information on the first row of the table may be verbalized as the following atomic facts.

SummerOlympics(OlympiadNr) 1 is assigned Year(CE:) 1896.

SummerOlympics(OlympiadNr) 1 was held.

Country(.Code) 'AU' competed in Sport(.Name) 'athletics' in SummerOlympics(OlympiadNr) 1.

Country(.Code) 'AU' competed in Sport(.Name) 'tennis' in SummerOlympics(OlympiadNr) 1.

For efficiency reasons, I've used Hindu-Arabic decimal numerals instead of Roman numerals for the Olympiad numbers. This allows them to be stored as integers rather than character strings. However, you could use Roman numerals instead or even in addition, if you wish. I've also identified each Summer Olympics directly by its Olympiad number. If desired, you could instead introduce Olympiad as an entity type identified by its number, and then identify each games by its relationship to an Olympiad.

As discussed previously, for display purposes *popular reference modes* have their names preceded by a dot (e.g. .Name, .Code). This ensures that the names of their underlying value types are understood to prepend the entity type name to the reference mode name (e.g. CountryCode, SportName).

In contrast, the reference mode OlympiadNr has no added punctuation marks. This classifies it as a *general reference mode*. This ensures that its underlying value type has the same name. For example, the reference scheme shown in compact form as SummerOlympics(OlympiadNr) is shorthand for an existential fact type with readings SummerOlmpics has / is of OlympiadNr.

The reference scheme shown in compact form as Year(CE:) uses the reference mode CE to indicate that years are numbered according to the Common Era convention. Long ago, this used to be called "AD" (for *anno domini*, the year of The Lord). Notice that a *colon* ":" is appended to this reference mode. This ensures that the underlying value type is named by appending "Value" to the reference mode name. So Year(CE:) is shorthand for an existential fact type with readings Year has / is of CEValue. For example, the year 1986 may now be expressed as "**the** Year **that** has CEValue 1986".

This appended colon notation for reference modes is also used for *unit-based reference modes*, where quantities are measured in terms of units. For example, the reference scheme Mass(kg:) references instances of the entity type Mass by relating them to instances of the value type kgValue.

The unary fact type SummerOlympics was held is used to explicitly record which games of the Summer Olympics have already been held. Adopting the Closed World Assumption for this fact type, the "No" entry in Table 2.3 for the games of Olympiads 6 and 32 is captured by the absence of these games in the population of the unary fact type. When mapped to a relational database, this fact type maps to a Boolean column with True and False entries for games that have or have not been held respectively.

The ternary fact type Country competed in Sport in SummerOlympics is used to record which countries competed in which sports in which Summer Olympics. This is an example of an *n*-ary fact type (a fact type with *n* roles, where *n* > 2). As discussed later, an alternative way to model this information is to use objectification (e.g. declare the binary fact type Country competed in SummerOlympics, then objectify that and attach another binary to record the sports). However, the ternary fact type approach is by far the most natural way to model this information.

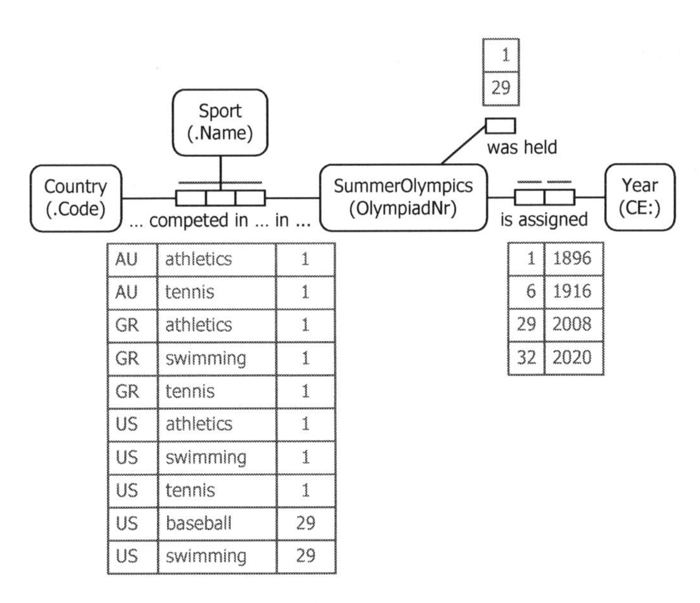

Figure 2.9 An ORM model for Table 2.3 (mandatory role constraints omitted)

A populated ORM schema for this example is set out in Figure 2.9, with mandatory role constraints yet to be added. Object type populations are omitted, but may be inferred from the fact type populations (the population of an object type that is not declared independent is the union of its elementary role populations).

As part of CSDP Step 4, uniqueness constraints have been added to the fact types. Notice that *no uniqueness bar is added to the unary fact type* SummerOlympics was held. This is because the population of each ORM fact type is a *set* of facts, not a bag (multiset), and duplicates are not allowed. Since each entry in the population of a unary fact type can appear there only once, a uniqueness constraint is implicitly assumed, so is not displayed.

The binary fact type SummerOlympics is assigned Year has a simple uniqueness constraint on each of its roles. This is called a *one-to-one* (1:1) fact type. These constrains verbalize as follows: **Each** SummerOlympics is assigned **at most one** Year; **For each Year**, **at most one** SummerOlympics is assigned **that** Year.

The ternary fact type Country competed in Sport in SummerOlympics has a uniqueness constraint spanning all its roles—this is called a *spanning uniqueness constraint*. Being set-based, all ORM fact types implicitly have a spanning uniqueness constraint, but for binary and longer fact types this is displayed only if no shorter uniqueness constraint applies. If you look at the sample population of the ternary fact type, you will see that duplicate entries appear for each individual role as well as each of the Country-Sport, Country-SummerOlympics, and Sport-SummerOlympics role pairs. So no 1-role or 2-role uniqueness constraint applies to this fact type.

Declaring a spanning uniqueness constraint on the ternary thus serves two purposes. Firstly, it indicates that no duplicate triples are allowed in its population. This verbalizes as follows:

In each population of Country competed in Sport in SummerOlympics,

each Country, Sport, SummerOlympics **combination occurs at most once**.

Secondly, it indicates that duplicate entries are allowed for each of its role pairs. This verbalizes as follows:

It is possible that for some Country **and** Sport,

that Country competed in **that** Sport in **more than one** SummerOlympics

and that for some Country **and** SummerOlympics,

that Country competed in **more than one** Sport in **that** SummerOlympics

and that for some Sport **and** SummerOlympics,

more than one Country competed in **that** Sport in **that** SummerOlympics.

For our next example, suppose we need to record the ranks of various countries in various sports, based on their collective medal tally over all the modern Summer Olympics. Table 2.4 shows a small extract of sample data for this universe of discourse. For an extensive coverage of the relevant data, please see http://en.wikipedia.org/wiki/Summer_Olympic_Games. As an exercise, you might like to try to model this example in ORM before reading on.

Table 2.4 An extract of country rankings in sports of the Summer Olympics

Sport\Country	AU	CU	KP	NE	US	...
baseball	5	1			2	
gymnastics			22	22	2	
swimming	2				1	
...						

The information is most naturally verbalized as ternary facts. For example, the 5 entry in the second column may be verbalized informally as "Australia is ranked 5th in baseball", and formally as "**The** Country **with** CountryCode 'AU' in **the** Sport named 'baseball' has **the** Rank numbered 5". All entries in the table may be verbalized similarly as instances of the ternary fact type Country in Sport has Rank. Alternatively, or in addition, you could have used other readings such as "Country has Rank in Sport" for this fact type.

Figure 2.10(a) shows a populated ORM model for this example, ignoring mandatory role constraints. The ternary fact type has only one uniqueness constraint, and this spans just its Country and Sport roles, as depicted by the uniqueness bar that spans both these roles, so no duplicate country-sport pairs are allowed in its fact table. This constraint verbalizes thus: **For each** Country **and** Sport, **that** Country in **that** Sport has **at most one** Rank.

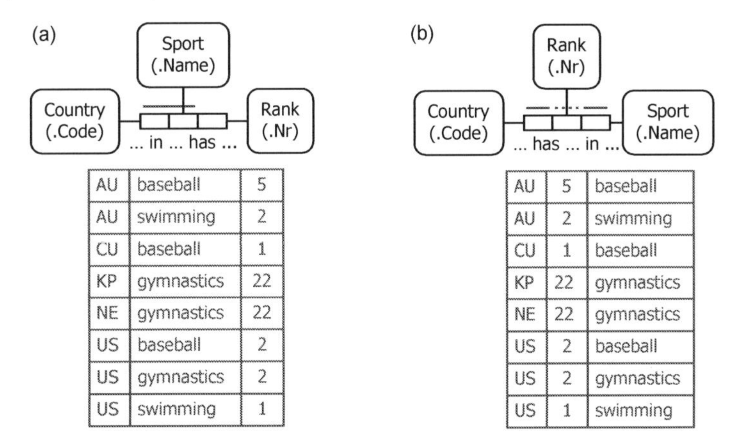

(a)

AU	baseball	5
AU	swimming	2
CU	baseball	1
KP	gymnastics	22
NE	gymnastics	22
US	baseball	2
US	gymnastics	2
US	swimming	1

(b)

AU	5	baseball
AU	2	swimming
CU	1	baseball
KP	22	gymnastics
NE	22	gymnastics
US	2	baseball
US	2	gymnastics
US	1	swimming

Figure 2.10 An ORM model for Table 2.4 (mandatory role constraints omitted)

Figure 2.10(b) shows an equivalent ORM model, using the fact type reading Country has Rank in Sport. In this case, the roles spanned by the uniqueness constraint are not contiguous, so a *dashed bar* is displayed over the other role to *exclude it from the constraint*. Here, the solid constraint bars are understood to cover roles restricted by the same, compound (multi-role) uniqueness constraint, rather than two simple (single role) uniqueness constraints. Note that the above Olympic sport rankings allow *ties*. For example, both North Korea (country code = KP) and the Netherlands (country code = NE) are ranked 22nd in gymnastics.

Now suppose that the rating system is changed so that *no tied rankings are allowed*. For example, suppose some new criterion is added that enables the Netherlands to be ranked in gymnastics just ahead (rank 22) of North Korea (rank 23), as shown in the ORM model population in Figure 2.11.

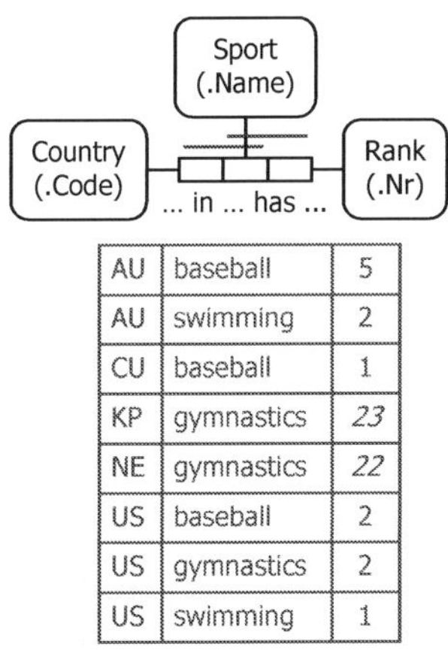

AU	baseball	5
AU	swimming	2
CU	baseball	1
KP	gymnastics	*23*
NE	gymnastics	*22*
US	baseball	2
US	gymnastics	2
US	swimming	1

Figure 2.11 A modified ORM model where no tied rankings are possible

To ensure that no ties are allowed, an additional uniqueness constraint is applied on the pair of roles hosted by Sport and Rank, so no duplicate sport-rank pairs are allowed in its fact table. This extra constraint verbalizes as follows: **For each** Sport **and** Rank, **at most one** Country in **that** Sport has **that** Rank. The ternary fact type in Figure 2.11 now has two, *overlapping uniqueness constraints*.

Once uniqueness constraints are added to an ORM schema, we can perform the second and final stage of CSDP Step 4 by performing an *arity check* on the fact types. The arity of a fact type is its number of roles. Recall that ORM schemas require all their asserted fact types to be atomic. So *if a fact type can be rephrased as a conjunction, it should be split* into smaller (lower arity) fact types. This captures the semantics in the simplest way, avoids the need for nulls, and relegates the task of grouping fact types into structures to the implementation level.

We can often use our common sense to determine whether some fact can be rephrased as a conjunction of smaller facts. However, the following *n*–1 *rule* can be used to detect many cases where a compound fact type should be split. Violation of this *n*–1 rule is a sufficient (but not necessary) condition for splittability.

- For each fact type with *n* roles (*n* > 2), its shortest uniqueness constraint must span at least *n*–1 roles.

Hence, each uniqueness constraint on a ternary (*n* = 3) fact type must span at least 2 roles. So if a ternary fact type has a simple uniqueness constraint (spanning just one role) it should be split. Recall our Figure 2.4 flight example. Suppose we modeled this using the ternary fact type Flight goes from Airport to Airport, as shown Figure 2.12(a). The uniqueness constraint spans just one role, thus violating the *n*–1 rule, so we must split the fact type as shown in Figure 2.12(b).

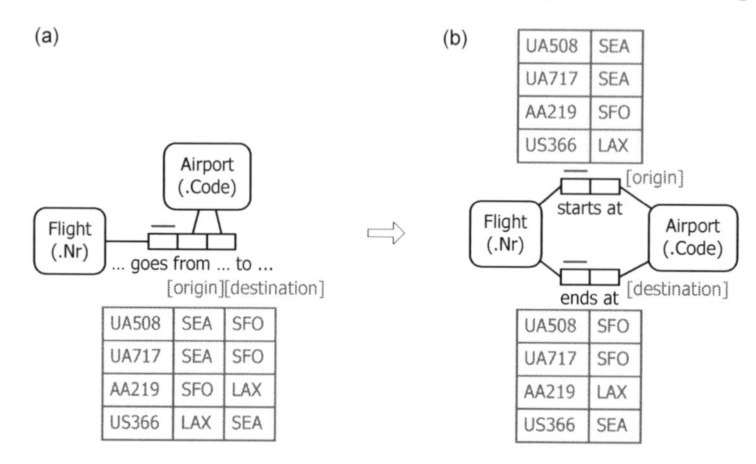

Figure 2.12 The ternary in (a) violates the *n*–1 rule, so should be split as in (b)

Table 2.5 summarizes the application of the n–1 rule for ternary (3-role), quaternary (4-role), and quinary (5-role) fact types. In practice, fact types of arity above 5 are rarely encountered in ORM models.

Table 2.5 Applying the n–1 rule for the most common n-ary fact type cases

Kind of fact type	*Arity*	*Minimum length of uniqueness constraint*
ternary	3	2
quaternary	4	3
quinary	5	4
...	...	...

Some fact types that do not violate the n–1 rule might still need to be split. For example, consider the ternary fact type Employee from Country speaks Language in Figure 2.13(a). Its uniqueness constraint spans two roles, so it does not violate the n–1 rule. Informally, we might verbalize its first fact entry as "Employee 101 from Australia speaks English". *Can this be rephrased as a conjunction of smaller facts without information loss?* Using our background knowledge, we should be able to see that it can be rephrased as the conjunction "Employee 101 comes from Australia, **and** Employee 101 speaks English". So the fact type should be split in two, as shown in Figure 2.13(b).

Another way to spot the problem with Figure 2.13(a) is to see that the role hosted by Country is *functionally dependent* on the role hosted by Employee (i.e. in this fact type, each Employee entry relates to at most one Country entry). We say that the first role *functionally determines* the second role. Though not part of the ORM notation, in Figure 2.13(a) this *functional dependency* (*FD*) is depicted as an arrow from the Employee role to the Country role.

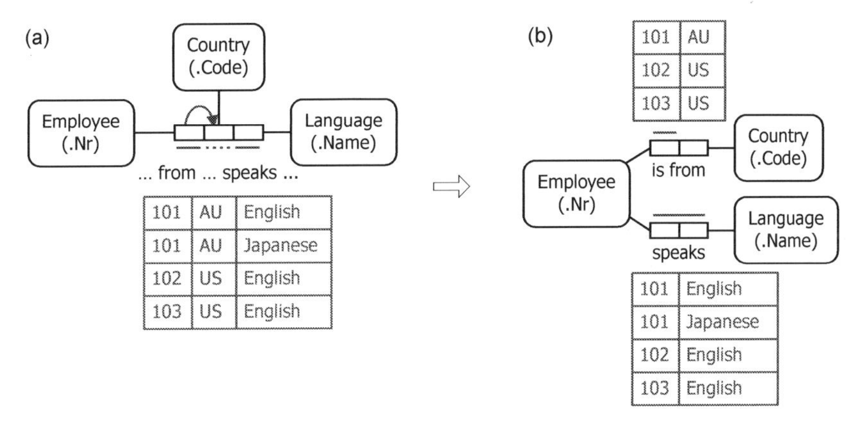

Figure 2.13 The ternary in (a) may be rephrased as a conjunction, so should be split as in (b)

In a correct ORM model, every functional dependency is implied by a uniqueness constraint, so the ORM notation does not include arrows for FDs as in Figure 2.13(a). Semantically, every functional dependency corresponds to a uniqueness constraint on a fact type, so it's best to expose it using a functional fact type such as the Employee is from Country fact type shown in Figure 2.13(b).

Another way to check for conjunctive facts is to perform a *redundancy check*. In ORM, redundancy means the *repetition of an atomic fact*. Looking at the fact table in Figure 2.13(a), we notice that the fact that employee 101 comes from Australia appears there twice, which indicates that the ternary should be split.

A uniqueness constraint that applies to one or more roles of the same fact type is said to be an *internal uniqueness constraint*, and is displayed as a bar beside the constrained roles of the fact type. All the uniqueness constraints considered so far have been internal.

A uniqueness constraint that applies to roles from different fact types is said to be an *external uniqueness constraint*. A simple example is provided by an ORM model for the report shown in Table 2.6. In this business domain, employees are primarily identified by their employee number, but the combination of their family name and extended given name is also unique. Here the term "extended given name" means a given name possibly extended by one or more initials or numbers to provide a distinct full-name for the employee. As a real example of this kind of naming convention, the US presidents known as George W. Bush and George H. W. Bush each have the same family name "Bush", but may be distinguished by adding their extended given names "George W." and "George H. W.".

Table 2.6 A report extract about employee identifiers

Employee Nr	*Family Name*	*Extended Given Name*
1001	Jones	Amanda
1002	Smith	John
1003	Smith	John T.
...	...	...

An ORM model for the Table 2.6 report (ignoring mandatory role constraints) is shown in Figure 2.14. Each of the two fact types Employee has FamilyName and Employee has ExtendedGivenName has an internal uniqueness constraint on its Employee role. The external uniqueness constraint on the roles hosted by FamilyName and ExtendedGivenName is displayed as a *circled uniqueness bar connected by dashed lines to the constrained roles*. This constraint verbalizes as follows:

For each FamilyName **and** ExtendedGivenName,

at most one Employee has **that** FamilyName **and** has **that** ExtendedGivenName.

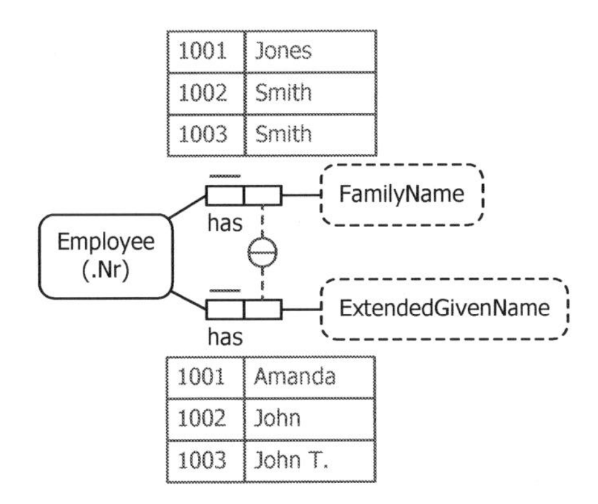

Figure 2.14 An ORM model for Table 2.6 (mandatory role constraints omitted)

In other words, each combination of family name and extended given name applies to at most one employee. In general, an external uniqueness constraint may be applied to two or more roles of different, typically binary fact types. As an example of an external uniqueness constraint involving a unary fact type, consider the report extract shown in Table 2.7. As an exercise, you may wish to model this yourself in ORM before reading on.

Table 2.7 Small extract of politician data

Politician	*Country Served*	*President?*
Barack Obama	US	✓
Joe Biden	US	✓
Joni Ernst	US	...
Pranab Mukherjee	IN	
...	...	

In this case, politicians are identified simply by their name. As usual, countries are identified by their ISO 2-character country codes—for a full list of these codes, seehttp://en.wikipedia.org/wiki/ISO 3166-1 alpha-2. The second column indicates the country served by the politician, and a check mark in the final column indicates that that politician holds the office of president. For example, the first row of data may be verbalized as the following atomic facts: the Politician named 'Barack Obama' serves the Country with country code 'US'; the Politician named 'Barack Obama' is a president.

The lack of a check mark in the final column indicates that that president is not a president. For example, the politicians Joe Biden and Joni Ernst do not hold the office of president.

Ignoring mandatory role constraints, the report may be modeled as shown in Figure 2.15. The external uniqueness constraint verbalizes as follows: **For each** Country, **at most one** Politician is a president **and** serves that Country. This is also called a *unique-where-true constraint*, because the constraint applies only where it is *true* that the politician is a president (as indicated in Table 2.7 by a check mark). For rows with no check marks (i.e. isaPresident is false), the same country (e.g. US) may be associated with many politicians (e.g. Joe Biden and Joni Ernst).

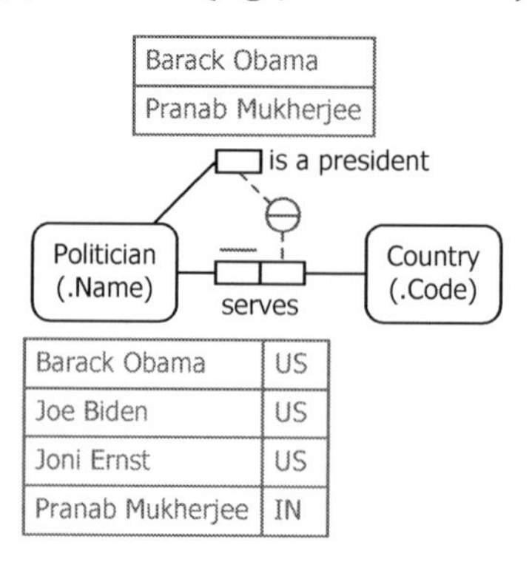

Figure 2.15 An ORM model for Table 2.7 (mandatory role constraints omitted)

2.3 CSDP Step 5

In CSDP Step 5 we add mandatory role constraints and check to see whether some fact types may be derived from others using a logical derivation rule. As discussed in the previous chapter, a *simple mandatory role constraint* applies to a single role, and is displayed as a solid dot at one end of the line that connects the role box to its object type shape. This indicates that for each state of the fact base, each instance in the population of that object type must play that role.

For example, consider the populated ORM model shown in Figure 2.16. This is an expanded version of the politician model just discussed. For each country, we record its name and whether or not it is a large country. We also make it optional whether to record a country's politicians. The role hosted by Politician in the fact type Politician serves Country has both a mandatory role constraint and a simple uniqueness constraint. Individually, these constraints verbalize as follows:

Each Politician serves **some** Country. -- simple mandatory role constraint

Each Politician serves **at most one** Country. -- simple uniqueness constraint

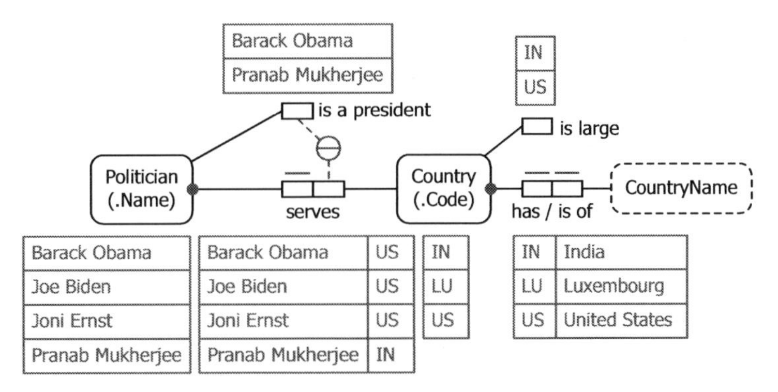

Figure 2.16 An ORM model including mandatory role constraints

The quantifier "**some**" means "**at least one**". The quantifier combination "**at least one and at most one**" may be compactly expressed as the quantifier "**exactly one**". Hence collectively, the combination of a simple mandatory role constraint and a simple uniqueness constraint on Politician's role in Politician serves Country may be expressed by the following single verbalization:

Each Politician serves **exactly one** Country. -- combined mandatory and unique

Similarly, the combination of mandatory role and uniqueness constraints on Country's role in the fact type Country has CountryName may be verbalized as: **Each** Country has **exactly one** CountryName. The NORMA tool allows you to configure such verbalizations to display in either individual or combined form, depending on your preference.

The role in each of the unary fact types Politician is a president and Country is large is *optional*, as shown by the absence of a mandatory role constraint on it. In this case, the role is *optional by nature*, as in the real world not all politicians are presidents and not all countries are large. In contrast, the role hosted by Country in the fact type Politician serves Country is *optional by choice*. In the real world, all countries are served by politicians, but in this UoD we chose to allow some countries to be recorded without also recording any of their politicians (as indicated by Luxembourg in the sample population).

In ORM, all *constraints are understood to apply to the model, not necessarily to the real world*. A role that is optional in the real world should be modeled as optional. However, a role that is mandatory in the real world may be modeled as mandatory or optional, depending on our information requirements.

A *functional role* is a role with a simple uniqueness constraint (spanning just that role). A role that is functional in the real world should be modeled as functional. However, a role that is non-functional in the real world may be modeled as functional or non-functional, depending on our information requirements. For example, the role hosted by Person in the fact types Person has Gender is functional in the real world, so should be modeled with a simple uniqueness constraint, to ensure that for each state of the fact base nobody is assigned more than one gender. In contrast, the role hosted by Person in the fact type Person has PhoneNr is typically non-functional in the real world, where a person may have more than one phone number. However, if we decide that one phone number for each person is enough to record, then we are free to model this role as functional (with a simple uniqueness constraint).

In Figure 2.16, the role hosted by CountryName in the fact type Country has CountryName is not marked as mandatory. However, if this is the only role hosted by CountryName in the global model, it is understood to be *implicitly mandatory*. This is because in ORM, top level object types are *not independent* unless explicitly declared to be independent (as indicated graphically by an exclamation mark after the object type's name). If an object type is top level (i.e. not a subtype) and is not independent, then for each state of the fact base, each instance in the population of that object type must play some elementary role.

One benefit of the implicit assumption in ORM is that it minimizes the need for the modeler to explicitly change the mandatory/optional status of roles as the model grows. For example, suppose we decide to extend our current model by recording the immediately previous name of countries that have changed their name over time (e.g. the country with country code 'MM' (Myanmar) was formerly called 'Burma'). Figure 2.17 shows an ORM model fragment for Country that includes the fact type Country has previous- CountryName. If we had previously declared the CountryName role in Figure 2.16 to be explicitly mandatory, we would now need to change its status to optional for the new version of the model.

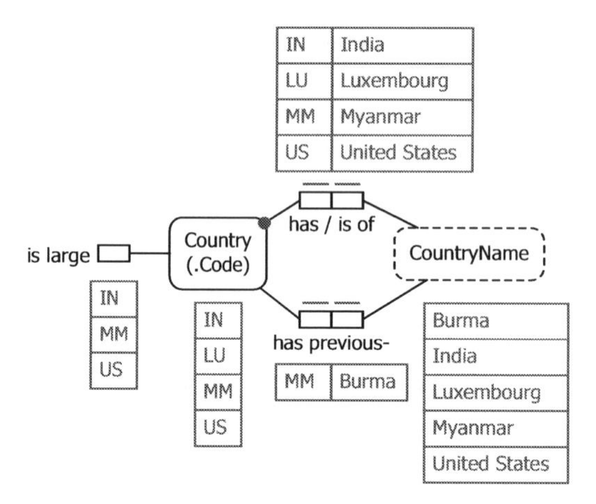

Figure 2.17 Adding another role for CountryName

Notice the use of the *hyphen* "-" in the fact type reading "Country has previous- CountryName". This improves the automated verbalization of constraints on the fact type by binding the adjective "previous" to the following object type name. For example, the uniqueness constraint on Country's role in this fact type verbalizes as "**Each** Country has **at most one** previous CountryName". Without this *hyphen binding*, this constraint verbalizes awkwardly as "**Each** Country has previous **at most one** CountryName".

Now consider the sample report extract shown in Table 2.8, which is an extended version of an earlier example. In this UoD, at least one contact detail (a phone number or e-mail address) must be recorded for each employee.

Table 2.8 A report extract about employee identifiers and contact details

Employee Nr	*Family Name*	*Extended Given Name*	*Contact Details (at least one is required)*	
			Phone Nr	*Email Address*
1001	Jones	Amanda	54371234	a.jones@gmail.com
1002	Smith	John	23451002	j.smith@live.com
1003	Smith	John T.	54371234	jt.smith@live.com
1004	Jones	John	...	...
...	...	...		

Figure 2.18 shows a populated ORM model for this report. The *circled mandatory role dot* ⊙ depicts an *inclusive-or constraint* over the roles hosted by Employee in the fact types Employee has PhoneNr and Employee has EmailAddress. This indicates the each employee must have a phone number or an email address, or both. This is also called a *disjunctive mandatory role constraint* because it applies to the logical disjunction of the two roles. This constraint verbalizes as follows: **Each** Employee has **some** PhoneNr **or** has **some** EmailAddress.

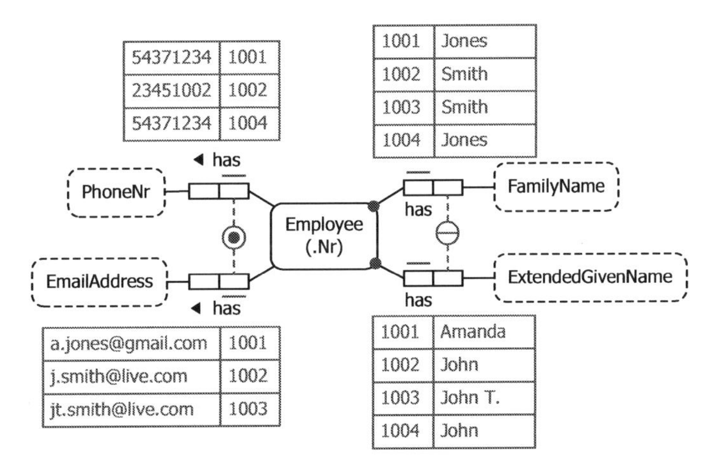

Figure 2.18 An ORM model for Table 2.8, including an inclusive-or constraint

Recall that if a top level object type that is not declared independent then each instance in the population of that object type must play some elementary role. In that case, if the object type hosts multiple elementary roles, an inclusive-or constraint is implicitly understood to apply over those roles. For example, consider the Figure 2.17 model discussed previously. If CountryName hosts no other roles in the global model, an inclusive-or constraint is implied between its two roles. As with implicit simple mandatory role constraints, it's better to leave this constraint as implied rather than declaring it unless you are absolutely sure that the constraint will still apply in any future version the model.

Now consider the report extract shown in Table 2.9, which shows the population of cities in the United States based on figures from the 2013 census. In this UoD, states are identified simply by their state code (e.g. OR for Oregon, and ME for Maine), but cities are identified by the combination of their city name and state, e.g. (Portland, ME) and (Portland, OR). This is an example of a *composite reference scheme* (i.e. a reference scheme with two or more components).

Table 2.9 Small extract of population data for US cities

City		
Name	*State*	*Population*
Eugene	OR	159,190
Portland	ME	66, 318
Portland	OR	609, 456
...	...	...

Figure 2.19 shows an ORM model for this example. For simplicity, I've used geometric shapes to denote the city entries in the reference fact types. In the elementary fact type table, cities are denoted by value pairs, e.g. (Eugene, OR). The *double uniqueness bar* in the external uniqueness constraint indicates that this provides the *preferred reference scheme* for City.

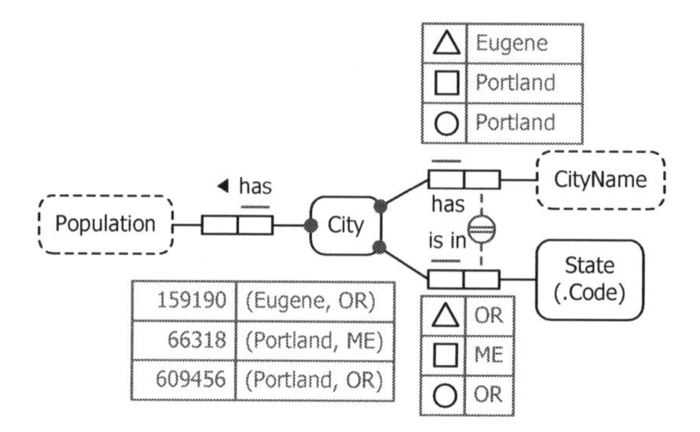

Figure 2.19 An ORM model for Table 2.9, including a composite reference scheme

This preferred external uniqueness constraint verbalizes as shown below. The first sentence verbalizes the basic external uniqueness constraint. The second sentence indicates that this constraint underpins the preferred reference scheme for City. Here City is said to be a *co-referenced object type*[12] because its preferred reference scheme is composite.

For each CityName **and** State,

at most one City has **that** CityName **and** is in **that** State.

This association with CityName, State **provides the preferred identification scheme for** City.

The final stage of CSDP Step 5 is to *check for logical derivations*. As an example, the ORM model in Figure 2.20 includes the derived fact type Politician is president of Country with its derivation rule shown at the bottom. This rule is classified as a *logical derivation rule* since it derives facts simply by applying logical operators (e.g. **and**) to other facts, rather than applying arithmetic operators/functions.

In the compact rule notation shown in Figure 2.20, "**iff**" denotes the logical equivalence operator "**if and only if**", and object variables in the head of the rule (here Politician and Country) are understood to be implicitly universally quantified. In expanded form, the derivation rule may be read as follows:

For each Politician **and** Country,

that Politician is president of **that** Country

if and only if

that Politician is a president **and** serves **that** Country.

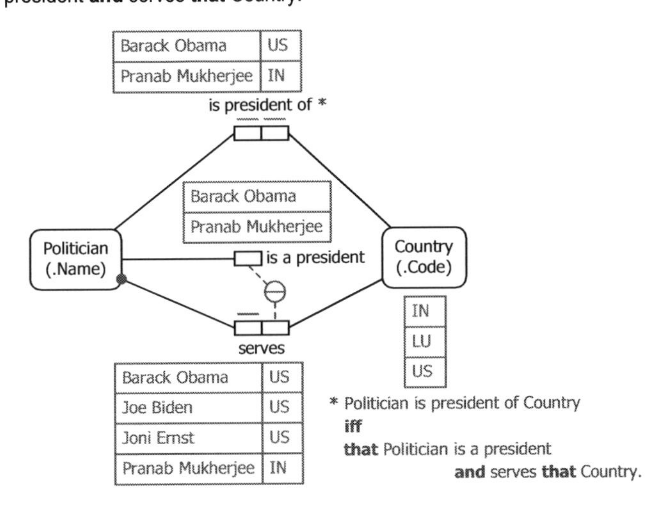

Figure 2.20 Politician is president of Country is a logically derived fact type

---

12 Here, "coreference" means reference by multiple components combined, rather than individually (as the term "coreference" is sometimes used in linguistics).

Constraints on derived fact types are typically implied by the combination of their derivation rule and constraints on the fact types used to derive it. For example, the uniqueness constraint on Politician's role in Politician is president of Country is implied by the derivation rule and the uniqueness constraint on Politician serves Country. The uniqueness constraint on Country's role in Politician is president of Country is implied by the derivation rule and the external uniqueness constraint. To emphasize that a constraint is derived rather than asserted, it may be colored green instead of the usual violet color, as shown in Figure 2.20.

2.4 Objectification

Consider the small extract of academic records shown in Table 2.10. The first two columns record which students enrolled in what courses. The third column records the course grades obtained by students, if known. Here, the question mark "?" indicates that a grade for the enrolment on that row is *unknown* (e.g. maybe the student has yet to sit the final exam for that course). In a relational database this entry corresponds to a *null* item (sometimes called a null value).

There are many correct ways to model this example. Informally, we might verbalize the first row of data as the ternary fact: Student 101 obtained an A for CS100. However, this kind of phasing won't work in ORM for the second row, because ORM requires all asserted facts to be atomic, so nulls aren't allowed. The second row may be informally verbalized simply as the binary fact: Student 101 enrolled in CS200.

Looking back at the first row, we see that it can be informally rephrased in two sentences as follows: Student 101 enrolled in CS100; *that enrolment* resulted in an A grade. Here, the second sentence uses a noun phrase ("that enrolment") to relate back to the verb phrase in the first sentence. Linguistically, this is an example of *nominalization*. More precisely, it is *situational nominalization*, because "that enrolment" refers to a situation or state of affairs, rather than a proposition.

Table 2.10 Small extract of academic records

Student Nr	*Course*	*Grade*
101	CS100	A
101	CS200	?
102	CS100	A
102	MA101	B
...	...	...

If the noun phrase referred instead to a proposition, we would instead have propositional nominalization, as demonstrated by the second sentence following: Student 101 enrolled in CS100; It's true *that student 101 enrolled in CS100*. Propositions are truth bearers (they are simply true or false). In contrast, situations or states of affairs (e.g. events) are truth makers (e.g. an enrolment can result in a grade, but a proposition cannot), and hence are treated as objects in ORM. In ORM, nominalization is always situational, and is known as *objectification*.

If we think about an enrolment first in terms of a binary relationship, and then as an object that results in a grade, we may model Table 2.10 as shown in Figure 2.21. The object type Enrolment is depicted as a soft rectangle enclosing the predicate shape for the fact type Student enrolled in Course, indicating that an enrolment *objectifies* an enrolment relationship. The exclamation mark appended to Enrolment marks it as an *independent* object type (so we can know about an enrolment without knowing the grade it results in). This is fairly typical for objectified relationships. It's also fairly typical for objectified relationships to have spanning uniqueness constraints, as in Figure 2.21. If you think about grades directly as letter grades, you can model Grade as a value type as shown. If you instead think of grades as entities referenced by letter values, use an entity type, e.g. Grade(.Letter).

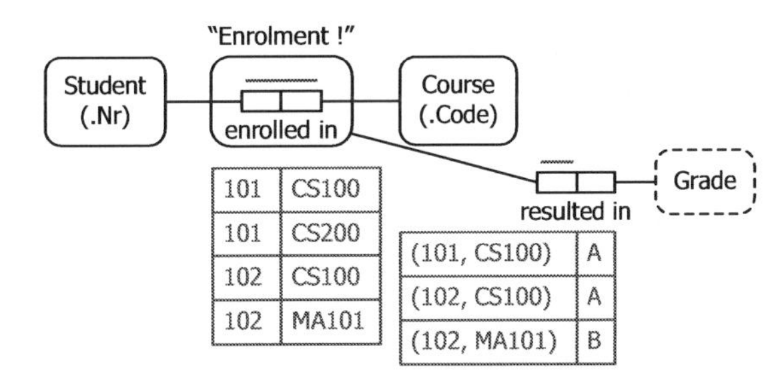

Figure 2.21 Student enrolled in Course is objectified as Enrolment

The envelope notation for objectification shown in Figure 2.21 is an abbreviation for the explicit notation shown in Figure 2.22. Here, Enrolment is a coreferenced entity type with its reference predicates displayed using dashed lines.

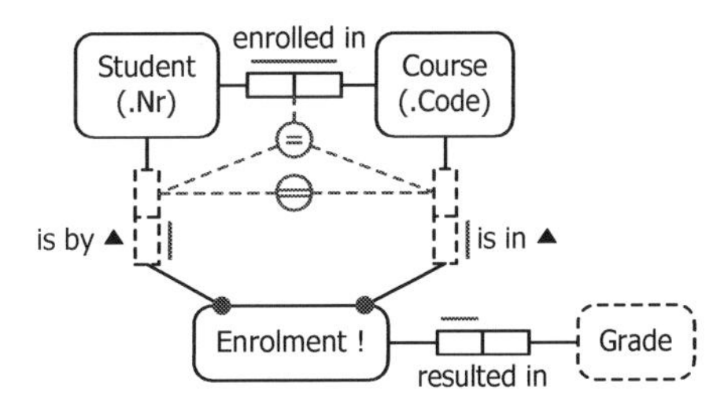

Figure 2.22 Expanded version of Figure 2.21 schema, showing link predicates

The reference predicates in Enrolment is by Student and Enrolment is in Course are called *link predicates*, because they link the objectification object type to the object types used to reference it. Objects are not relationships, so instances of the Enrolment object type are not identical to instances of the Student enrolled in Course fact type. However, the enrolment objects are in *one-to-one correspondence* with the facts they objectify. The 1:1 correspondence is enforced by the *equality constraint* depicted by a circled equals sign "=" connecting the enrolment relationship to the roles hosted by Student and Course in the link predicates. Equality constraints are discussed in CSDP Step 6.

The envelope notation for objectification is more compact and convenient than the explicit notation, so is used by default for objectified fact types in the NORMA tool. However, NORMA does allow you to display the expanded version as well if you so wish.

To simplify things, I've left it until now to discuss objectification. However, verbalizing facts using objectification is really an activity that belongs to CSDP Step 1. Note that objectification is used only if you wish to talk about some aspect of the UoD in terms of both a relationship and an object. If you don't want to talk about that aspect using a relationship, you can simply use a coreferenced object type by itself, as shown in Figure 2.23. This model would be the natural result of informally verbalizing the first row of Table 2.10 as follows: "There is an enrolment by student 101 in course CS100; that enrolment resulted in an A grade". In this case, enrolments are always talked about as objects, not relationships.

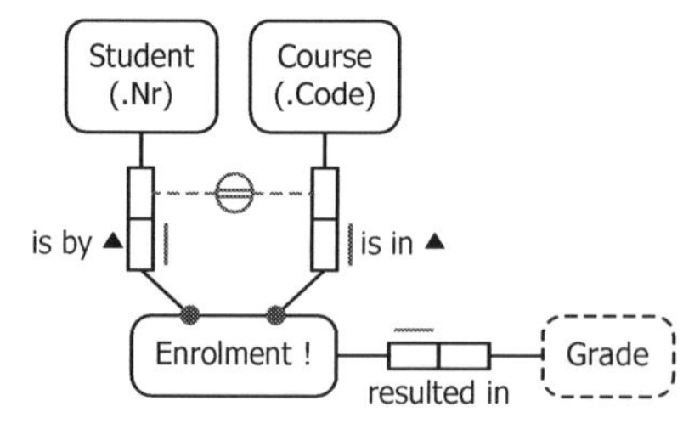

Figure 2.23 An ORM schema for Table 2.10 that does not use objectification

Often there is more than one correct way to model the same UoD. Yet another alternative for modeling Table 2.10 would be to use the binary fact type Student enrolled in Course for enrolments with no grades, and use the ternary fact type Student in Course obtained Grade for enrolments with known grades. If you model things this way, you also need to specify a subset constraint from the binary fact type to the Student-Course role pair in the ternary fact type. Subset constraints are discussed as part of CSDP Step 6.

In the examples just discussed, at most one grade may be recorded for a student in a course. If instead we allow a student to enroll multiple times in the same course, and we wish to be able to record a grade result for each enrolment occurrence, we need to distinguish between different enrolments of the same student in the same course. For example, we could include the date of each enrolment, or the number of times enrolled so far by the student in the course. The model in Figure 2.24 incorporates the date within the objectification.

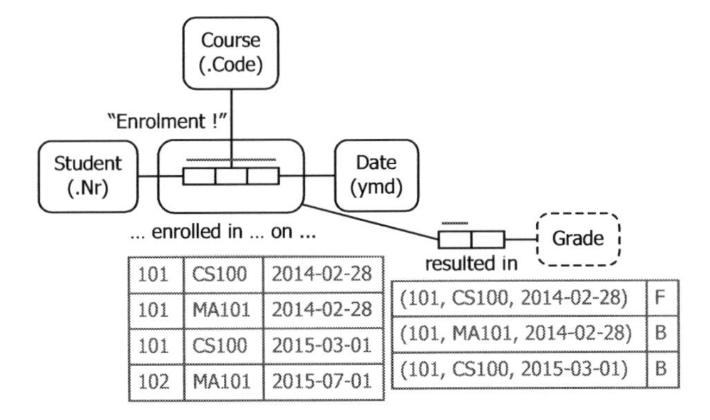

Figure 2.24 Enrolments now include a date in their identification scheme

Without using objectification, enrolments may be modeled using a coreferenced entity type, as shown in Figure 2.25(a). If we wish to avoid a three-part identifier as the preferred reference scheme for enrolments, we can introduce an artificial, simple identifier such as an enrolment number, as shown in Figure 2.25(b). Here, the three-part identifier is still maintained as a secondary reference scheme. The external uniqueness constraint now displays with a single bar, indicating it is not used for the primary reference scheme.

For a detailed discussion on modeling temporal aspects of information systems, see section 10.3 of Halpin & Morgan (2008).

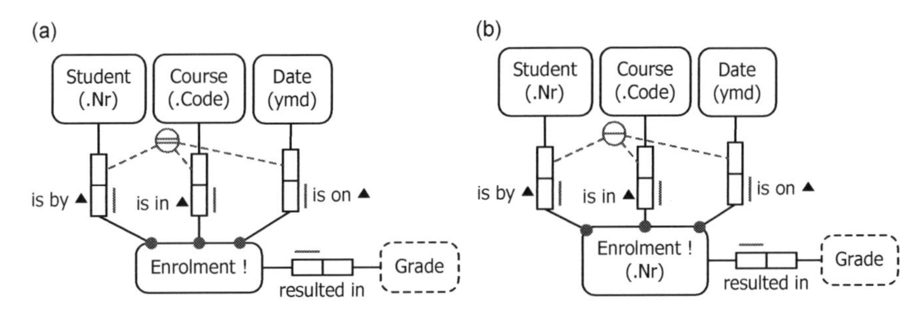

Figure 2.25 Modeling enrolments without using objectification

2.5 NORMA Lab 2

Figure 2.26 shows an ORM schema that illustrates most aspects of the ORM graphical notation discussed in this chapter. This diagram was drawn using the ORM2 stencil for Microsoft Visio, but for this lab we'll see how to enter this schema in the NORMA tool.

Note the *shadows* around the Sport and Rank object type shapes. These indicate that the shape appears multiple times in the diagram. The ability to duplicate shapes on a diagram is useful for avoiding line crossings. Although line crossings are allowed, they tend to make the diagram appear cluttered, so are best avoided for aesthetic reasons.

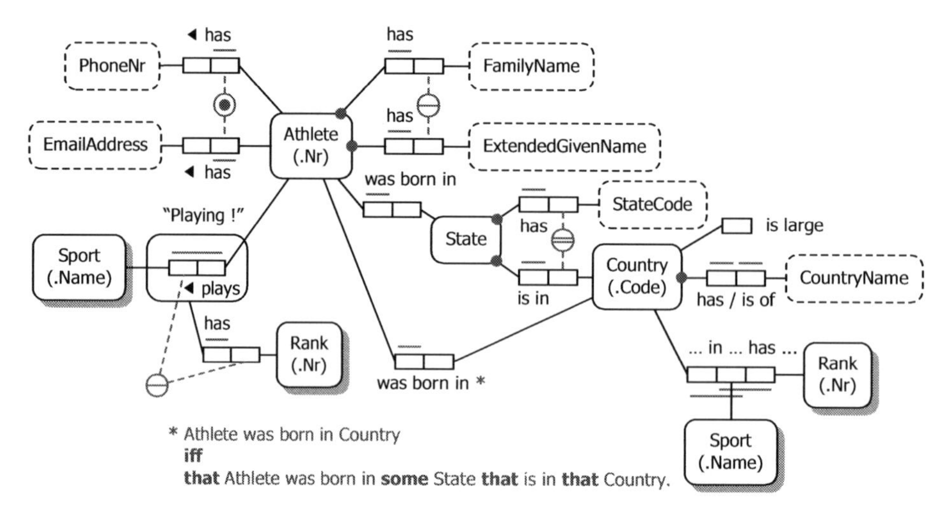

Figure 2.26 A Visio diagram of the ORM schema to be entered in NORMA

If needed, please review the NORMA Lab 1 for the basics on the NORMA tool. Now open Visual Studio, press File > New > File to open the New File dialog. Then select General > Object-Role Modeling File and press Open. In the Fact Editor, type "Athlete(.Nr) has FamilyName()" and press Ctrl+Enter to have the fact type drawn on screen.

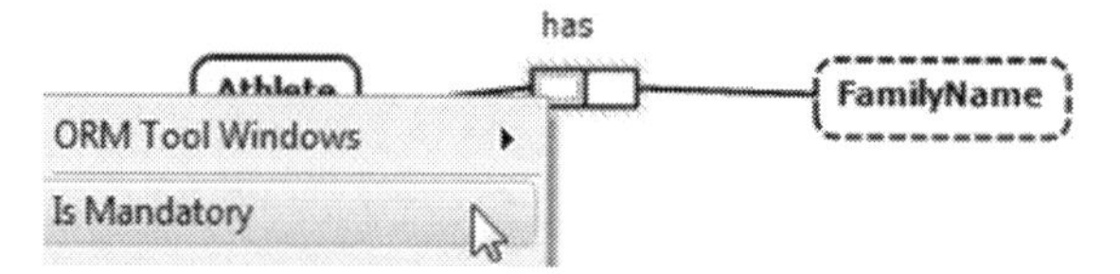

To declare Athlete's role in that fact type *mandatory*, right-click that role and select IsMandatory from its context menu. A mandatory role dot now appears.

Now right-click the same role, and select Add Uniqueness Constraint. A uniqueness constraint bar now appears.

Select FamilyName and set its DataType property to Text:Variable Length with a maximum length of 30 characters. Select and move predicate text and shapes as desired to lay them out in your preferred position.

Select Athlete to display Athlete(.Nr) in the Fact Editor, then append the rest of the fact type reading " has ExtendedGivenName()" and press Ctrl+Enter. Right-click its first role and select isMandatory, then right-click the role again and select Add Uniqueness Constraint. Select ExtendedGivenName and set its DataType property to Text:Variable Length with a maximum length of 30 characters.

Now select the External Uniqueness Constraint shape in the Toolbox, and drag it to a position near the FamilyName and ExtendedGivenName roles.

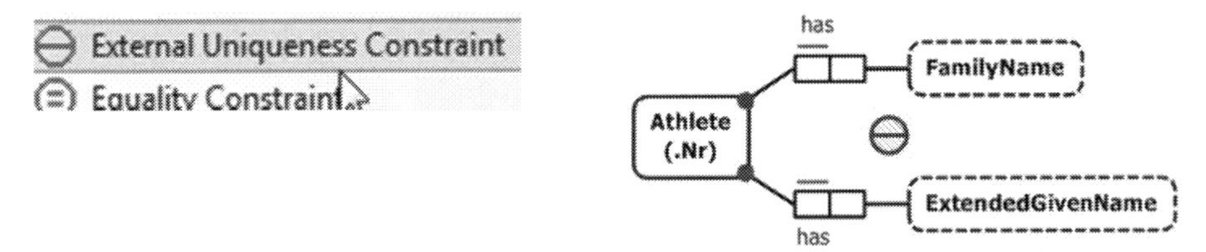

Double-click the constraint shape. A tool tip on how to add the constraint appears. Click FamilyName's role. A "1" appears in the role box indicating it is the first role in the constraint's argument. Click ExtendedGivenName's role. A "2" appears in its role box indicating it is the second role in the constraint's argument. Double-click to commit the constraint.

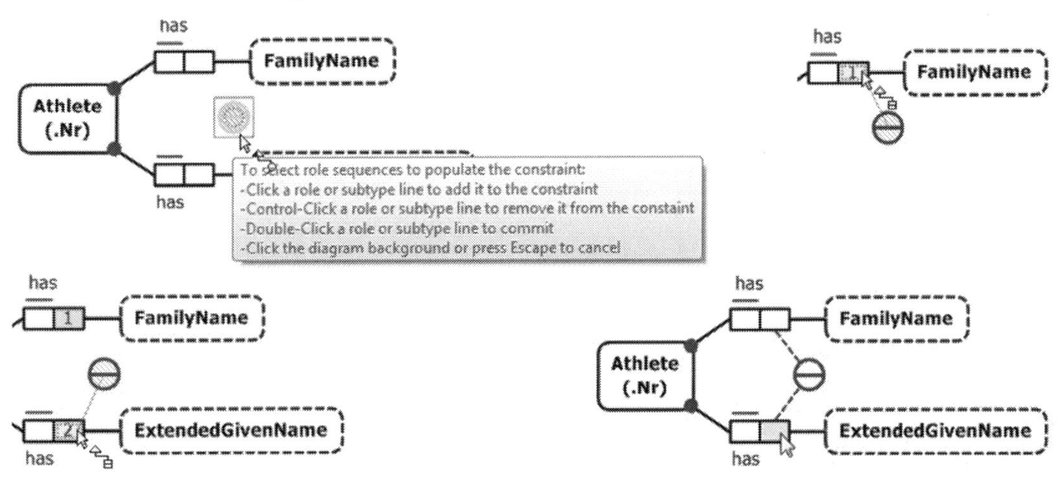

Now enter the fact type Athlete has PhoneNr() in the Fact Editor, right-click its Athlete role and select Add Uniqueness Constraint, then select PhoneNr and set its DataType to Text: Variable Length with a length of 10 characters. The automated layout of this fact type will look something like that shown below.

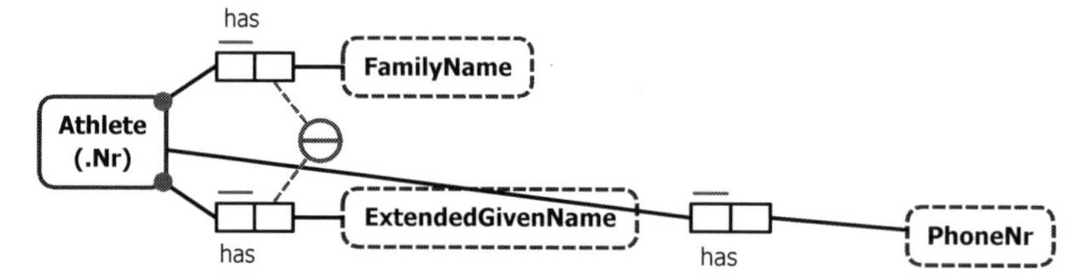

Drag the PhoneNr and predicate shapes to the left of the Athlete shape, then right-click the predicate shape and select Orientation > Reverse Role Order from its context menu. The predicate shape now flips its direction, and a left-arrow-tip is added to the predicate reading to indicate that it should be read from right to left.

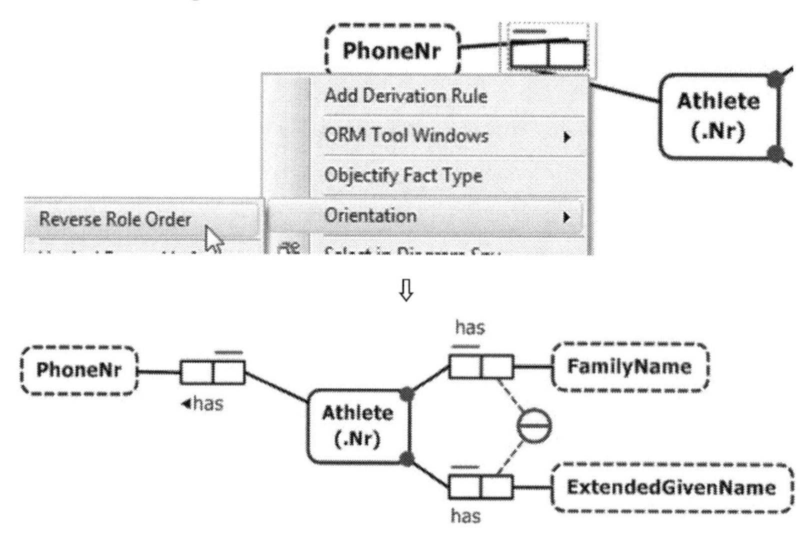

Similarly, add the fact type Athlete has EmailAddress(), add a uniqueness constraint to its Athlete role, lay it out to the left of Athlete as shown below, and set the datatype for EmailAddress to Text: Variable Length with a length of 30 characters.

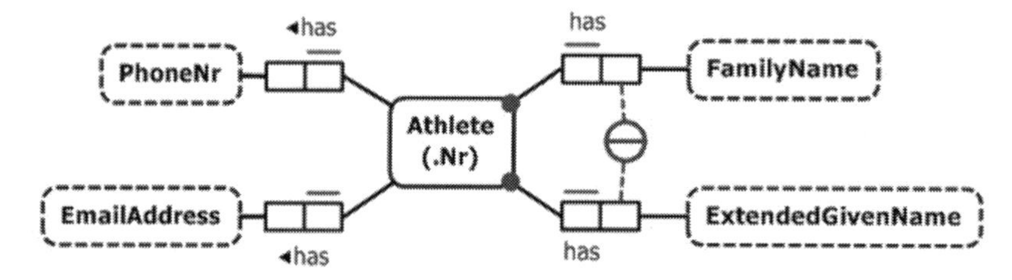

Drag the Inclusive Or Constraint shape from the Toolbox to position it between Athlete's roles in the fact types just added.

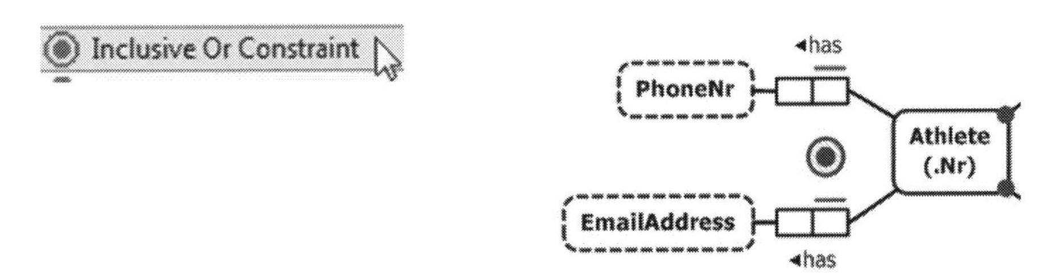

Double-click the constraint shape, select Athlete's role in Athlete has PhoneNr, then select Athlete's role in Athlete has EmailAddress, then double-click to commit the constraint. Make sure that the role position number (1 or 2) is displayed at the time that you click or double-click the role. The inclusive-or constraint is now displayed.

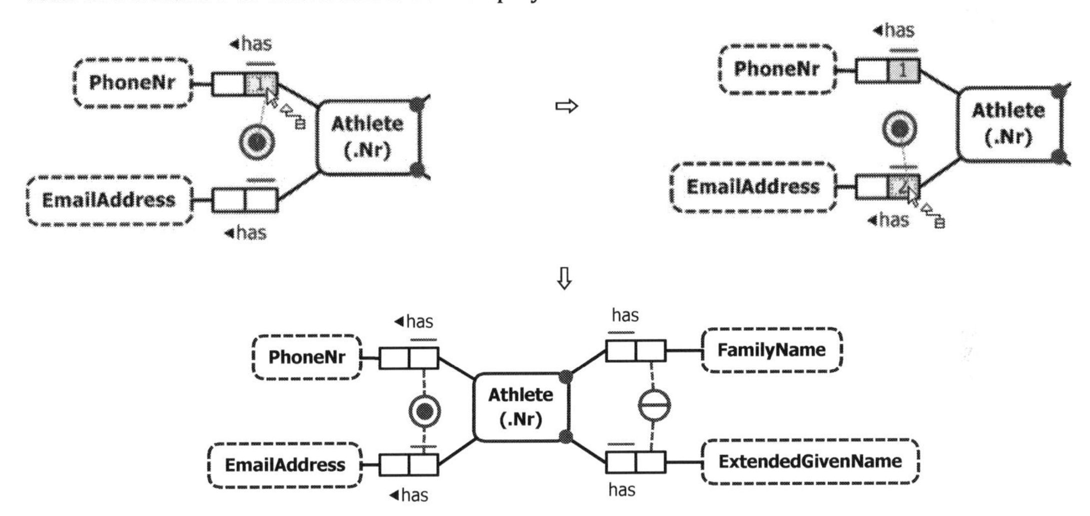

If you select all of the diagram, its full verbalization is displayed in the Verbalization Browser. A representative selection of this verbalization is shown below. Object types with predefined reference modes have predefined data types. For example, by default Athlete(.Nr) has Numeric: Signed Integer for its data type. You can change the data type for any object type by selecting the type and editing its data type setting in the Properties window.

Athlete **is an entity type.**
Reference Scheme: Athlete has Athlete_Nr.
Reference Mode: .Nr.
Data Type: Numeric: Signed Integer.

FamilyName **is a value type.**
  Data Type: Text: Variable Length (30).

ExtendedGivenName **is a value type.**
  Data Type: Text: Variable Length (30).

PhoneNr **is a value type.**
  Data Type: Text: Variable Length (10).

EmailAddress **is a value type.**
  Data Type: Text: Variable Length (30).

Fact Types:

Athlete has FamilyName.
  Each Athlete has **exactly one** FamilyName.
  It is possible that more than one Athlete has **the same** FamilyName.

Athlete has ExtendedGivenName.
  Each Athlete has **exactly one** ExtendedGivenName.
  It is possible that more than one Athlete has **the same** ExtendedGivenName.

Athlete has PhoneNr.
  Each Athlete has **at most one** PhoneNr.
  It is possible that more than one Athlete has **the same** PhoneNr.

Athlete has EmailAddress.
  Each Athlete has **at most one** EmailAddress.
  It is possible that more than one Athlete has **the same** EmailAddress.

For each FamilyName **and** ExtendedGivenName,
  at most one Athlete has **that** FamilyName **and** has **that** ExtendedGivenName.

Each Athlete has **some** PhoneNr **or** has **some** EmailAddress.

Before going any further, let's save the work we've done so far by pressing the Save icon in the main menu to open the Save File As dialog, then entering Lab2 as the FileName, and pressing the Save button.

Select Athlete to make Athlete(.Nr) appear in the Fact Editor, then complete the entry of the fact type reading Athete(.Nr) was born in State. In the Document Window, the entity type State appears in an error state because it has no reference scheme. Now select State, and in the Fact Editor enter the fact type readings State has StateCode() and State is in Country(.Code). Then add the simple uniqueness and mandatory role constraints in Figure 2.26 to these fact types in the usual way by right-clicking the role and selecting Add Uniqueness Constraint or IsMandatory as needed.

Adjust the layout of the shapes similar to that shown in Figure 2.26 by selecting and dragging, and by aligning selected shapes using the Layout Toolbar (if this is not shown, choose

View > Toolbars > Layout from the main menu). For example, the Align Middles layout option shown opposite aligns selected shapes horizontally.

At this stage, your diagram should look something like the diagram shown below.

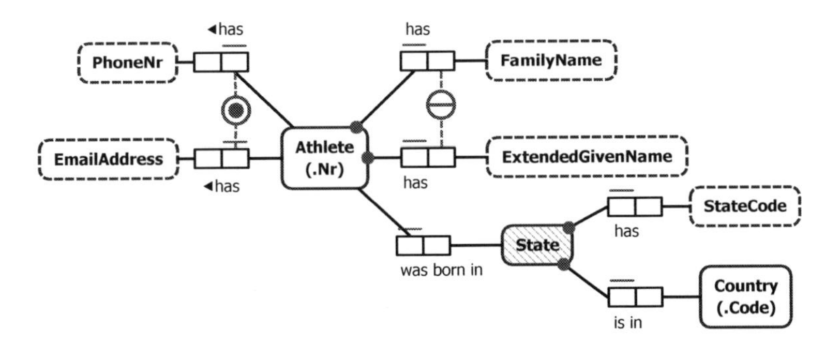

Now drag the External Uniqueness Constraint shape from the Toolbox to position it as shown below, then click the roles hosted by StateCode and Country and double-click to commit the constraint. Now select the constraint, and in the Properties Window double-click its IsPreferredIdentifier property to toggle its value from False to True.

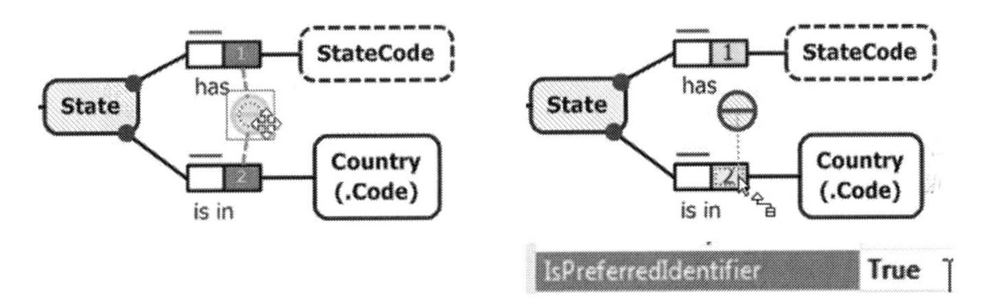

The external uniqueness constraint now displays with a double bar indicating it provides the preferred reference scheme for State. Since State is now properly identified, the red hashing fill on the State shape indicating an error is removed.

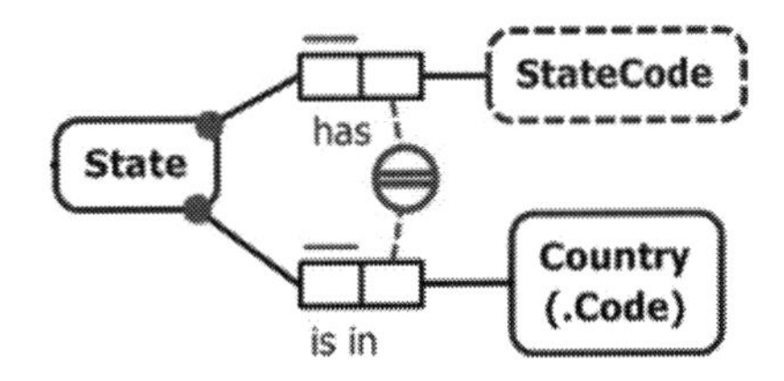

Select Country and in the Fact Editor enter the fact type readings Country is large and Country has/is of CountryName(). Then add mandatory role and uniqueness constraints in the usual way to obtain the schema fragment shown opposite.

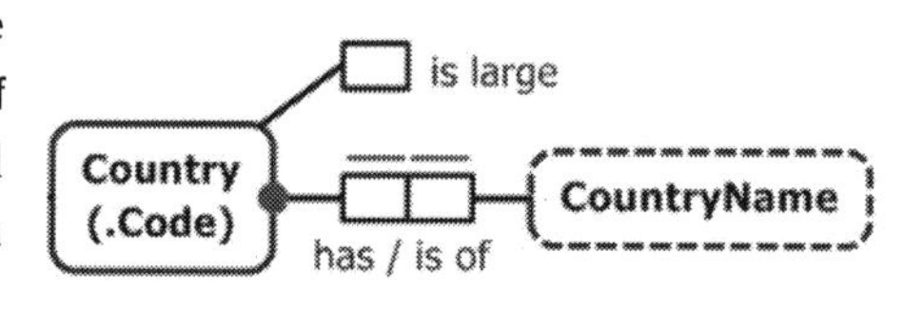

Select Country and enter the fact type reading Country(.Code) in Sport(.Name) has Rank(.Nr) in the Fact Editor. Now *hold the Shift key down* as you click the roles hosted by Country and Sport in this fact type, then right-click and select Add Uniqueness Constraint from the context menu. This adds a composite uniqueness constraint over those roles.

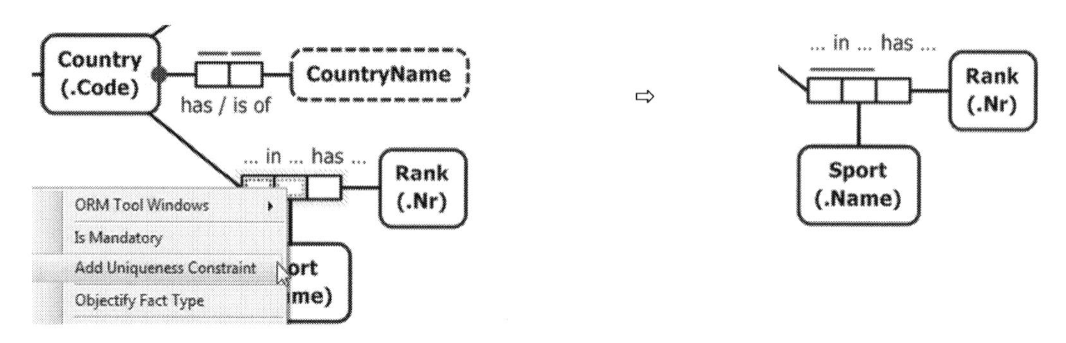

Similarly, add a composite uniqueness constraint to the roles hosted by Sport and Rank in this fact type. The two overlapping uniqueness constraints are now displayed on the ternary fact type, as shown opposite.

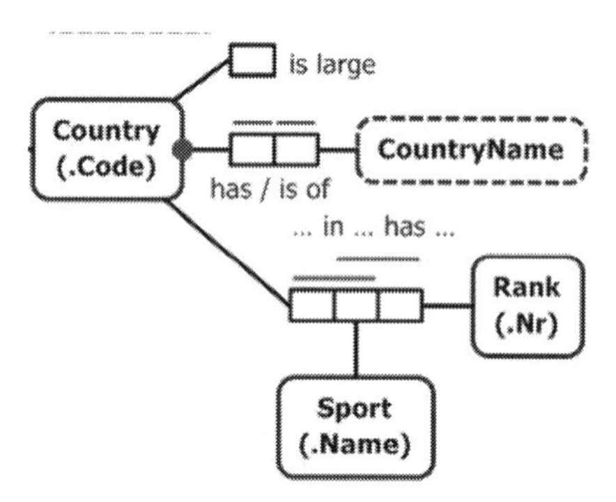

Select the Sport shape and *hold the Ctrl key down* as you *drag* it to a position on the lower right of the diagram as shown below. An *object type shadow* now appears around both instances of the Sport shape indicating that it is *displayed multiple times* in the schema.

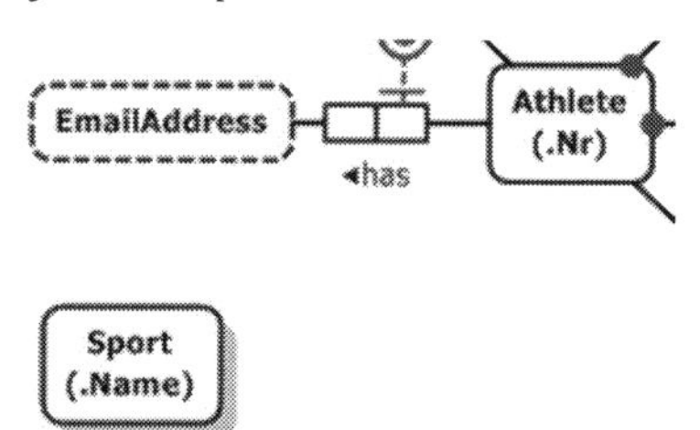

Hold the shift key down as you select Athlete then Sport, to make both their terms appear in the Fact Editor. Place the cursor between them, type " plays " and press Ctrl+Enter to add the fact type Athlete plays Sport to the model.

Move the plays predicate shape to the position shown below, then right-click the predicate shape and choose Orientation > Reverse Role Order from its context menu.

Hold the shift-key down as you select both roles of the predicate, then right-click and choose Add Uniqueness Constraint. A uniqueness bar now appears over the roles. Right-click the fact type and choose Objectify Fact Type from its context menu.

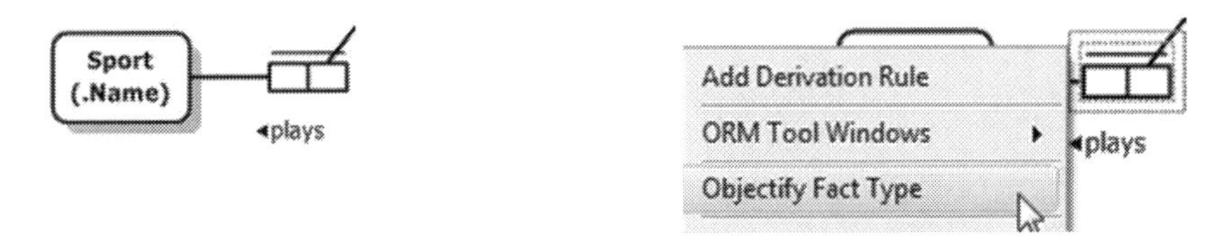

The objectifying entity type now appears with the name "AthletePlaysSport" as shown. Select the fact type shape and edit its Name property to Playing in the Properties Window and press Enter. The entries in the Name property and the two properties below it are now updated to Playing, and this shorter name now appears on the diagram. Alternatively, you could have selected "AthletePlaysSport" on the diagram and updated its Name property to Playing.

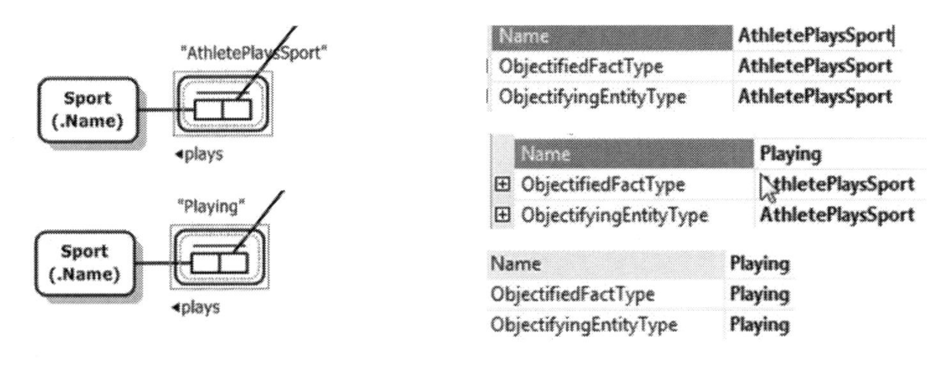

With the fact type shape still selected, double-click its IsIndependent property to toggle its value from False to True. An exclamation mark now appears on the diagram after the name of the entity type to indicate that it is an independent object type (in this UoD, we can know that an athlete plays a given sport without knowing anything else about that playing (e.g. the athlete's rank in that sport).

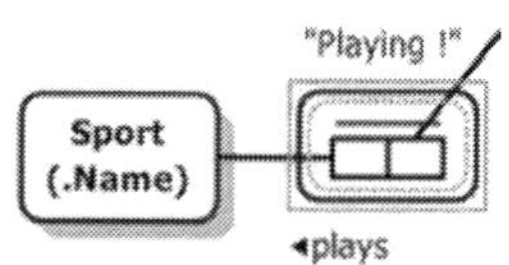

Select the text "Playing !" on the diagram to display Playing in the Fact Editor (don't select the fact type shape, as that would instead display the reading of the fact type that is objectified). Now append " has Rank" and press Ctrl+Enter to enter the Playing has Rank fact type. There is no need to append "(.Nr)" to Rank, as this entity type was already in the model.

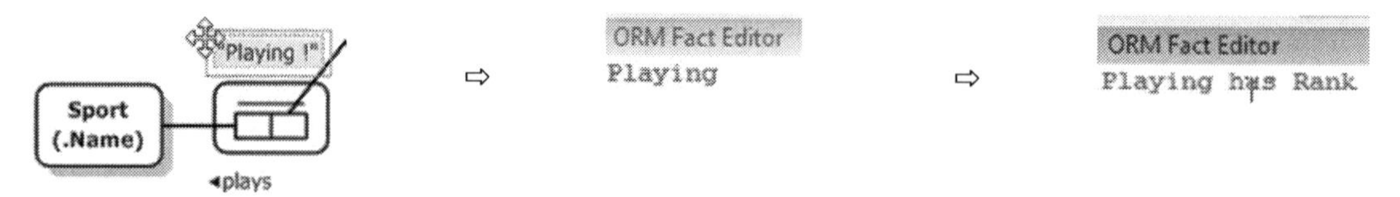

The auto-layout of the Playing has Rank fact type is messy, because the predicate shape is connected to the Rank shape at the right of the diagram.

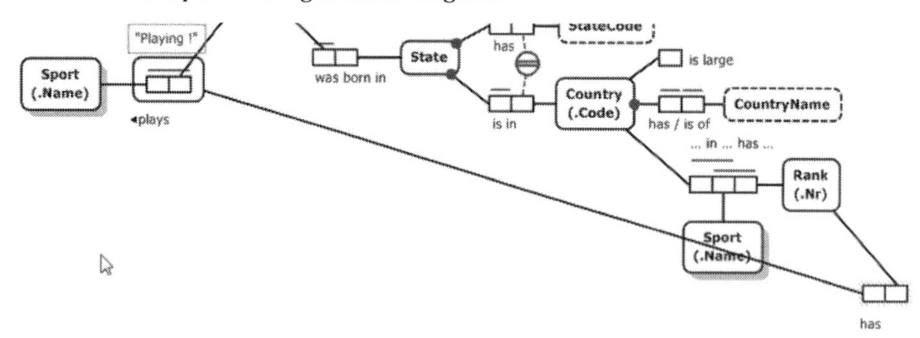

Select Rank and *Control drag* (hold the Ctrl key as you drag) it close to Playing, as shown below. Then drag the "has" predicate shape near it as shown below. The predicate now connects to the nearest Rank shape as shown. Both Rank shapes now display with a shadow indicating duplicated display.

Right-click the left role of the predicate and choose Add Uniqueness Constraint.

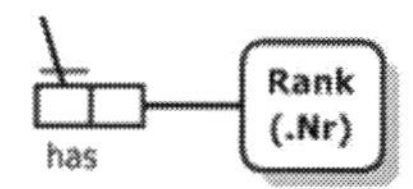

Drag the External Uniqueness Constraint shape from the Toolbox to position it as shown below. Double-click the constraint, then click the role hosted by Sport and then click the role hosted by Rank and then double-click to commit the constraint.

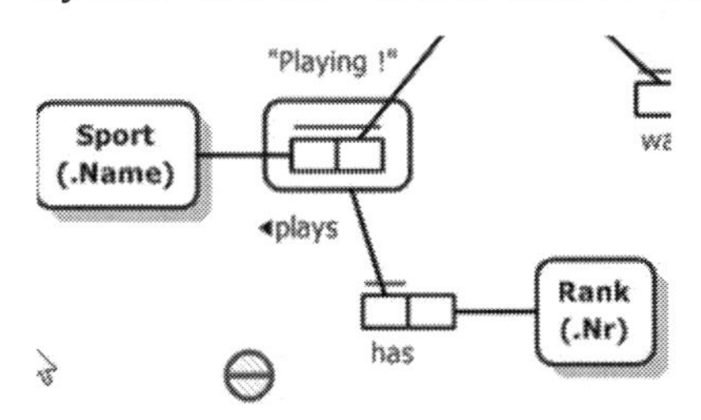

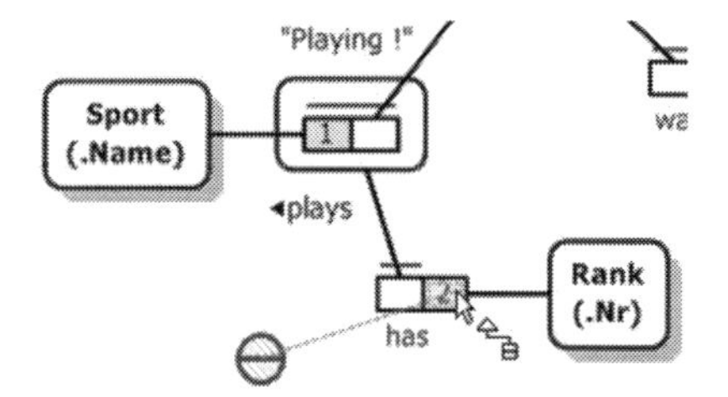

Select the external uniqueness constraint shape and view its verbalization in the ORM Verbalization Browser as shown below. As each Playing is by only one athlete, this constraint ensures that no ties in rank are allowed for a given sport.

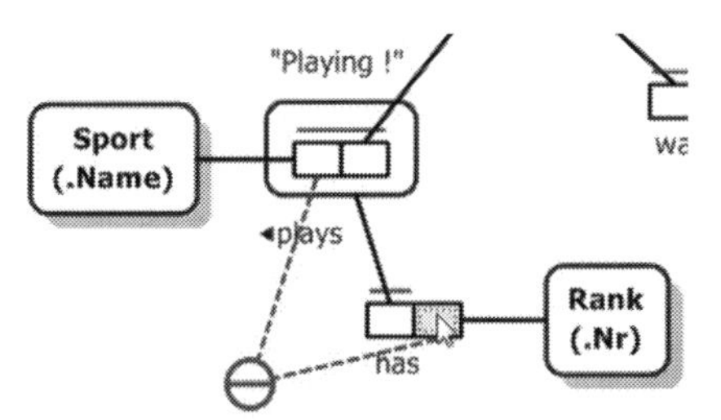

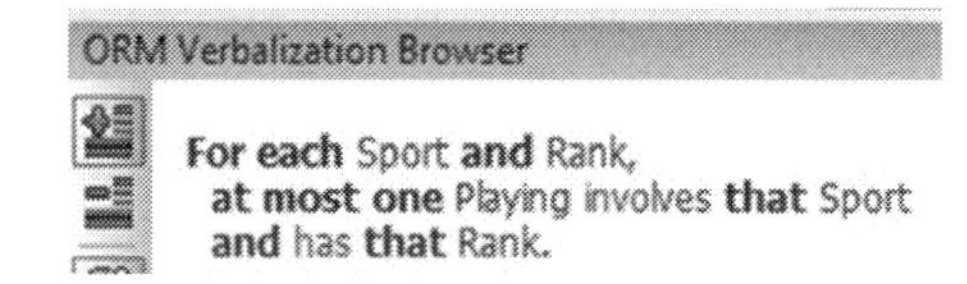

We have now entered all the object types, but have not set the data types for some of them. The quickest way to ensure all the data types are set is to check that each value type listed in the ORM Model Browser has its data type properties correctly set in the Properties Window.

If the ORM Model Browser is not already visible, open it by right-clicking an empty space in the Document Window and selecting ORM Tool Windows > ORM Model Browser. Expand the Object Types section by clicking its expand button ("+"). The expand button changes to a contract button ("–"), and the object type list appears as shown opposite. Each value type is displayed with a dashed line border, and should have its data type (including length where relevant) set correctly.

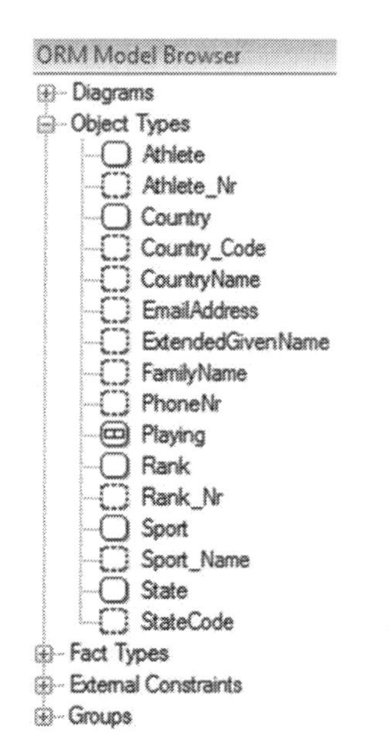

Click each value type in the list, and where needed edit its data type properties in the Properties Window as now discussed. Set the data type for Country_Code to Text: Fixed Length, with length 2. Set the data type for CountryName to Text: Variable Length, with length 30. Set the data type for Rank_Nr to Numeric: Unsigned Small Integer. Set the data type for Sport_Name to Text: Fixed Length, with length 20. Set the data type for StateCode to Text: Fixed Length, with length 2.

On the diagram, hold the shift down as you select Athlete then Country to have their terms appear in the Fact Editor. Enter the predicate reading " was born in " between them, and press Ctrl+Enter to add the fact type Athlete was born in Country. Right-click Athlete's role in this fact type and choose from the context menu.

Now select the fact type, and in the Properties Window press the down-arrow icon at the right of its DerivationNote property, type "* Athlete was born in Country" then press Ctrl+Enter to move to the next line. Then type " iff" and press Ctrl+Enter to move to the next line. Then type " that Athlete was born in some State" and press Ctrl+Enter to move to the next line. Then type "   that is in that Country." and press Enter to enter the derivation note

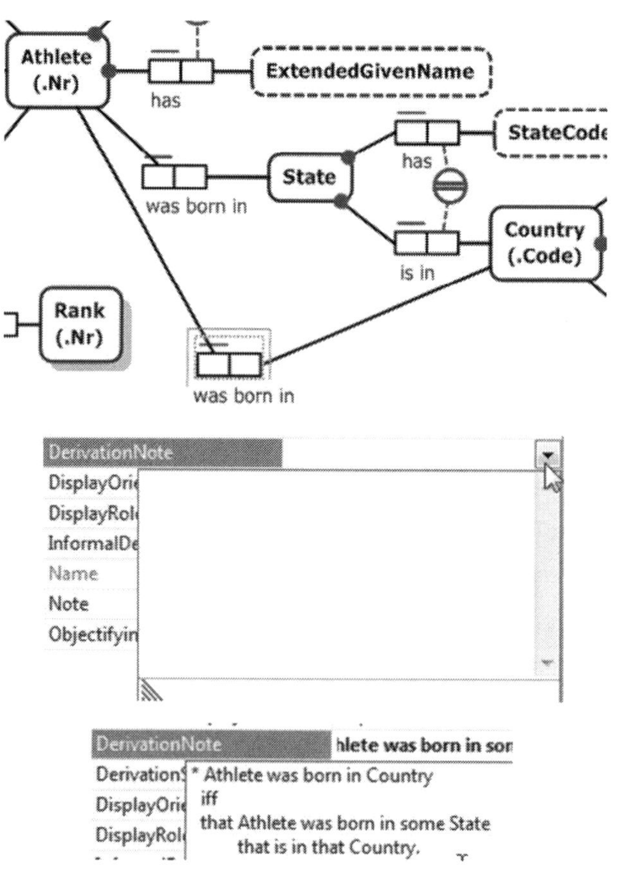

An asterisk appears after the predicate reading on the diagram indicating that the fact type is derived. Select the fact type and look in the ORM Verbalization Browser. The derivation note is included in the verbalization.

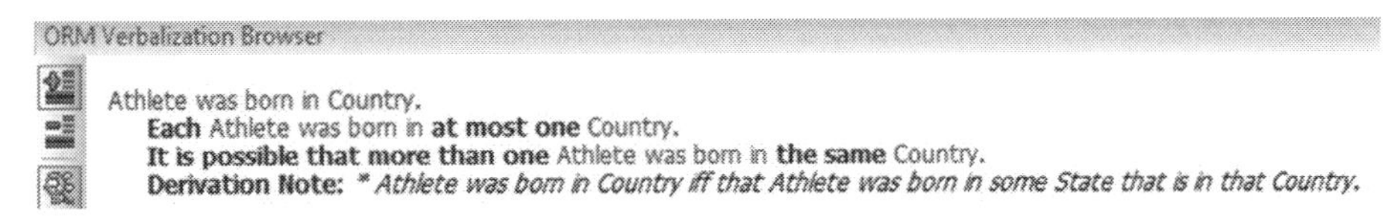

If you wish to have the derivation rule displayed with the diagram, drag a *Model Note* shape from the Toolbox to place it below the derived fact type. Then select the derived fact type, open its Derivation Note property, select all of its text and press Ctrl+C to copy it to the clipboard. Then select the Model Note shape, press Ctrl+V to paste the clipboard text into it, and press Enter. The derivation rule now appears in the Model Note. If you wish to connect the model note to the derived fact type shape, drag a Model Note Connector shape from the Toolbox, then drag to connect it to the fact type shape. A dotted line connector now appears, as shown below.

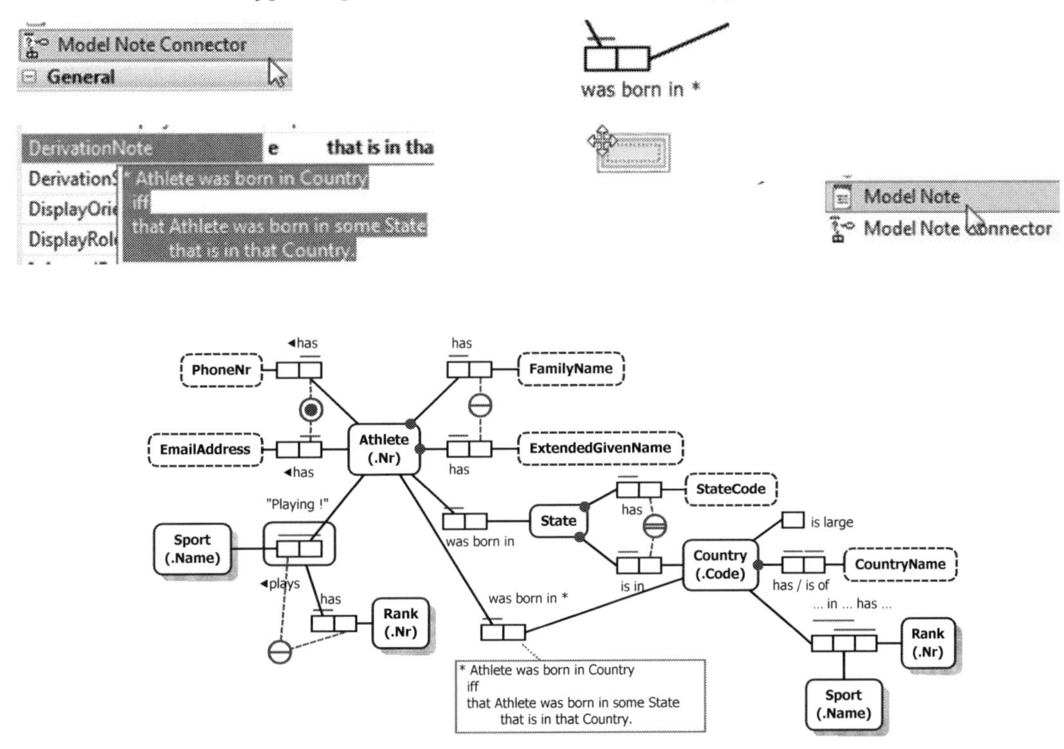

Now right-click an empty space in the Document Window and select Extension Manager ... > Relational View and press OK. Select the Relational View tab to view a diagram for the relational schema that is automatically generated from the ORM schema, as shown below.

By default, NORMA generates a fully normalized relational schema. Table schemes appear as boxes with the table name at the top, and column names listed below along with their data types. Columns with names in bold type are not nullable. Primary key columns are marked "**PK**", foreign keys are marked "**FK*n***", and other columns with a uniqueness constraint are marked "**U*n***", where ***n*** is a positive integer. If two FK*n* columns in the same table have the same number *n* they are components of the same foreign key. If two U*n* columns in the same table have the same number *n* they are constrained by the same, compound uniqueness constraint. Arrowed lines between tables depict foreign key relationships.

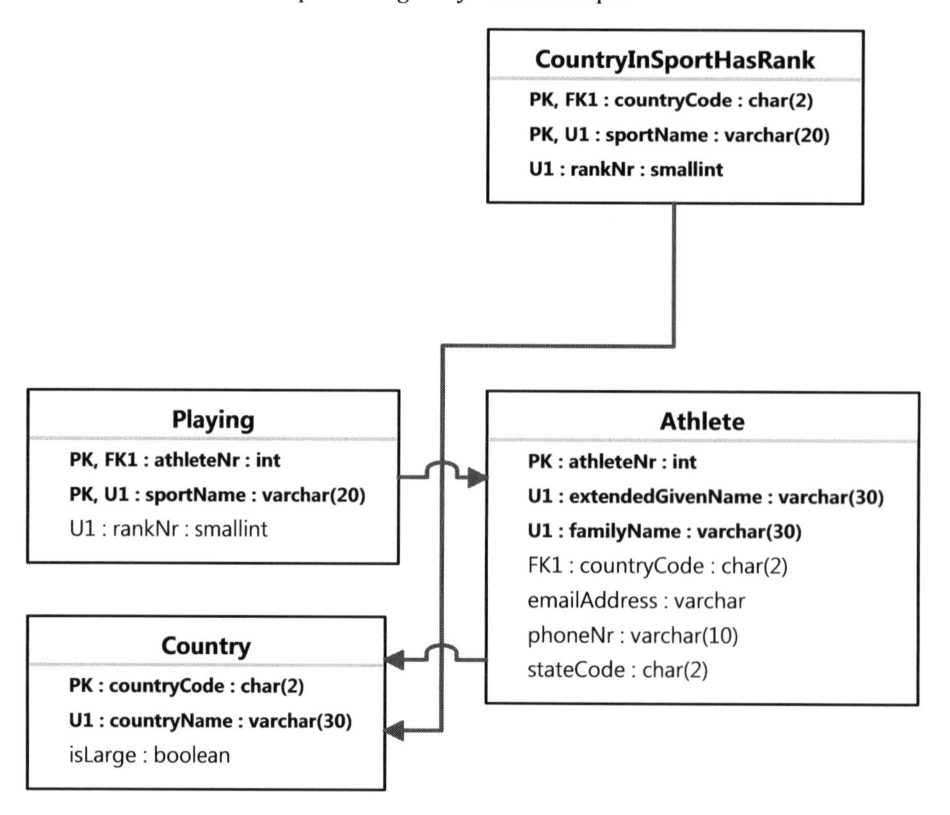

To improve the layout, you can reposition any table by dragging it to a new location. For example, to avoid edge crossings of the foreign key relationship lines select the CountryInSportHasRank table shape and move it down below the Athlete table shape, to obtain the following diagram.

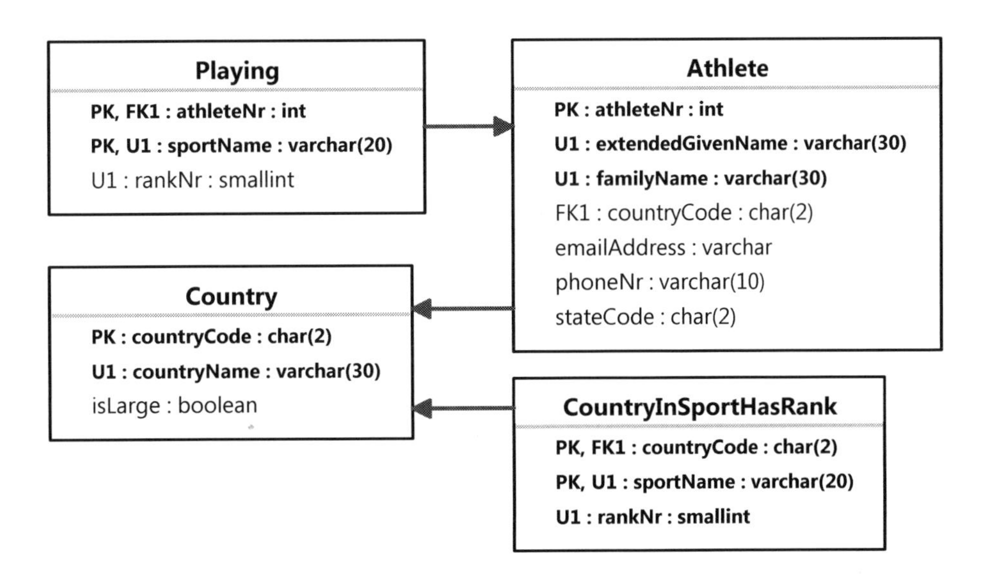

Although the order of columns in a table has no bearing on the semantics, for readability it may sometimes be preferable to reorder the columns from where NORMA places them. To reorder a column in a table simply select the column name in the relational view and drag it to the desired position. Do this now for the stateCode and countryCode columns in the Athlete table to obtain the following diagram.

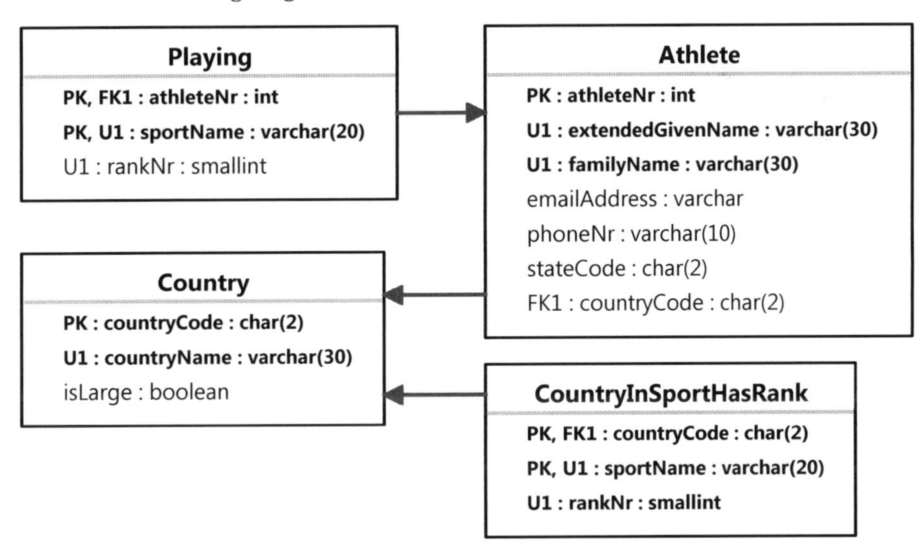

NORMA provides many ways to control the text of table and column names. For example, NORMA automatically supplies default names for *m:n* fact types, *n* -ary fact types (*n* > 2), and objectified types. These names become the names of the tables generated from these fact types (assuming the objectified predicate has a spanning uniqueness constraint). To change any of these names, select the fact type, open its Properties Window (press F4 if needed), edit the Name property and press Enter.

Also, role names may often be used to control the names of columns generated from the roles. Lab 4 includes some examples in this regard. For this example however, the automatically generated names are reasonable, so let's leave them as-is.

I prefer to remove the underscore character "_" (as well as dots "." and colons ":" if used) in value type names when generating column names. To change this setting, choose Tools > Options > ORM Designer from the main menu and edit the entry for the Object Type Name Removed Characters option as you wish.

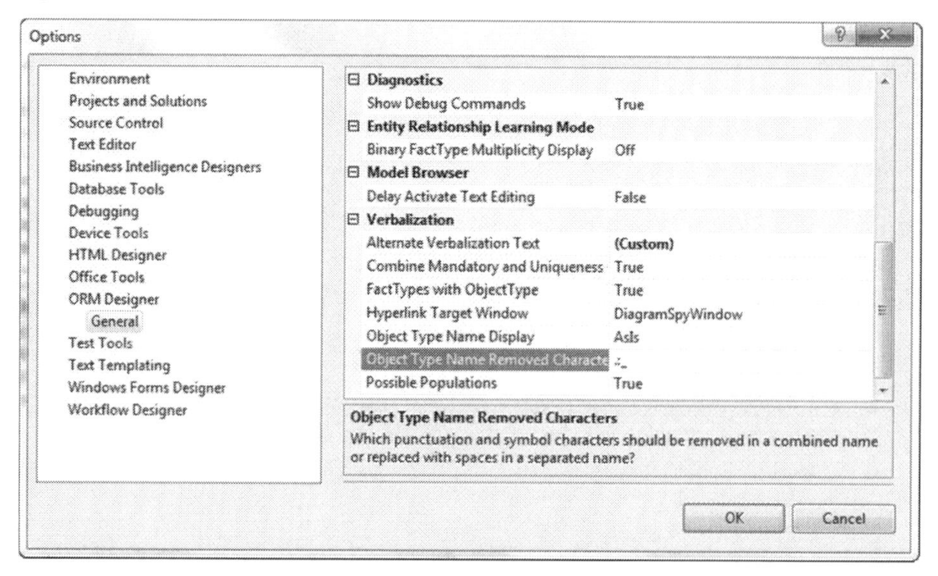

The derived fact type Athlete was born in Country was declared to be simply derived, not derived and stored, so by default NORMA does not generate a table column for it. The public domain version of NORMA discussed in this book has no formal support for derivation rules, so it is left up to you how to implement the derivation rule (e.g. by editing the SQL code that NORMA generates from the relational view). For this table, there is little point in doing anything in this regard, as the countryCode column would normally be interpreted to denote the birth country.

To complete this Lab, save your work by pressing the Save icon in the main menu.

As an optional exercise, and to see how a small change in the ORM schema can result in a significant change in the relational schema, you could change the simple uniqueness constraint on the fact type Athlete has PhoneNr to a spanning uniqueness constraint, so the fact type is now a many-to-many relationship, allowing an athlete to have many phone numbers and allowing many athletes to share the same phone number. The modified relational scheme that is now generated will store phone number details in a separate table rather than as an attribute of the Athlete table.

3 CSDP Step 6

The previous chapters covered the first five steps of the Conceptual Schema design Procedure (CSDP), in which we verbalized examples of the required information as atomic facts, drew the fact types, performed a population check, checked for object types that should be combined, noted any arithmetic derivation rules, added uniqueness and mandatory role constraints, and noted any logical derivation rules.

This chapter discusses *CSDP Step 6*, in which we perform the following tasks:

- Add value constraints
  - object type value constraints
  - role value constraints
- Add set-comparison constraints
  - subset constraints
  - equality constraints
  - exclusion constraints
- Add subtyping

3.1 Value Constraints

A *value constraint* restricts the set of values that are allowed for instances of an object type or role. To reduce the need for continual schema updates, value constraints should be declared only if the list of possible or permitted values is fixed, or at least reasonably stable over time. As an example where value constraints should be specified, consider the report extract about top pole-vaulters shown in Table 3.1. As an exercise, you might wish to model this in ORM before reading on.

Table 3.1 Small extract of data about top pole-vaulters

Athlete	*Gender*	*Country*		*Height (cm)*	*Pole Vault Mark (cm)*
		Code	*Name*		
Jennifer Suhr	F	US	United States	183	502
Renaud Lavillenie	M	FR	France	177	616
Sergey Bubka	M	UA	Ukraine	183	615
Yelena Isinbayeva	F	RU	Russia	174	506
...	...	...	...	...	...

Figure 3.1 shows an ORM schema for this example. In this specialized UoD, athlete are identified simply by their name. As usual, we reference genders by their gender codes, and countries by their country codes. As a secondary reference scheme, countries may also be identified by their country name. Heights are measured in centimeters, as indicated by the unit-based reference mode (cm:). The uniqueness and mandatory role constraints are all simple in this example.

The four value sets listed in braces (curly brackets) depict value constraints. *Object type value constraints* restrict the allowed values of a value type, and are displayed next to the value type, or (as in this example) the entity type that is referenced by the value type. So the {'M', 'F'} next to Gender(.Code) restricts the allowed gender codes to be represented by just 'M' and 'F'. This is an example of a value type *enumeration*, because all the allowed values are enumerated (listed).

The {0..} next to Height(cm:) restricts centimeter values that denote heights to be represented by non-negative numbers (zero or above). The 0 indicates the minimum value, and the two dots ".." with nothing following before the closing brace indicates that no maximum value is specified. This is an example of a value type *range* constraint.

The {50..300} notation attached by a dashed line to the role hosted by Height in the fact type Athlete has Height is a *role value constraint* that restricts the allowed instances of this role to heights in the range from 50 cm to 300 cm inclusive. This is a range constraint where both the minimum and maximum values in the range are specified. I've chosen 50..300 here as a pretty safe estimate, given that the shortest and tallest adult humans on record were 54.6 cm and 272 cm in height respectively.

The {450..700} notation attached by a dashed line to the role hosted by Height in the fact type Athlete pole vaulted Height is another role value constraint. This restricts the allowed instances of this role to heights in the range from 450 cm to 700 cm inclusive. I've chosen these values based on typical figures for pole vault data, and allowing some room for expansion at either end for the future.

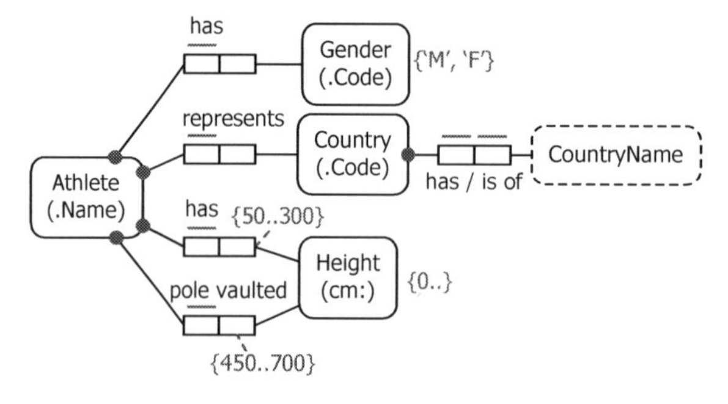

Figure 3.1 An ORM schema for Table 3.1, including value constraints

In principle, value constraints could be declared for CountryCode and CountryName, but the value lists would be very large (about 240 values in each list), and they would be somewhat unstable, since countries sometimes change their name, and over time some countries can be removed from or added to the official lists. So we'll leave the conceptual schema as shown in Figure 3.1. When this is mapped to a relational schema, the code and name fact types for Country map to the table scheme *Country*(countryCode, countryName) with CountryCode as the primary key, and CountryName as a secondary key. We can now populate this table with the relevant data (e.g. based on country codes and names from the ISO 3166 standard). Such a table may be used in many databases, and is often called a *reference table*.

Although value constraints may seem fairly trivial, they are useful for picking up data entry errors, especially those that result from accidentally hitting the wrong key. Figure 3.2 provides a more comprehensive sample of value constraint settings for object types. These value constraint settings may also be applied to roles.

Ranges specified as *n..m* are assumed to be closed, so the end values *n* and *m* are included. For example, 0..100 includes 0 and 100 as well as the numbers in between. To exclude the start value *n* from the range, prepend a left parenthesis, and to exclude the last value *m* from the range, append a right parenthesis. So a range of the form (*n..m* excludes *n* but includes *m*; a range of the form *n..m*) includes *n* but excludes *m*; and a range of the form (*n..m*) excludes both *n* and *m*. This is useful if the underlying data type is a real number (e.g. float or decimal). On an ORM diagram, ranges are always displayed inside braces. For example, the range displayed as {(0..100} covers the positive (above 0) numbers up to 100. If desired, a square bracket may be used to explicitly indicate inclusion (the default). For example, "(0..100" and "(0..100]" mean the same. You may also combine enumerations and/or ranges into a single constraint, as in Figure 3.2(c).

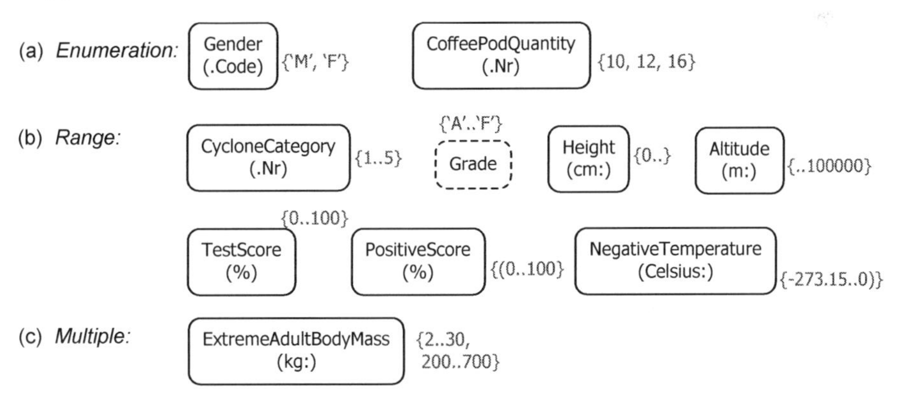

Figure 3.2 Examples object type value constraints

Short value constraint expressions can be conveniently displayed in full on a single line. For longer value lists, you can control the number of values displayed per line in NORMA by selecting the displayed list and setting its MaxColumns property. For example, for Month(.Name) we might specify the value list {'January', 'February', March', 'April, 'May', 'June', 'July', 'August', 'September', 'October', 'November, 'December'}. Setting MaxColumns to 3 displays the list with 3 values per line, as shown in Figure 3.3(a).

You can also choose to display just some leading values in the value list by setting its MaxValues property. A trailing ellipsis "..." then indicates that the display of later values is suppressed. For example, if you select the displayed list and set its MaxValues property to 2, just the first two values will be displayed, as shown in Figure 3.3(b). You can still see all the values by looking in the Verbalizer or the Properties sheet for the object type.

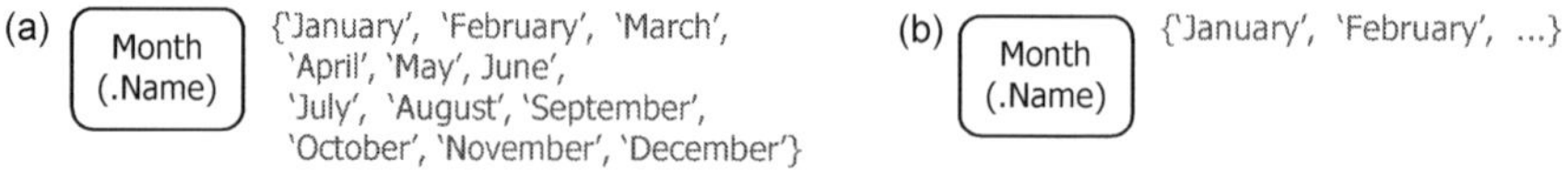

(a) Month (.Name) {'January', 'February', 'March',
'April', 'May', June',
'July', 'August', 'September',
'October', 'November', 'December'}

(b) Month (.Name) {'January', 'February', ...}

Figure 3.3 Controlling how many values are displayed (a) per line, or (b) in total

3.2 Set-Comparison Constraints

Set-comparison constraints place restrictions on how the population of one role, or a sequence of multiple roles, may relate to the population of another role or multi-role sequence. The population of a single role is always a set of objects. The population of a multi-role sequence is a set of object sequences. Sequences of objects are also known as ordered *n*-tuples, or simply *tuples*. The ORM constraints considered in this book are all *static constraints*, so they apply to each individual state of the database, including the empty state. For that reason, the only set-comparison constraints of interest are subset, equality and exclusion constraints. As a simple example with subset and equality constraints, consider the report shown in Table 3.2. As an exercise, you may wish to model this before reading on.

Table 3.2 Small extract of data about hospital patients

Patient Nr	*Patient Name*	*Smokes?*	*Cancer-prone?*	*BP (mm Hg)*		*Drugs Taken*	*Dosage (mg)*
				Systolic	*Diastolic*		
101	Smith, J	No	No	120	80	?	—
102	Smith, J	Yes	Yes	160	100	Irbesartan	30
103	Jones, A	No	Yes	?	?	Amlodopine	30
104	Wang, S	Yes	Yes	150	95	Amlodopine	?
...	...	...	...	...	...	Hydralazine	25
						...	...

In this domain, patients are identified by patient numbers, but may have the same patient name (stored as a single value). If a patient's latest blood pressure (BP) is recorded, both the systolic pressure (taken when the heart is beating) and diastolic pressure (taken when the heart is resting between beats) readings are recorded.

In this report, a question mark entry "?" denotes a simple null, indicating that an actual value is *unknown* (maybe it doesn't exist in the real world, or maybe it does exist in the real world but is not recorded). In contrast, a dash entry "—" indicates *inapplicable.* For example, patient 101 is not recorded to take any drugs, so there is no point in trying to specify a dosage.

Notice that each patient who smokes is also recorded as being cancer-prone. Let us suppose that after checking with the domain expert this dependency is confirmed as always the case. The data for patient 103 indicates that it is possible for a patient to be cancer-prone even if he or she doesn't smoke (e.g. the hospital may determine that a patient is cancer-prone based on evidence not recorded here).

Figure 3.4(a) shows an ORM schema for this domain. Figure 3.4(b) populates Patient and the unary fact types Patient smokes and Patient is cancer-prone with the sample data. The circled subset operator "⊆" over a dashed arrow directed from the role in Person smokes to the role in Person is cancer-prone depicts a simple *subset constraint* between these roles. This subset constraint verbalizes as follows:

If some Patient smokes **then that** Patient is cancer-prone.

So for each state of the database, the set of patients populating the Patient smokes fact type is always a subset of the set of patients populating the Patient is cancer-prone fact type. The arrow notation reminds us that subset constraints are *directional.* If we were to reverse the direction of the arrow, the altered constraint would declare incorrectly that each cancer-prone patient smokes.

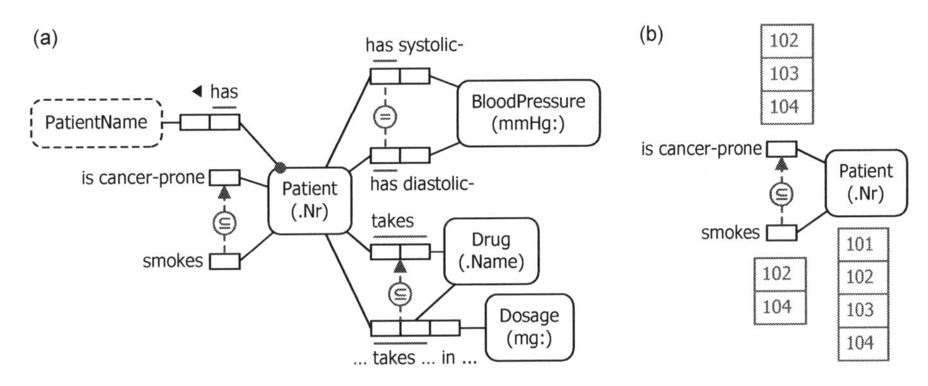

Figure 3.4 (a) An ORM schema for Table 3.2, with a populated fragment (b)

Figure 3.5 populates the fact types Patient as systolic- BloodPressure and Patient has diastolic- BloodPressure with the sample data. The hyphens appended to "systolic" and "diastolic" bind these adjectives to BloodPressure for verbalization purposes. So the uniqueness constraints on these facts types verbalize as **Each** Patient has **at most one** systolic BloodPressure and **Each** Patient has **at most one** diastolic BloodPressure. The circled equality operator "=" connected by dashed lines to the Patient roles in these fact types depicts a simple *equality constraint* between these roles. This equality constraint verbalizes as follows:

For each Patient,

that Patient has **some** systolic BloodPressure **if and only if**

that Patient has **some** diastolic BloodPressure.

So for each state of the database, the set of patients populating Patient's role in the systolic blood pressure fact type equals the set of patients populating Patient's role in the diastolic blood pressure fact type. In other words, either both systolic and diastolic readings are recorded or neither is. Unlike subset constraints, equality constraints are non-directional, so the order in which roles are selected for the constraint doesn't matter.

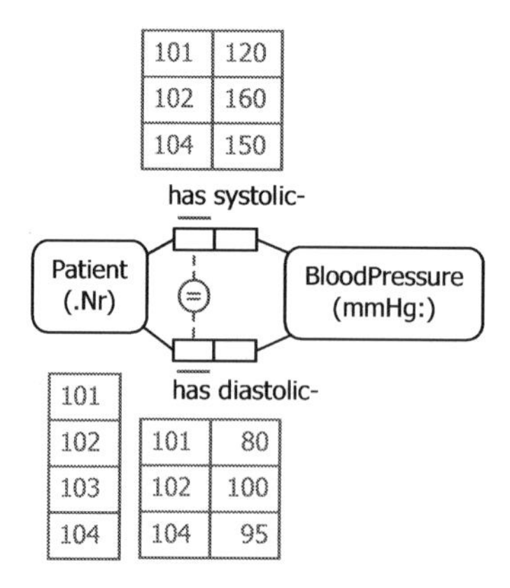

Figure 3.5 A fragment of the ORM model for Table 3.2, with an equality constraint

Figure 3.6 populates the fact types Patient takes Drug and Patient takes Drug in Dosage with the sample data. In this case, the subset constraint is directed from the pair of Patient, Drug roles in the ternary fact type to the pair of Patient, Drug roles in the binary fact type. Connecting an end of the constraint arrow to the junction of two roles indicates that that role pair is an argument of the constraint. This constraint an example of a *pair-subset constraint*, and verbalizes as follows:

If some Patient takes **some** Drug in **some** Dosage

then that Patient takes **that** Drug.

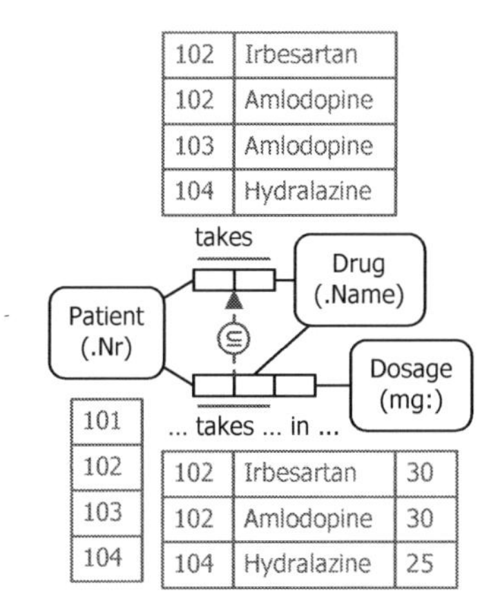

Figure 3.6 A fragment of the Table 3.2 ORM model, with a pair-subset constraint

So for each state of the database, the set of (Patient, Drug) pairs populating the first two roles of the ternary fact type is always a subset of the set of (Patient, Drug) pairs populating the binary fact type. The sample population is consistent with this constraint.

As you might have realized, there are other correct ways to model the patient drug details. For example, the ORM schema fragment in Figure 3.7 objectifies the binary fact type as DrugTaking, and attaches a binary fact type for the dosage. Here, DrugTaking is declared independent, so that we can record that a patient takes a drug without knowing the dosage—this aspect was catered for in Figure 3.6 by using a subset constraint rather than an equality constraint.

The schema fragments in Figure 3.6 and Figure 3.7 are said to be *semantically equivalent*, as each provides a correct way of modeling the same state of affairs. ORM schemas have an underlying formalization that enables them to be mapped to logical formulae where schema equivalence results can be formally proved. Although the schemas in Figure 3.6 and Figure 3.7 are semantically equivalent, the objectified version leads to a more efficient relational schema when mapped by NORMA. For further details on schema equivalence, schema transformation and schema optimization in ORM, see chapter 14 of Halpin & Morgan (2008).

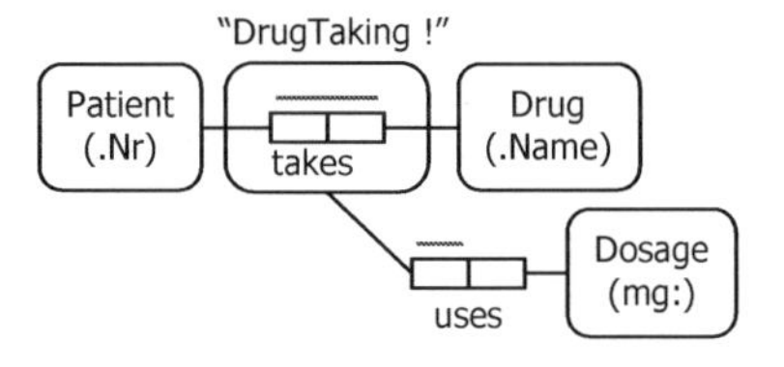

Figure 3.7 An alternative way of modeling the patient drug details

Figure 3.8 shows the schema from Figure 2.3 of the previous chapter, but this time with constraints added. In this academic UoD, only employees with degrees can be tenured. This restriction is captured by the subset constraint from Employee's role in Employee holds Degree to the role in Employee is tenured. Because Employee's role in Employee has Gender is mandatory, the following subset constraint is *implied*: **If some** Employee holds **some** Degree **then that** Employee has **some** Gender. The other roles hosted by Employee are also mandatory, so the following equality constraint is also *implied*: **For each** Patient, **that** Patient has **some** FamilyName **if and only if that** Patient has **some** GivenName.

If you are viewing this book in color, you'll notice that I've colored the two implied constraints in green rather than the usual violet color used for asserted constraints. *Implied constraints over asserted fact types should normally be omitted.* If you try to add such implied constraints over asserted fact types in the NORMA tool, an error message will appear to tell you that they are implied. However, it's normally helpful to display implied constraints on *derived* fact types.

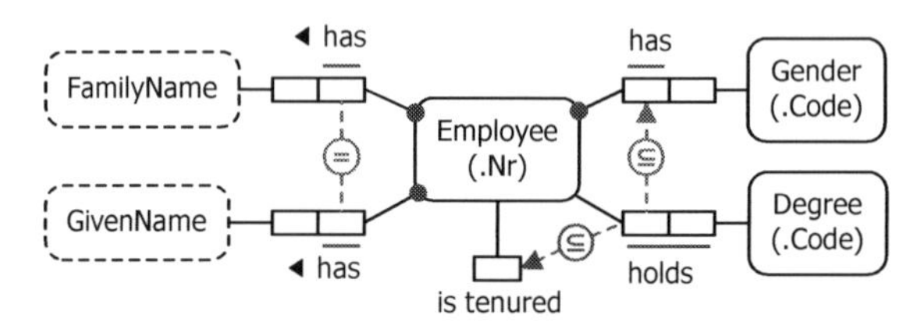

Figure 3.8 Two of the constraints are implied, and should normally be omitted

The third and last kind of set-comparison constraint is an *exclusion constraint*. The ORM model depicted in Figure 3.9(a) includes a simple exclusion constraint between the roles of the fact types Planet is moonless and Planet has multiple moons. This exclusion constraint, depicted as a *circled cross* ⊗ connected by dashed lines to the constrained roles, verbalizes as follows:

For each Planet, **at most one of the following holds**:

that Planet is moonless;

that Planet has multiple moons.

So for each state of the database, the set of moons instantiating the role in Planet is moonless is mutually exclusive with the set of planets instantiating the role in Planet has multiple moons. (i.e. the populations have no instance in common).

Note that if the model were to also include the fact type Moon orbits Planet, as discussed in chapter 1, then these two unary fact types would be derived, and hence marked with an asterisk. Although the exclusion constraint would then be derivable, for clarity it's still best to display it.

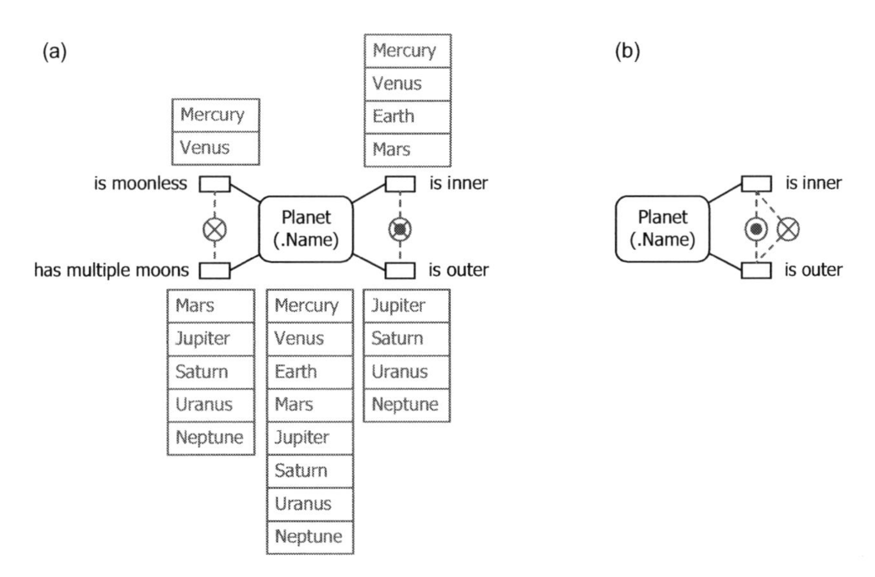

Figure 3.9 A simple exclusion constraint, and an exclusive-or constraint

The ORM model depicted in Figure 3.9(a) includes an *exclusive-or constraint* between the roles of the fact types Planet is inner and Planet is outer. This exclusive-or constraint, depicted as a *circled lifebuoy symbol* connected by dashed lines to the constrained roles, verbalizes as follows:

For each Planet, **exactly one of the following holds**:

that Planet is inner;

that Planet is outer.

So each planet is inner or outer but not both. An exclusive-or constraint is also known as an *xor constraint* or a partition constraint.

For compact display, an exclusive-or constraint is usually displayed using the lifebuoy symbol. However, an exclusive-or constraint is actually the combination of an inclusive-or constraint ⊙ with a simple exclusion constraint ⊗, and the lifebuoy shape is composed of these two constraint shapes superimposed. Via a context menu option for the constraint, the NORMA tool allows you to display an exclusive-or constraint's two components separately, as in Figure 3.9(b).

In ORM, subset, equality and exclusion constraints may be declared between role sequences of any length, so long as the corresponding roles in those sequences are *compatible*. Basically, roles are compatible if they are hosted by the same object type, or by object types belonging to the same subtype graph (subtyping is discussed in the next section). Each constrained role sequence is said to be an *argument* of the constraint. Subset constraints have only two arguments, while equality and exclusion constraints may have two or more arguments.

Figure 3.10 adds constraints to the direct flight model considered earlier in Figure 2.6. Each argument of the exclusion constraint is a role pair, so this is a *pair-exclusion constraint*. This compound exclusion constraint verbalizes as follows:

For each Flight **and** Airport, **at most one of the following holds**:

that Flight starts at **that** Airport;

that Flight ends at **that** Airport.

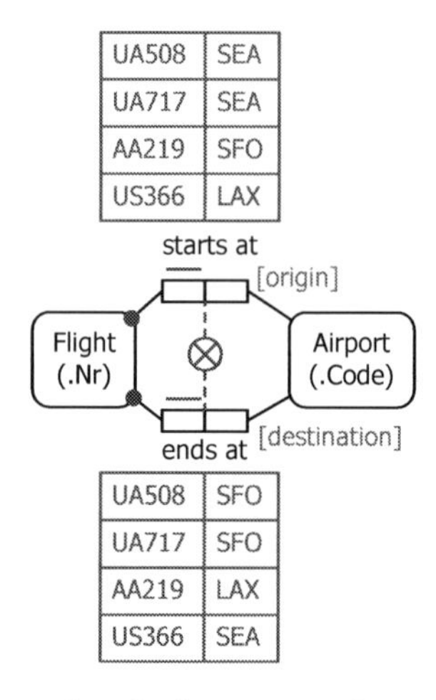

Figure 3.10 An example of a compound exclusion constraint

Now consider the ORM schema and sample population shown in Figure 3.11. In this UoD, each politician is either a president or vice-president, but not both (as shown by the inclusive-or constraint). Each country is identified by a country code and also has an identifying country name. Not all countries have a president or vice-president (e.g. Australia instead has a prime minister and deputy prime minister).

If a country has a vice-president, then it also has a president (as shown by the subset constraint). However a country may have a president without also having a vice-president (e.g. this is the case for Ireland).

The pair-exclusion constraint indicates that no president of a country can be vice-president of *the same* country. However this *pair-exclusion constraint is implied by the simple exclusion constraint* that is part of the exclusive-or constraint. The simple exclusion constraint ensures that no president of a country can be vice-president of *any* country, so implies the weaker pair-exclusion constraint. As the pair-exclusion constraint applies to asserted fact types, it should be omitted.

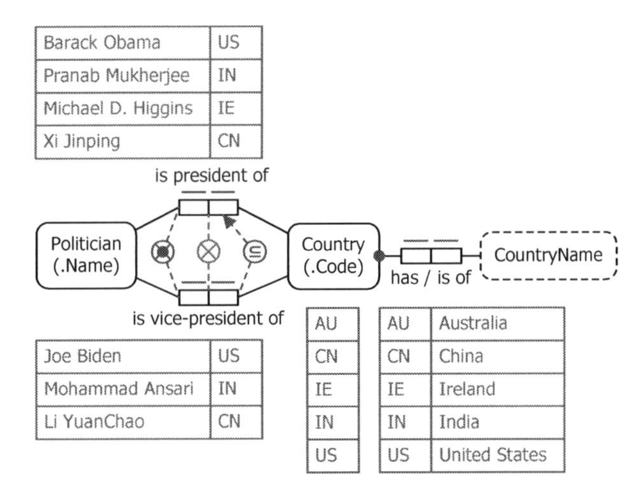

Figure 3.11 The pair-exclusion constraint is implied, and should be omitted

An argument of a set-comparison constraint may include roles from different fact types, so long as a *join-path* can be determined to join the predicates involved. For simple cases, NORMA can detect such join paths automatically. For example, in Figure 3.12 the first argument of the subset constraint is the (Employee, Program) role pair in the fact type Employee is a developer for Program. The second argument is the (Employee, Program) role pair projected from the path that runs from the fact type Employee is fluent in ComputerLanguage through the fact type ComputerLanguage is used for Program, performing a *conceptual join* on the roles of ComputerLanguage where their values match.

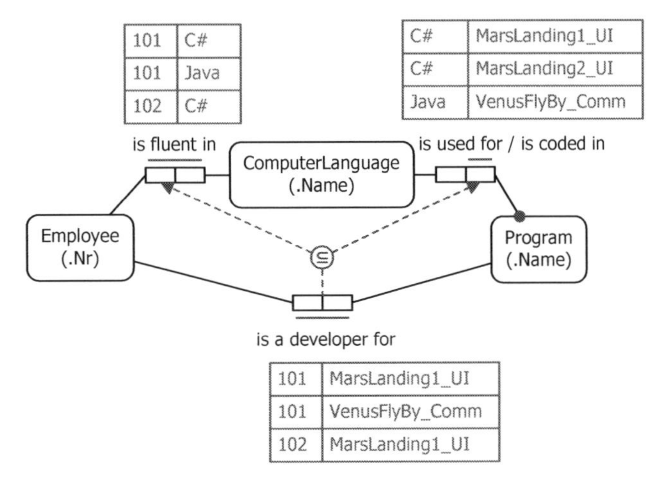

Figure 3.12 Example of a join-subset constraint

This is an example of a *join-subset constraint*. It has the following verbalization:

If some Employee is a developer for **some** Program

then that Employee is fluent in **some** ComputerLanguage **that** is used for **that** Program.

Given the population shown, if we were to add a fact assigning employee 102 to the VenusFly-By_Comm program, this would violate the join-subset constraint, because employee 102 is not fluent in Java, which is the only language used for that program.

3.3 Subtyping

To help organize the way we think about objects in the world, we classify them into object types, like Person, Country, Planet, Book etc. Sometimes we specialize some instances of an object type into a more specific type. For example, for legal reasons we might further categorize some persons as adult persons. In that case, the object type AdultPerson is said to be a *subtype* of Person. Equivalently, Person is said to be a *supertype* of AdultPerson. On an ORM diagram, this subtyping relationship is depicted as a *solid arrow* from the subtype shape to the supertype shape, as shown in Figure 3.13(a).

Figure 3.13(b) depicts the same subtyping relationship on an Euler diagram, by placing the shape for AdultPerson inside the shape for Person. Although Euler diagrams are more intuitive for simple cases, they are unwieldy for complex cases involving multiple overlapping subtypes, so they are not used in ORM.

ORM makes a clear distinction between types and populations. A *type* includes all its possible instances, past, present and future. A *population* is the set of instances recorded in a given state of the fact base. In ORM, subtyping is understood to mean *proper subtyping*, so the ORM schema in Figure 3.13(a) classifies Adult Person as a proper subtype of Person. This implies the following:

1. For each state of the fact base, the *population* of AdultPerson is a subset of the *population* of Person.
2. The *type* AdultPerson is not identical to the *type* Person.

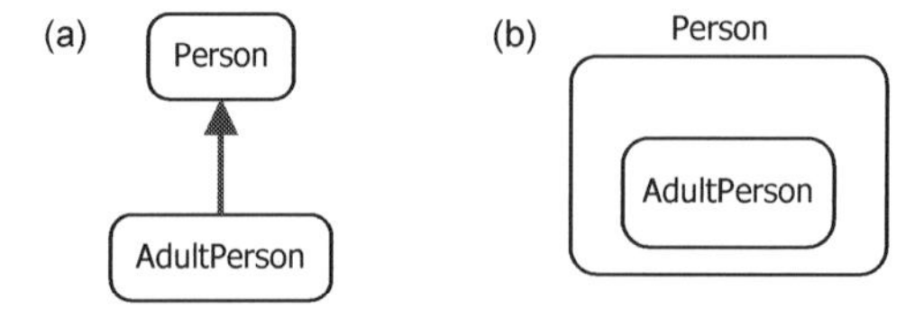

Figure 3.13 AdultPerson is a subtype of Person

Given any sets A and B, the expression $A \subseteq B$ (read as "A is a subset of B") means that each member of A is also a member of B. So condition 1 above ensures that each adult person known to the information system is also known to be a person. This includes any state in which the only recorded persons are adult persons (the populations of the two types are then equal—this includes the case when the information system is empty). Condition 2 declares that the subtyping is proper, so it is possible for a person to be recorded who is not an adult person.

An object type may have multiple subtypes declared. In this case, we need to indicate whether any *subtyping constraints* apply between the subtypes. These constraints are depicted using the *inclusive-or*, *exclusion*, and *exclusive-or* constraint notations discussed earlier.

By default in ORM, subtypes of the same supertype are assumed to overlap (i.e. it is possible for their populations to share a common instance). For example, Figure 3.14(a) has no subtyping constraints declared, so it's possible that some state of the fact base records some person to be both adult and female. In Figure 3.14(b), the inclusive-or constraint ensures that each team member is either a player or a coach or both. Since the union of the populations of Player and Coach always equals the population of TeamMember, the subtypes are said to be exhaustive for their supertype. In Figure 3.14(c), the exclusion constraint ensures that no cat is ever a dog.

In Figure 3.14(d), the exclusive-or constraint ensures that no male person is a female person, and that each person is male or female. Since the subtypes MalePerson and FemalePerson are both mutually exclusive and collectively exhaustive, they form a *partition* of their Person supertype. In this case, the exclusive-or constraint is also called a partition constraint.

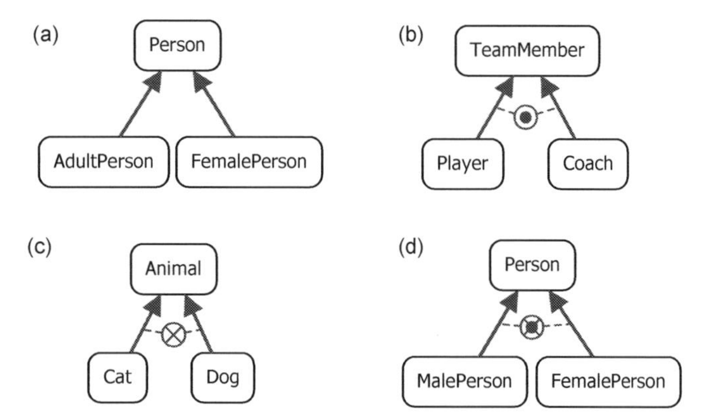

Figure 3.14 Subtypes that are (a) overlapping but not exhaustive, (b) overlapping and exhaustive, (c) mutually exclusive but not exhaustive, (d) mutually exclusive and exhaustive (hence forming a partition of their supertype)

Though depicted as a relationship between types, in ORM a subtyping relationship is actually an identity (equals) relationship between instances[13] of the types, with "is" used for both forward and inverse predicate readings. Connecting a constraint to a subtyping arrow corresponds to connecting the constraint to the role hosted by the supertype in this instance-level equality relationship. For example, the ORM schema in Figure 3.15(a) is internally implemented using the implicit identity relationships in Figure 3.15(b), depicted here with dashed lines.

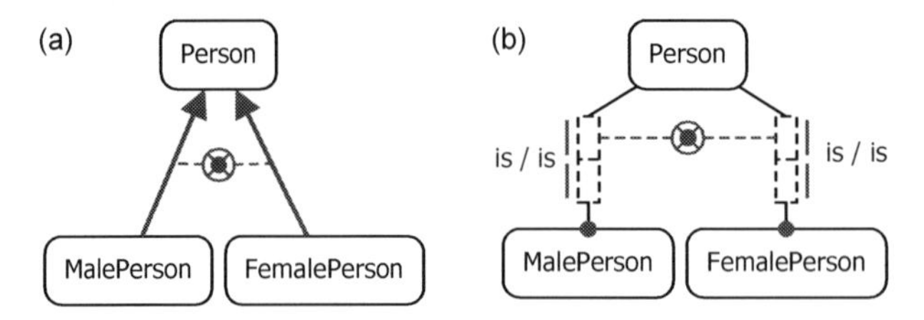

Figure 3.15 Instance-level identity relationships underlie subtyping relationships

Using the forward reading "is" for the implicit, identity relationships underlying the subtyping, the inclusive-or, exclusion, and exclusive-or constraints in the subtyping examples in Figure 3.14 have the following verbalizations respectively.

Each TeamMember is **some** Player **or** is **some** Coach.

For each Animal, **at most one of the following holds:**
that Animal is **some** Cat;
that Animal is **some** Dog.

For each Person, **exactly one of the following holds:**
that Person is **some** MalePerson;
that Person is **some** FemalePerson.

Set-comparison constraints may also be applied between normal fact type roles and a supertype's role in the instance-level identity relationship underlying a subtyping link. For example, the subset constraint in Figure 3.16 runs from Employee's role in the implicit identity fact type Employee is Executive to Employee's role in the fact type Employee is assigned CompanyCar. This constraint verbalizes as follows: **If some** Employee is **some** Executive **then that** Employee is assigned **some** CompanyCar.

This subset constraint performs the function of a *"restricted mandatory role constraint"* on Employee's role in the company car assignment fact type, by requiring that role to be mandatory for a restricted subset of employees (the executives). For employees who are not executives, that role is optional.

[13] ORM's formalization is based on first-order logic, where predication and quantification is over individuals only, not types.

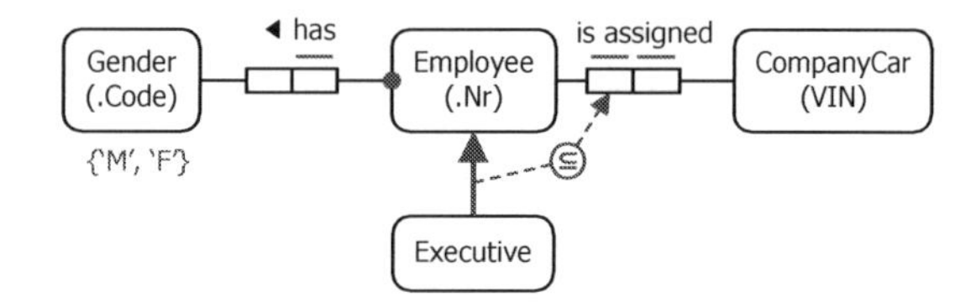

Figure 3.16 A subset constraint to enforce a restricted mandatory role constraint

In this model, the reference mode for CompanyCar is VIN (standing for Vehicle Identification Number). This is a general reference mode, since a VIN may also be used to identify some vehicles other than cars, such as motorcycles and scooters (see http://en.wikipedia.org/wiki/Vehicle_identification_number).

Typically, a subtype is included in an information model to perform at least one of the following actions:

- Declare that one or more specific roles are hosted only by the subtype
- Reuse existing model components by inheriting from the supertype
- Specify a small taxonomy for the supertype

For example, only males have prostate glands, so if we wish to record the prostate status of hospital patients, we would include a MalePatient subtype of Patient, and attach the fact type MalePatient has ProstateStatus to record this information. Similarly, we might use a FemalePatient subtype for recording pregnancy data.

Rather than adding fact types to MalePatient and FemalePatient to record gender-neutral details such as name, gender, birthdate etc., we record those details on the Patient supertype so that is available to each of its subtypes. The subtypes then *inherit* such information from their supertype.

If a subtype has two or more direct supertypes, this is known as *multiple inheritance*. For this to happen in ORM, the supertypes involved must overlap. For example, in the Figure 3.17 schema, FemaleCancerPatient is a direct subtype of both FemalePatient and CancerPatient. If FemalePatient and CancerPatient had instead been declared mutually exclusive, FemaleCancerPatient would necessarily be empty, which is illegal because ORM requires object types to be populatable.

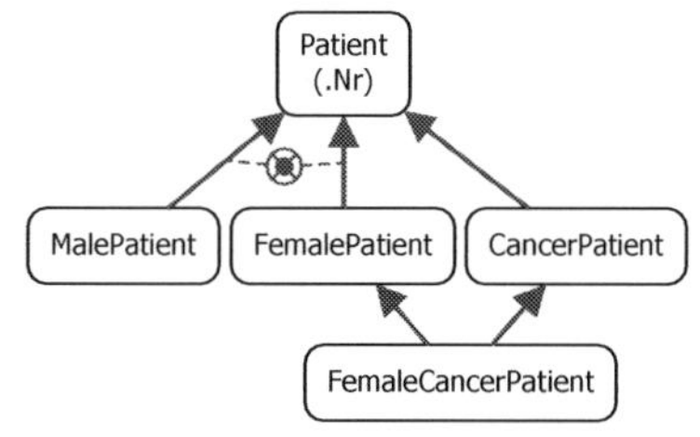

Figure 3.17 FemaleCancerPatient exhibits multiple inheritance

Subtyping is a transitive relationship, so if we know that FemaleCancerPatient is a subtype of FemalePatient, and that FemalePatient is a subtype of Patient, then it's implied that FemaleCancerPatient is a subtype of Patient. For exposition purposes, this indirect subtyping relationship is depicted with an asterisk in Figure 3.18, but in an actual ORM schema it should not be shown.

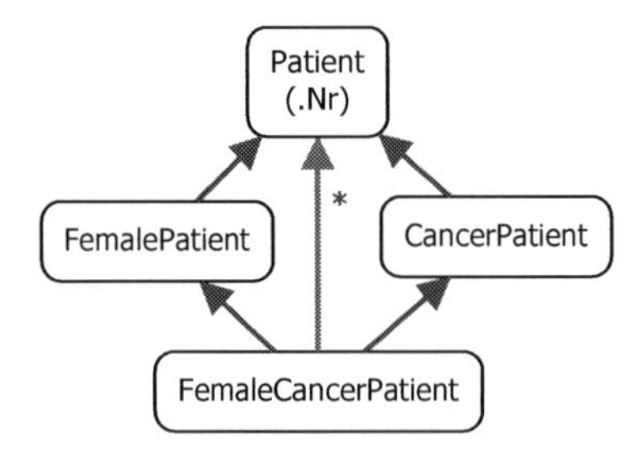

Figure 3.18 The indirect subtyping from FemaleCancerPatient to Patient is implied, and should be omitted

In general, when considering relationships other than subtyping, a sequence of direct links implies indirect links, so when needed such indirect linkages should be derived rather than asserted.

If an object type can be partitioned into a small number of subtypes, we sometimes use subtyping simply to display the taxonomy, or classification scheme used in the business domain. For example, the ORM schema in Figure 3.19(a) partitions Patient into MalePatient and FemalePatient, simply by asserting these subtypes and adding the exclusive-or constraint.

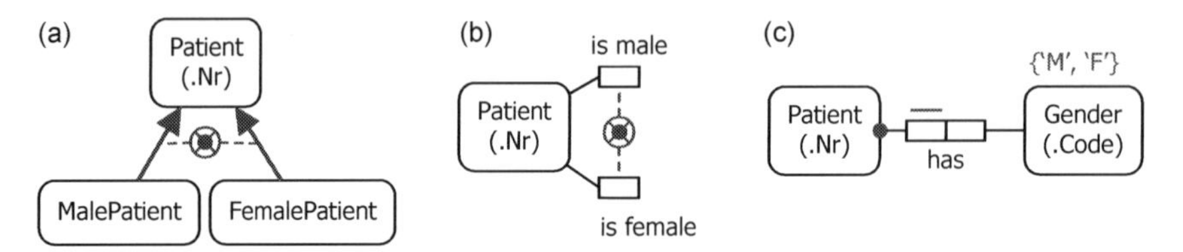

Figure 3.19 Some different ways to assert gender details

If the number of subtypes is small, and we have nothing specific to record for the subtypes, we could model the taxonomy instead using a set of unary facts types and an exclusive-or constraint, as shown in Figure 3.19(b). Alternatively, we could model the information using a binary fact type and a value constraint, as shown in Figure 3.19(c)—in this case, we could also use gender names ('male', 'female') instead of or in addition to gender codes.

If the size of the taxonomy is large, the subtyping and unary solution becomes impractical, so the binary solution is often preferred. If the size of the taxonomy is very large (e.g. a botanical classification scheme), the possible values are stored as data (e.g. instances of PlantKind) rather than as a value constraint.

If there are roles specific to the subtypes, it's often best to use a fact type to capture the taxonomy then *derive* the subtypes from this fact type by means of a derivation rule. On an ORM diagram, *derived subtypes* are marked with an *asterisk* "*" after their name, as shown in Figure 3.20. The exclusive-or constraint between the subtypes is derivable from the derivation rules displayed next to the schema diagram. As the reference mode for Gender is declared separately, there is no need to repeat it in the subtype definitions.

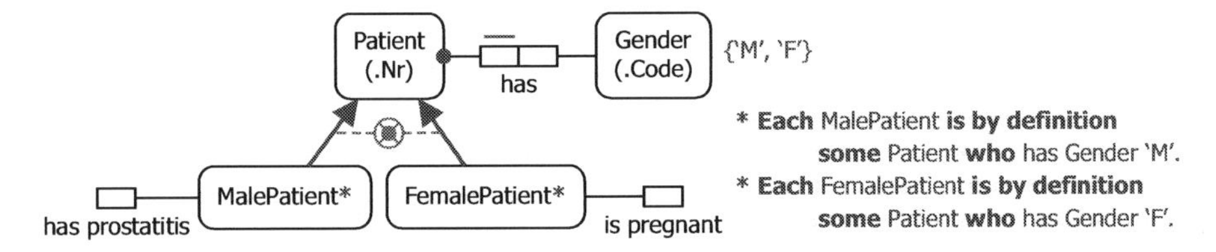

Figure 3.20 The subtypes are now derived from the gender fact type.

Often we have a choice about whether to model some feature using subtyping or set-comparison constraints. For example, if we model gender facts using unaries, the domain schematized in Figure 3.20 can be modeled using subset constraints instead of subtyping, as shown in Figure 3.21. As another example, consider the report extract in Table 3.3. Here "?" is a simple null, whereas "—" means inapplicable. You may wish to try modeling this before reading on.

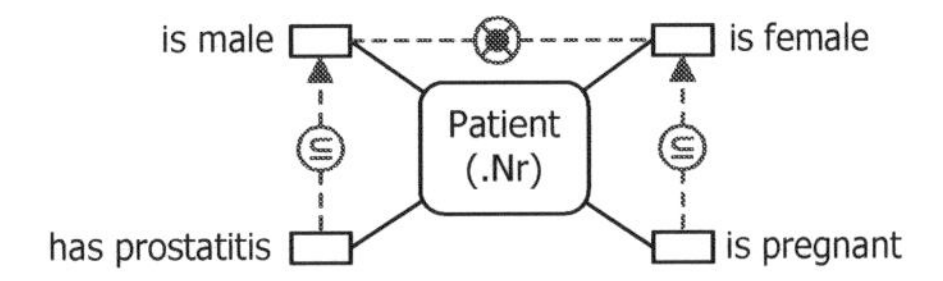

Figure 3.21 An alternative to the schema in Figure 3.20.

Table 3.3 Small extract of data about employees

Employee Nr	*Employee Name*	*Company Car VIN*	*Driver License#*	*Driver Insurance#*	*Parking Bay*
101	Smith, John	JM0ER103190114925	ABC123	CGU00246	B1
102	Jones, Ann	?	—	—	—
103	Smith, Sue	IB0XY123456789012	XYZ246	?	?
104	Evans, Bill	IB0AA012345678901	DEF012	CGU000123	?
105	Wang, Sue	JM0FE246802468024	GHI123	?	A2

In the UoD for Table 3.3 only some employees are assigned a company car. Anyone who is assigned a company car must have his/her driver license number recorded, and optionally may have his/her driver insurance policy number recorded. Only employees assigned a company car may be assigned a parking bay.

Figure 3.22(a) models this example using subset and equality constraints, while the model in Figure 3.22(b) using subtyping. Instead of simply using value types for the license and policy numbers, I've used entity types for DriverLicense and DriverInsurancePolicy to allow for other facts that might be recorded about them.

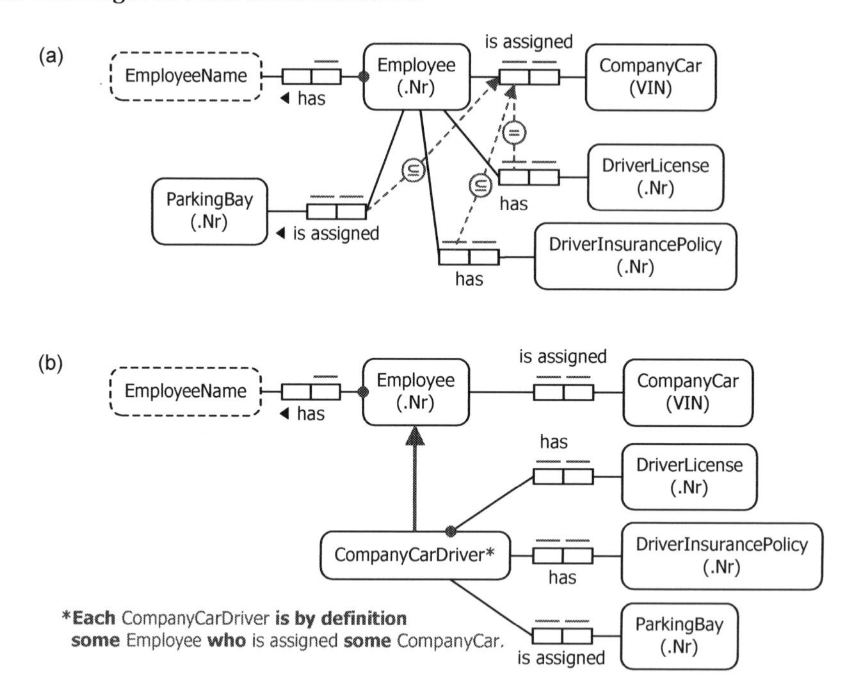

Figure 3.22 Two ways of modeling the report extract in Table 3.3

Of these two solutions, I prefer the subtyping approach because it seems tidier, and is easier to extend if we wish to add more facts about company car drivers. In general, if there any many roles specific to a subtype it's usually better to introduce the subtype explicitly rather than rely on set-comparison constraints to do the job.

Moreover, subtype definitions are often stronger than mere subset constraints, so the subset constraint approach can be too weak as an alternative to subtyping unless you include a unary fact type (possibly derived) corresponding to membership in the subtype as the target of the subset constraint.

So far, the subtypes discussed have been either asserted or derived. Just as with normal fact types, it is also possible to have subtypes that are semiderived, although this is fairly rare in practice. A *semiderived subtype* may have some instances that are simply asserted, and some other instances that are known only by deriving them by means of a derivation rule.

On an ORM diagram, semiderived subtypes are marked with a plus superscript "+" after their name, and their FORML derivation rule begins with "+" and includes the word "**derived**" before the subtype name. Figure 3.23(b) shows a classic example. If our knowledge of parenthood facts is complete, we can fully derive the grandparents using the rule shown in Figure 3.23(a). However, if our knowledge of parenthood facts is incomplete, we can still know and assert that someone is a grandparent without knowing a chain of two parenthood facts that implies grandparenthood.

For example, suppose the following three facts are asserted for the schema in Figure 3.23(b): Norma Halpin is a parent of David Halpin; David Halpin is a parent of Sam Halpin; Tony Morgan is a grandparent. Given the derivation rule, the two parenthood facts imply that Norma Halpin is a grandparent. The population of Grandparent now includes two instances, one derived (Norma Halpin) and one asserted (Tony Morgan).

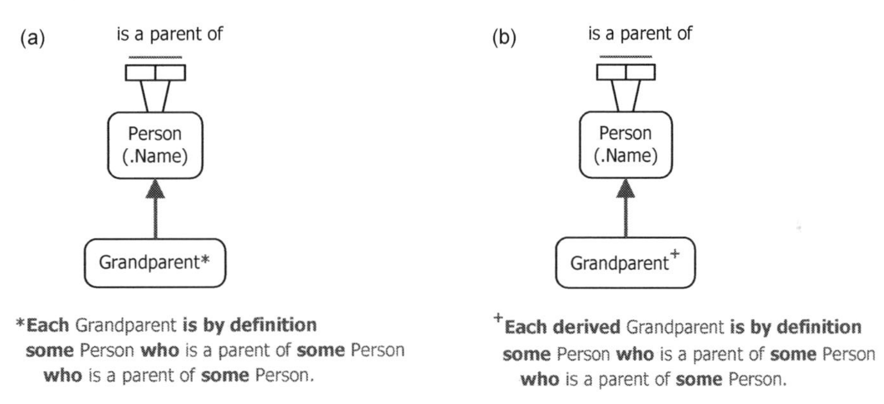

Figure 3.23 Modeling the Grandparent subtype as (a) derived or (b) semiderived

Inspection of realistic sample data often suggests the relevant constraints that apply. However, sample data might not be fully representative, so strictly speaking it can't be used to prove which constraints apply, even though it can show that certain constraints don't apply. If in doubt about a constraint or derivation rule, it's always best to check with the domain expert. This is especially the case with determining derivation rules for subtyping, since for any finite set of data there are always an infinite number of patterns that fit the data.

20. Are you an Australian citizen who was born in Australia?

No ☐ ▶ *Go to next question*

Yes ☐ ▶ ***Go to 25***

21. What is your country of birth? ☐

22. In what year did you start living in Australia? ☐

23. If this year is before 1965, give details below, *else go to next question.*

Name of ship or airline on which you arrived. ☐

Name of city where you arrived. ☐

24. What is your country of citizenship?

Australia ☐ ▶ Date granted [/ /] ▶ ***Go to 25***

Other country ☐

25. How often do you wish to receive the pension?

Fortnightly ☐ Quarterly ☐

Figure 3.24 Simplified extract from an Australian age pension application form

Sometimes, the relevant subtyping can be determined directly from instructions on sample input forms. For example, Figure 3.24 shows a simplified extract from an age pension application form used in Australia. Notice that the form instructions specify conditions to determine which questions must be answered. Though not shown here, assume that each applicant is identified by a Centrelink Reference Number (CRN) assigned to them in person before they can apply for the age pension—a CRN is roughly analogous to a social security number in the USA. You may wish to try modeling this example before reading on.

Figure 3.25 shows one way to model this example, using the term "Immigrant" to cover applicants who are not Australian citizens born in Australia. I've used the terms "EarlyImmigrant" and "ImmigrantAustralian" in the sense provided by their subtype definitions.

Here, countries are identified by name, but you could use country codes instead or in addition. I've identified cities by name assuming these are unique for ports of entry into Australia. If this is not the case, replace the city arrival fact type by the fact type EarlyImmigrant arrived in a city with CityName. Even though dual citizenships are possible in the real world, the application form allows at most one country of citizenship, so I've modeled it that way.

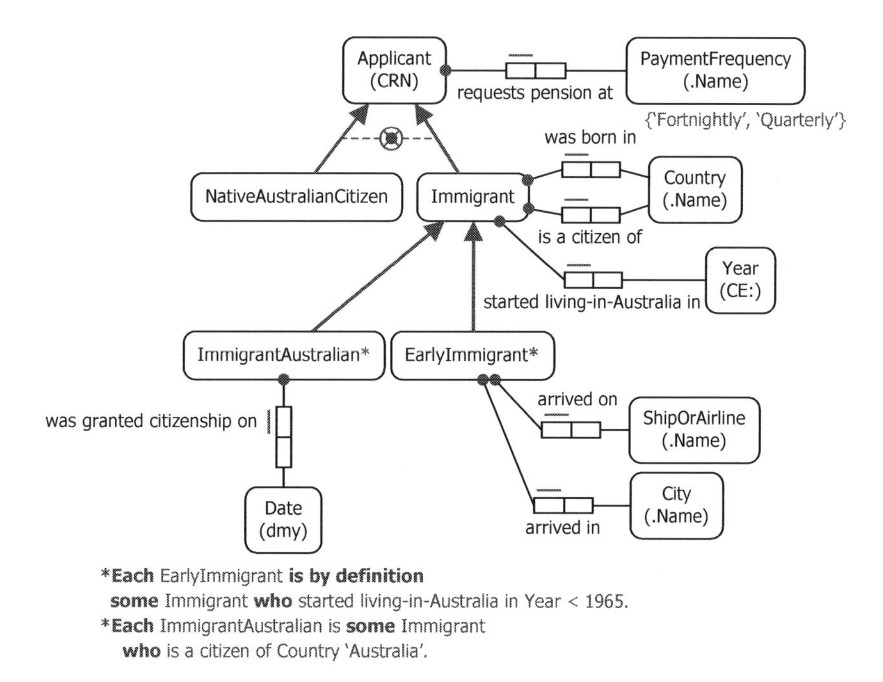

Figure 3.25 One way of modeling the age pension form extract in Figure 3.24

I often use object type names that are concatenated, such as "EarlyImmigrant". To include spaces in a name when typing it into NORMA's Fact Editor, enclose the name in square brackets, e.g. "[Early Immigrant]". Square brackets may also be used in the Fact Editor to start an object type with a lower case letter, e.g. "[early Immigrant]". You can also use spaces and initial lowercase in NORMA if you drag an object type shape from the Toolbox and edit its name directly. As a configuration option, you can also choose to have spaces inserted in concatenated names for verbalization purposes by setting the ObjectTypeNameDisplay option to SeparateCombinedNames.

NORMA's Fact Editor does not allow words that start with a capital letter (e.g. "Australia") as part of a predicate reading. So if you tried to enter "started living in Australia in" as a predicate reading in the Fact Editor, "Australia" would be parsed as an object type name. Hence, I've hyphenated the predicate reading as "started living-in-Australia in". To avoid such hyphenation when using NORMA, you can edit the predicate reading to "started living in Australia in" in the ORM Reading Editor.

The subtyping examples discussed so far have introduced a subtype either to constrain certain roles to be played only by instances of that subtype, or to simply declare that subtype for taxonomic reasons. As discussed earlier, another reason for using subtypes is to have subtypes inherit common properties of their supertype(s) without needing to specify those properties separately for individual subtypes. We now discuss an example of this situation.

Suppose we need to model details about famous batters who are either baseball players or cricketers. Figure 3.26 shows an extract of the required data.

Famous baseball batters

	Birth			*Home*
Name	*Country*	*Year*	*Died*	*runs*
Babe Ruth	US	1895	1948	714
Willie Mays	US	1931	?	660

Famous cricket batsmen

	Birth			*Batting*	*Top*
Name	*Country*	*Year*	*Died*	*Average*	*Test Score*
Donald Bradman	AU	1908	2001	99.94	334
Sachin Tendulkar	IN	1973	?	53.78	248

Figure 3.26 Extract from a report on famous baseball batters and batsmen

If you model the tables in this report separately and then combine your schemas you could arrive at a schema like that shown in Figure 3.27. Notice that the birth country, birth year and death year details are modeled separately for both FamousBaseballBatter and FamousBatsman. Although there is nothing semantically wrong in doing this, such repetition can lead to inefficiencies (e.g. if we wish to group both kinds of batters together in a single query on a relational database we need to access two tables).

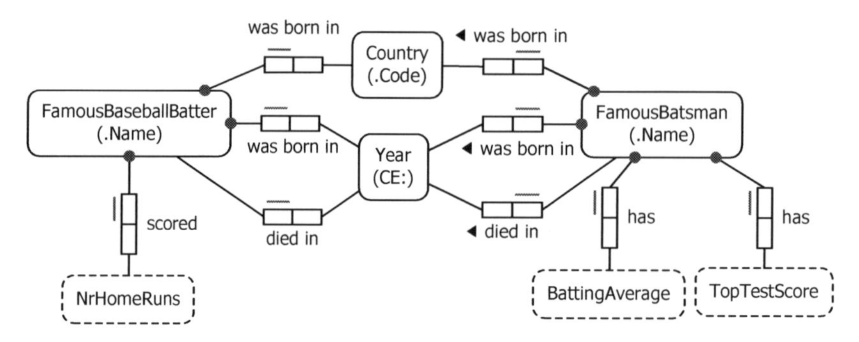

Figure 3.27 One way to model the report in Figure 3.26

Recall that CSDP Step 3 includes a check to see whether entity types should be combined into a more general type. Entity types that overlap must be combined if we wish to know about such overlap (e.g. Origin and Destination in the Airport example discussed in the previous chapter). In that case, no details are recorded only for origin airports or only for destination airports, so the original Origin and Destination types were removed once they had been generalized into Airport.

However, the schema pattern in Figure 3.27 is different for two reasons. Firstly, the FamousBaseballBatter and FamousBatsman types are mutually exclusive. Secondly, each of these types has at least one role specific to it only. Because of their common properties (birth country, birth year, death year) we may generalize FamousBaseballBatter and FamousBatsman to a more general type, e.g. FamousBatter. However, the original types must now be retained as subtypes, to constrain their specific roles only to them, as shown in Figure 3.28. When using NORMA to map this ORM schema to a relational schema, we can choose to map the whole ORM schema to a single table. This mapping option is not available for the ORM schema in Figure 3.27, which will always map to two relational tables.

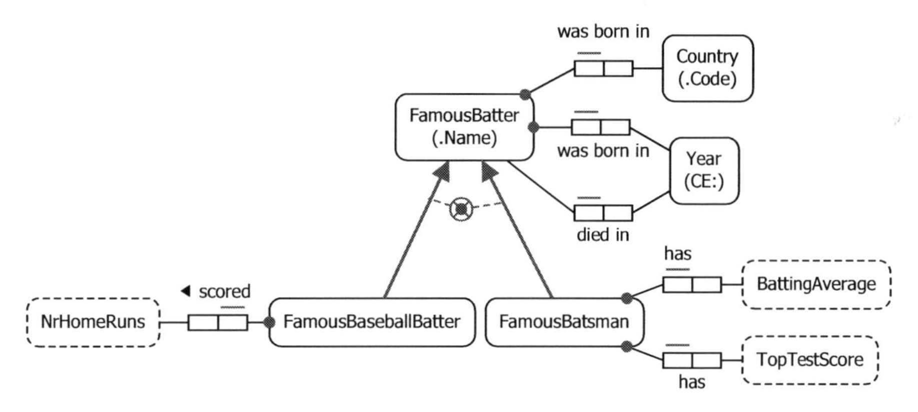

Figure 3.28 Applying generalization to the schema in Figure 3.27

In Figure 3.27, the FamousBaseballBatter and FamousBatsman entity types are referenced by the value types FamousBaseballBatterName and FamousBatsmanName. Although these value types are distinct, an instance of each value type could be represented by the same character string. For example, the Figure 3.27 schema would allow a baseball batter and a batsman to each have a name represented by the character string "John Smith".

In Figure 3.28, FamousBatter is referenced by the value type FamousBatterName, so the same character string cannot be used to represent both the name of a baseball batter and the name of a batsman. Hence the merging of the two naming schemes into one requires additional restrictions on how the entities are named. If such additional restrictions do not in fact apply in the domain being modeled, a new reference scheme should be introduced for the supertype. The original reference schemes for the subtypes can also be retained as a secondary reference scheme for them if desired.

If you wish, you can even use the original reference schemes for the subtypes as their preferred reference scheme within the context of the fact types directly attached to them. This is known as *context-dependent reference*, since the preferred reference scheme for an object depends on the context. This capability can be particularly useful when merging or federating formerly separate systems, in case we wish to retain the local identifiers as primary in their local context.

As an example consider the schema in Figure 3.29, which models a simplified fragment of an information system resulting from the merging of an employee record system and a student record system at a university. Here each person is either an employee or student, or both. In the original employee record system, employees were identified by employee numbers, and in the original student record system students were identified by student numbers.

In the combined system we wish to know which employees are students (e.g. to ensure that no employee teaches a course in which he or she is enrolled, and to record whether an employee receives a staff education grant to help with his/her studies). A new global identifier (PersonNr) is introduced for each person. Massive data already exists using the old identifiers (EmployeeNr and StudentNr) and the combined system retains these as preferred identifiers in the context where they were used.

A *dashed subtyping arrow* indicates that that subtyping relationship does not provide a path to the preferred identifier of the subtype. In this case, the subtype must either introduce its own preferred reference scheme (as with Employee and Student) or inherit its identification scheme from another subtyping path (as with StudentEmployee).

A *solid subtyping arrow* is used for a subtyping relationship that points the way to a supertype from which the subtype inherits its preferred reference scheme. For example, in the schema shown in Figure 3.29, when we populate the fact type StudentEmployee receives StaffEducationGrant, the student employees are identified by their employee numbers rather than their student numbers.

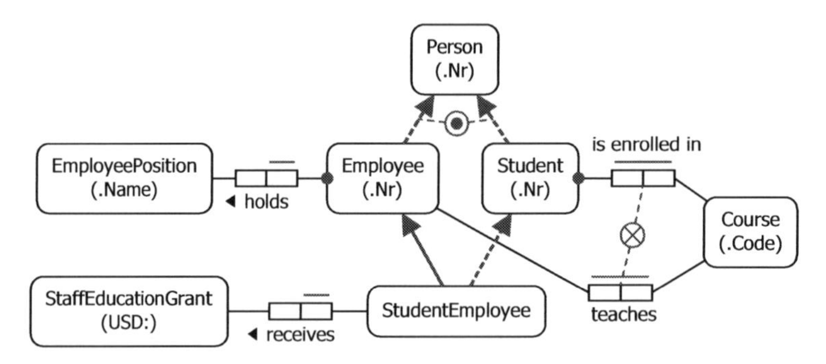

Figure 3.29 An example of context-dependent reference

Suppose that the person number 357 is assigned to the employee with employee number 203 who is also the student with student number 1005. This information can be asserted as instances of the instance-level identity relationships Employee is Person and Student is Person underlying the subtyping relationships from Employee and Student to Person.

The pair-exclusion constraint between the role pairs in Student is enrolled in Course and Employee teaches Course applies semantically to the actual entities (in this case, persons) involved, so this constraint ensures that nobody is enrolled in a course that they teach. This exclusion constraint verbalizes as follows:

For each Person **and** Course, **at most one of the following holds**:

some Student **who** is **that** Person is enrolled in **that** Course;

some Employee **who** is that Person teaches **that** Course.

Notice the use of the pronoun "**who**" instead of "**that**" when referencing some student or employee. To automate this pronoun choice when using NORMA to do the verbalization, set the isPersonal property of the Person object type to true.

3.4 NORMA Lab 3

Figure 3.30 shows an ORM schema that illustrates most aspects of the ORM graphical notation introduced in this chapter. This diagram was drawn using Microsoft Visio, but for this lab we'll enter the schema in the NORMA tool.

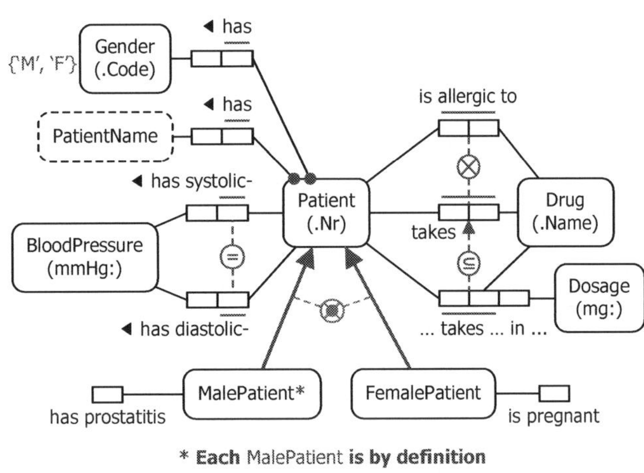

Figure 3.30 A Visio diagram of an ORM schema to be entered in NORMA

If needed, please review NORMA Labs 1 and 2. Now open Visual Studio, press File > New > File to open the New File dialog. Then select General > Object-Role Modeling File and press Open. In the Fact Editor, enter the gender, patient name and blood pressure fact types shown below in the usual way. Then move the fact types to the left of the Patient shape, right-click the predicates and choose Orientation > Reverse Role Order to reverse their direction, and use the Layout Toolbar to better align the shapes. For each of the four fact types, right-click its Patient role and choose the relevant options from its context menu to add the uniqueness and mandatory role constraints displayed below.

Select the Gender shape, open its Properties sheet, and enter M, F in its ValueRange property. Don't include the braces "{}", because NORMA adds those for you. The {'M', 'F'} *value constraint* on GenderCode is now displayed next to the Gender shape. Select this value constraint shape, and move it to the left of the Gender shape as shown on the right below.

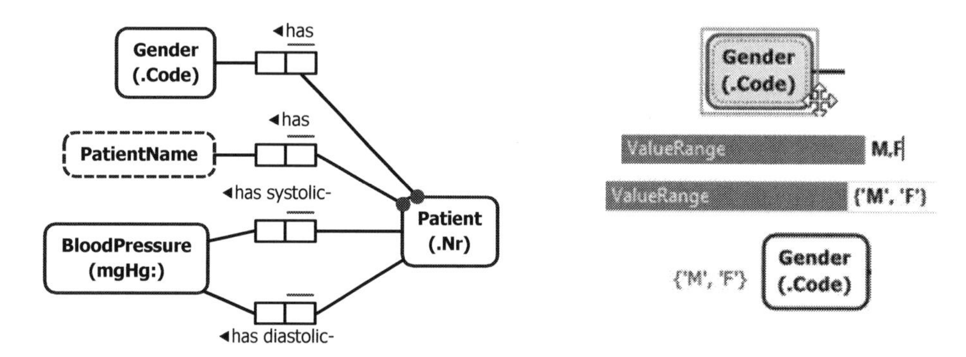

Drag the *Equality Constraint* shape from the toolbox to a place between the two blood pressure predicates. Double-click the constraint shape to active the constraint pointer, and click Patient's role in the "has systolic-"predicate (the role is now numbered 1). Double-click to commit this first role sequence (the roles is now numbered 1.1). Now click Patient's role in the "has diastolic-" predicate (the roles is now numbered 1). Double-click to commit this second role sequence (the roles are now numbered 1.1 and 2.1).

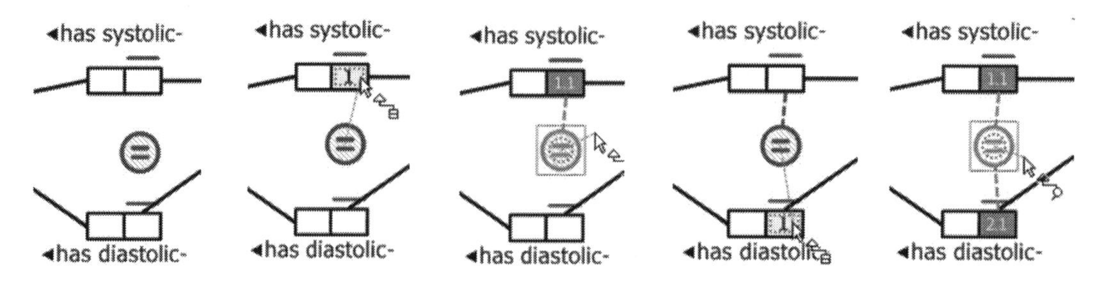

No further role sequences are involved in the constraint, so commit the constraint by pressing the escape key (Esc) or by clicking outside the shapes. If you wish, select the equality constraint shape and the constrained roles and use the Layout Toolbar to align them vertically. This part of the schema should now appear as shown below.

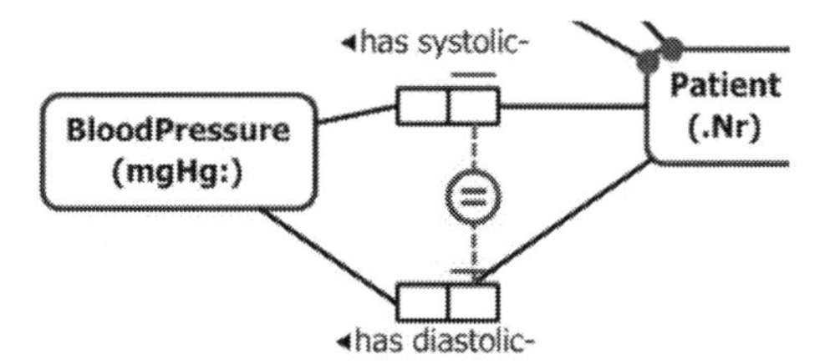

Use the Fact Editor to add the two drug fact types shown below, then select each Patient-Drug role pair and add a uniqueness constraint to it as shown. Drag the *Exclusion Constraint* shape from the toolbox to a place between the two predicates. Double-click the constraint shape to active the constraint pointer, and slowly click each role of the Patient is allergic to Drug fact type (the roles are now numbered 1 and 2). Double-click to commit this first role sequence (the roles are now numbered 1.1 and 1.2).

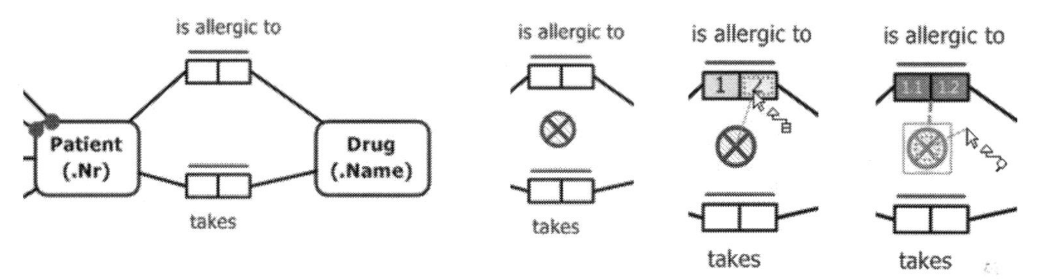

Now slowly click each role of the Patient takes Drug fact type (the roles are now numbered 1 and 2). Double-click to commit this second role sequence (the roles are now numbered 2.1 and 2.2). No further role sequences are involved in the constraint, so commit the constraint by pressing the escape key (Esc) or by clicking outside the shapes. The exclusion constraint ensures that no patient takes a drug he or she is allergic to. Use the Layout Toolbar to align the shapes vertically.

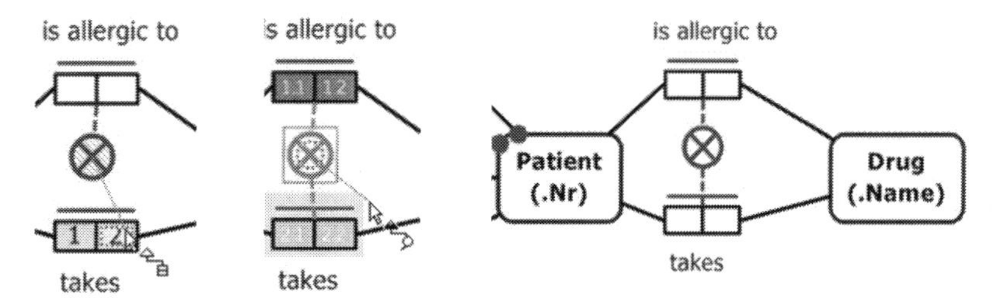

Now use the FactEditor to enter the ternary fact type shown below, right-click its Patient and Drug roles and add a uniqueness constraint to them as shown.

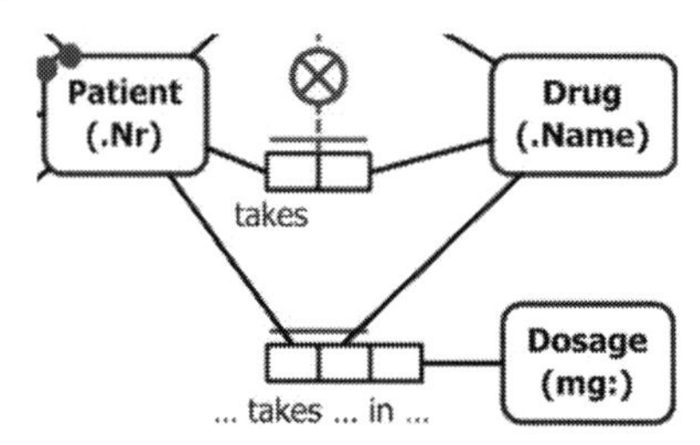

Drag the *Subset Constraint* shape from the toolbox to a place between the two predicates. Double-click the constraint shape to active the constraint pointer, and slowly click the Patient and Drug roles of the Patient takes Drug in Dosage fact type (the roles are now numbered 1 and 2). Double-click to commit this source role sequence (the roles are now numbered 1.1 and 1.2).

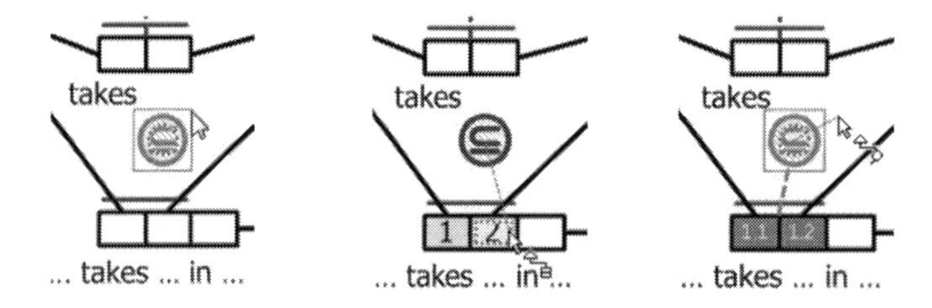

Now slowly click each role of the Patient takes Drug fact type (the roles are now numbered 1 and 2). Double-click to commit the constraint. Unlike equality and exclusion constraints, a subset constraint always applies to exactly two role sequences. If you now select the subset constraint shape, the roles in the target role sequence are numbered 2.1 and 2.2. Now select the subset constraint shape then the binary predicate and use the Layout Toolbar to align the shapes vertically.

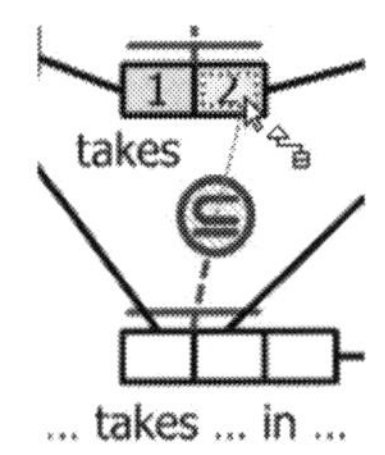

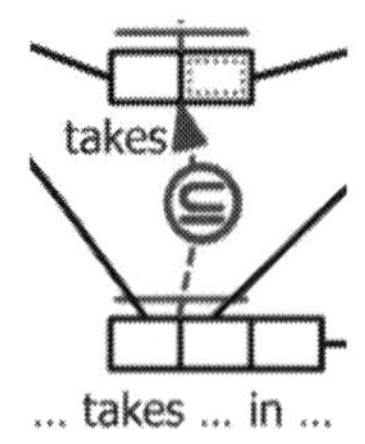

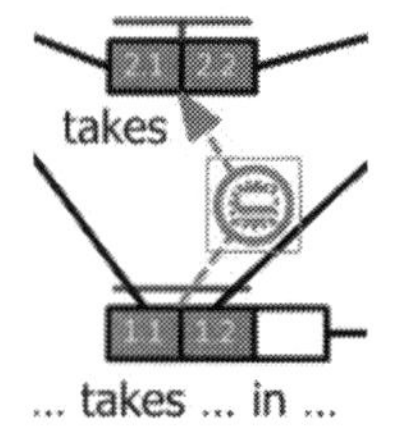

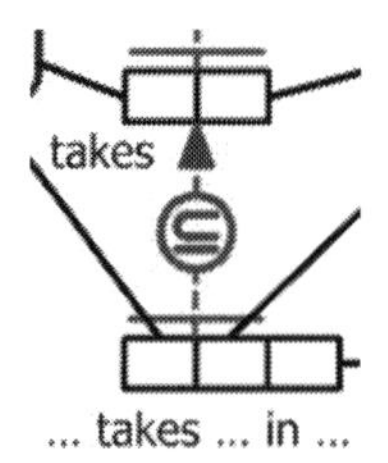

Individually select each set-comparison constraint shape and view its verbalization in the ORM Verbalization Browser. The equality, exclusion and subset constraints verbalizations display respectively as shown below.

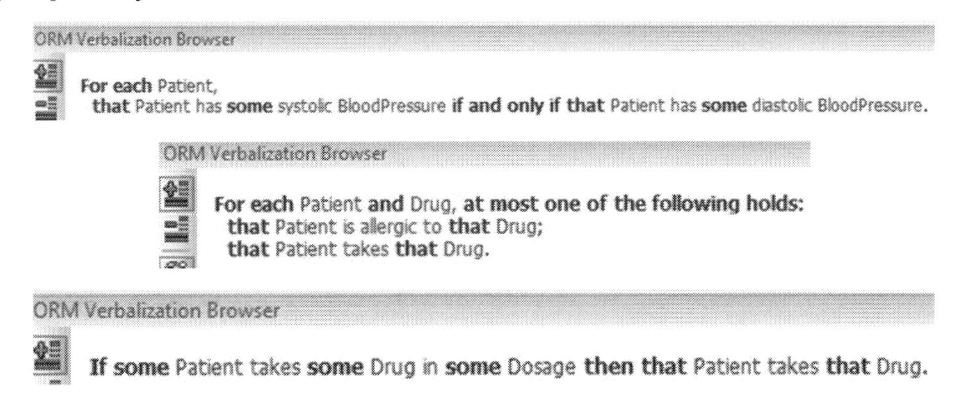

Now drag an Entity Type shape from the Toolbox and position it below the Patient shape as shown. By default, this is named "EntityType1". Select the shape, and change its name to "MalePatient" either by typing inside the shape or by editing its Name property in the Properties sheet. The MalePatient shape is displayed with red fill indicating an error state. To view the error message, right-click the shape then select Validation Errors from its context menu. This indicates that the entity type MalePatient requires a reference scheme. You can also view a detailed error message in the Verbalization Browser.

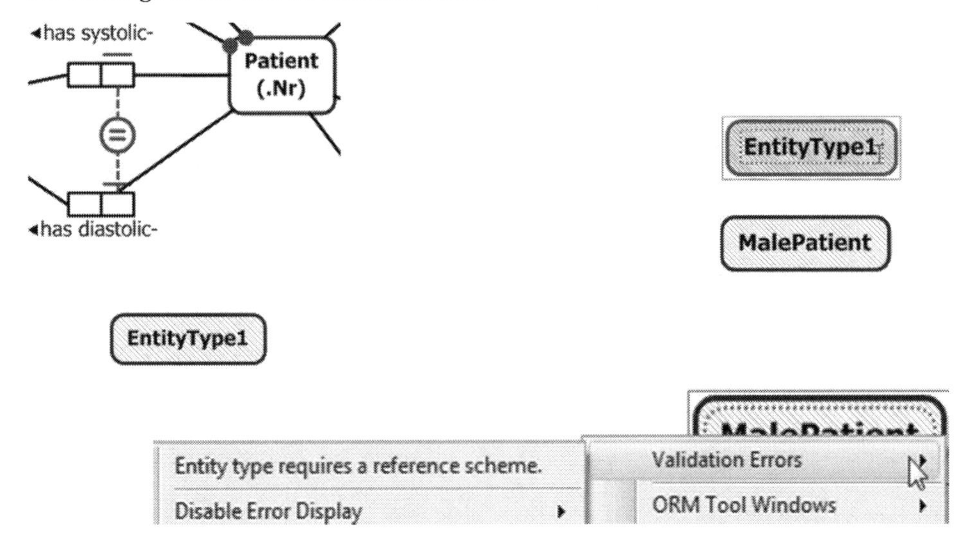

To remove this error, we will declare MalePatient as a subtype of Patient from which it will inherit its reference scheme. Drag the *Subtype Connector* shape from the Toolbox, then drag the connector shape from MalePatient to Patient (alternatively, with the connector click MalePatient then click Patient). A subtyping relationship arrow is now displayed as shown, and the error fill on MalePatient is removed.

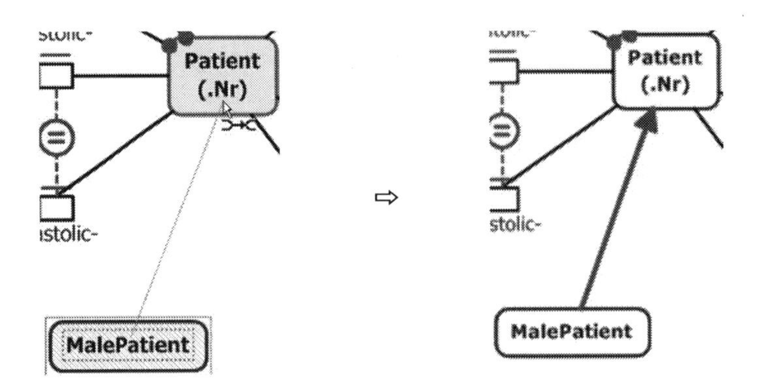

At this stage, the subtype MalePatient is simply asserted. To make it a derived subtype, select MalePatient, and in the DerivationNote property in the Properties sheet click the down-arrow and enter the following derivation rule, pressing Ctrl+Enter at the end of the first line of the subtype definition:

*Each MalePatient is by definition

some Patient who has Gender 'M'.

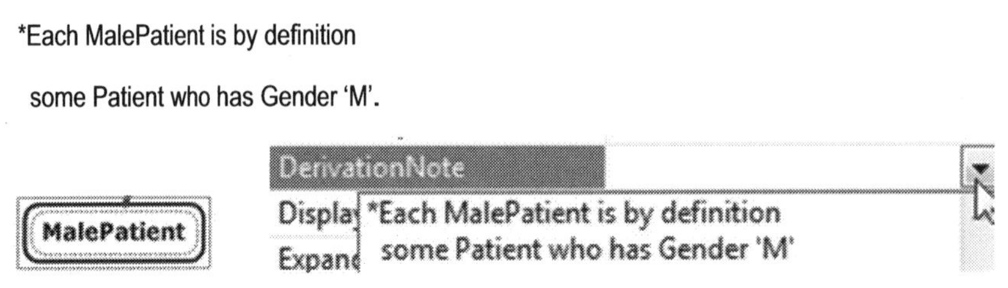

An asterisk is now appended to the subtype name, indicating that it is derived. Now drag a Model Note shape from the Toolbox, copy the subtype definition into the Model Note, drag a Model Note Connector from the Toolbox, and connect the note to the subtype shape as shown below.

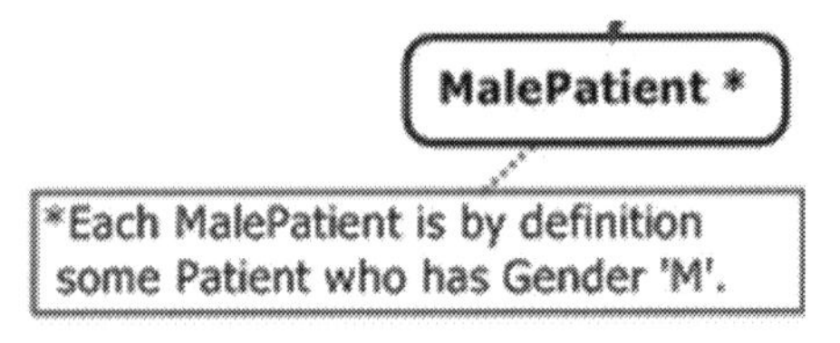

Now go through a similar procedure to add the FemalePatient subtype and its derivation rule. The subtyping graph should now display as shown.

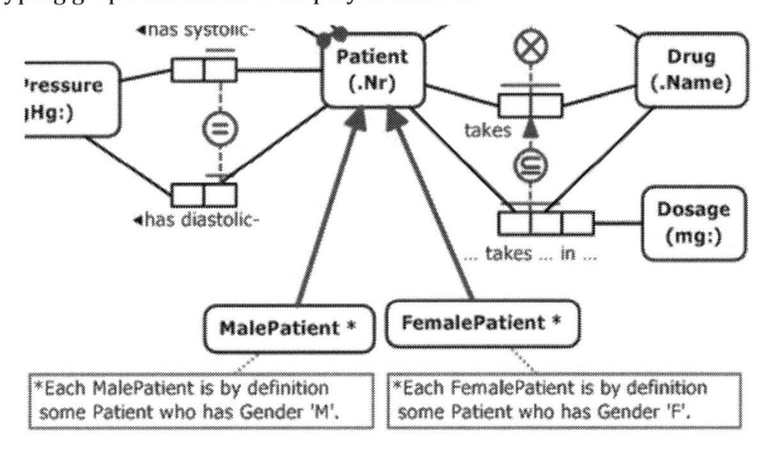

Now drag an *Exclusive-Or Constraint* shape from the Toolbox, and position it between the two subtyping arrows as shown below. Double-click the constraint, then click the left-hand subtyping arrow, then click the right-hand subtyping arrow, then double-click to commit the constraint.

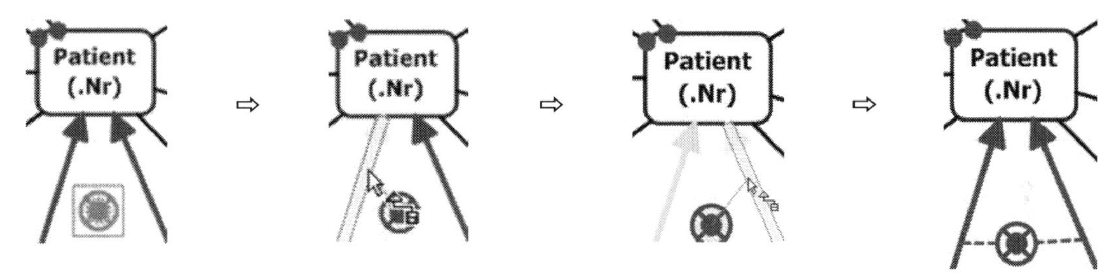

Although this exclusive-or constraint is derivable from the formal subtype definitions, in the public domain version of NORMA the subtype definitions can be entered only as informal, derivation notes. So here the xor constraint needs to be asserted and its shape displays in violet color rather than green.

Now select the xor constraint shape and view its verbalization in the ORM Verbalization Browser.

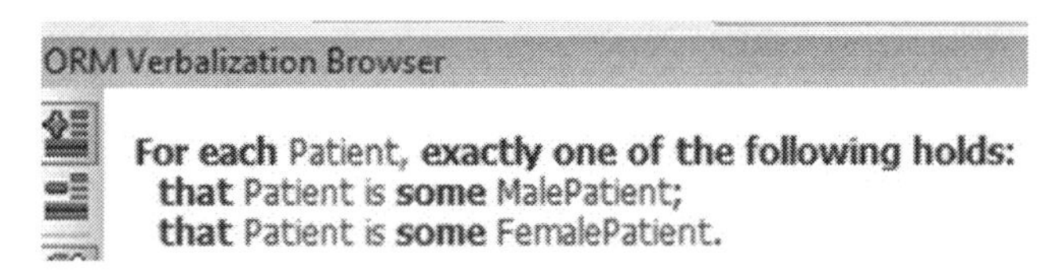

Our subtype definitions used the personal pronoun "**who**" instead of the impersonal pronoun "**that**" when referring to patients. To ensure this pronoun choice where relevant in verbalization of rules and constraints, select the Patient shape and double-click its IsPersonal property to toggle its value from False to True.

Now use the Fact Editor to add the unary fact types Malepatient has prostatitis and FemalePatient is pregnant. The full diagram should now appear as shown below.

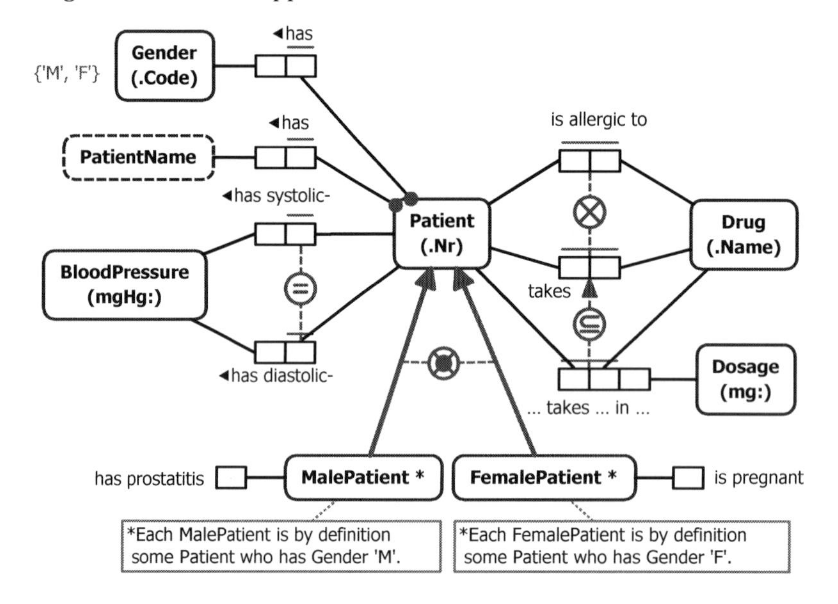

Now expand the Object Types section in the ORM Model Browser, then select each value type and set its datatype entries in the Properties sheet as follows:

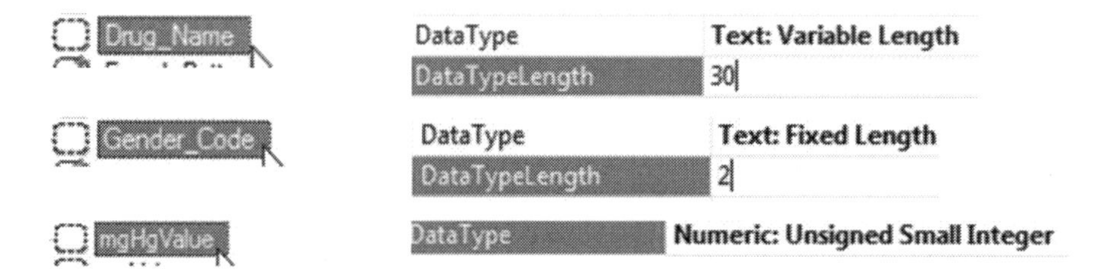

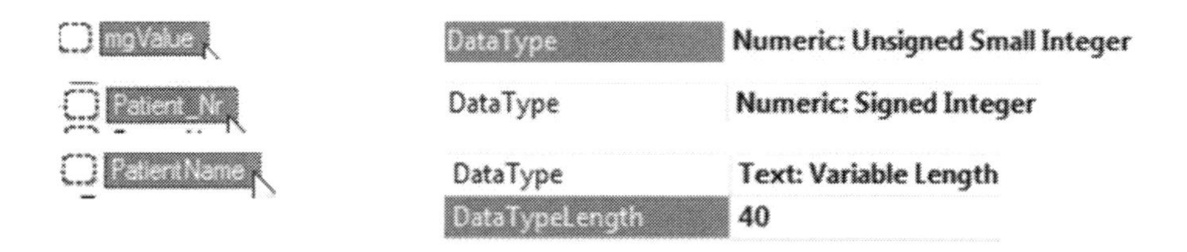

By default, NORMA includes an underscore "_" when generating the value type names "Drug_Name", "Gender_Code" and "Patient_Nr" from the reference mode names. Our current setting for relational mapping will remove these underscores when generating relational table or column names.

You could remove these underscores from the ORM value type names as well, by selecting the value type and editing its Name property (e.g. edit "Drug_Name" to "DrugName"), but this is inadvisable as it breaks the former link between reference mode names and value type names, so that reference mode names would now display simply as the long value type name. To retain the compact display of short reference mode names on the diagram, we should leave the value type names with underscores unaltered.

When mapping an ORM schema to a relational schema, NORMA currently generates a separate table for each fact type with a compound internal uniqueness constraint. For example, fact types Patient takes Drug and Patient takes Drug in Dosage map to two different tables.

A more efficient relational schema can be obtained by mapping these drug taking details into a common table. This can be achieved by applying the step in ORM's conceptual optimization procedure that recommends remodelling subsetting patterns such as that of Figure 3.31(a) by objectification, as in Figure 3.31(b). NORMA will then map the objectified design to a single table, with a nullable column for the dosage.

For further discussion of ORM conceptual optimization procedure, see section 14.5 of Halpin & Morgan (2008).

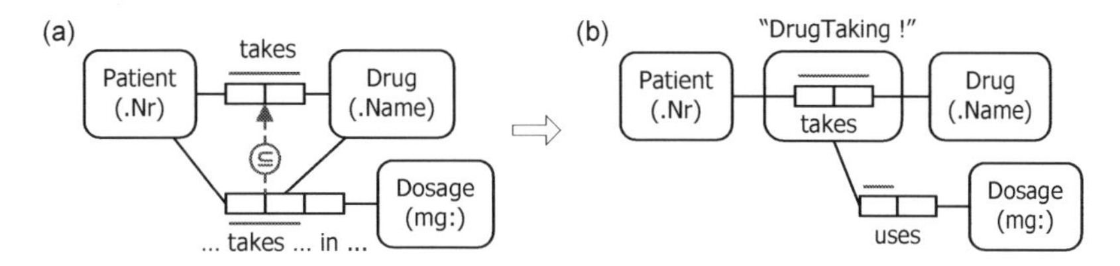

Figure 3.31 The ORM schema fragment (a) is optimized to schema fragment (b)

To modify our ORM schema accordingly, first delete the ternary fact type by selecting its shape, pressing the Delete key (or selecting Delete Fact Type from the context menu) and pressing the Yes button on the dialog shown below.

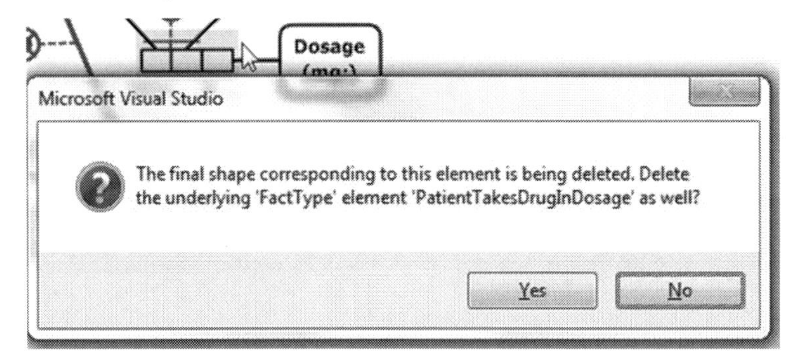

Now select the subset constraint shape, press the Delete key, then press the Yes button in the deletion dialog.

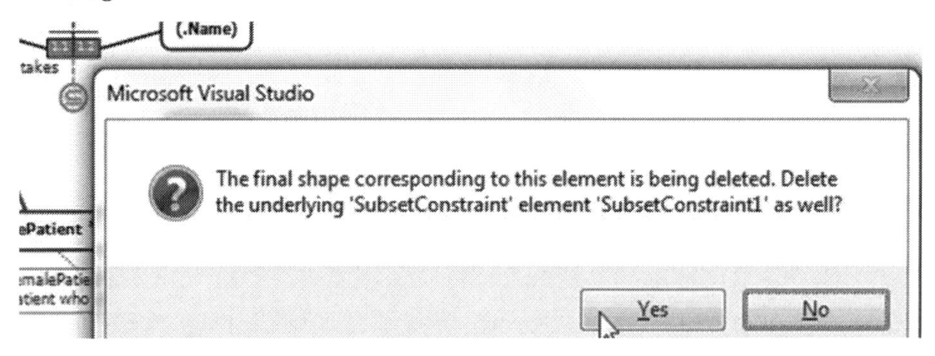

Now right-click the predicate shape in the fact type Patient takes Drug, and choose Objectify Fact Type from its context menu. The fact type is now objectified as "Patient takes Drug". Drag this label to the right of the shape as shown below, then double click its IsIndependent property to toggle its value from False to True (this setting allows us to record that a patient takes a drug without also recording the dosage).

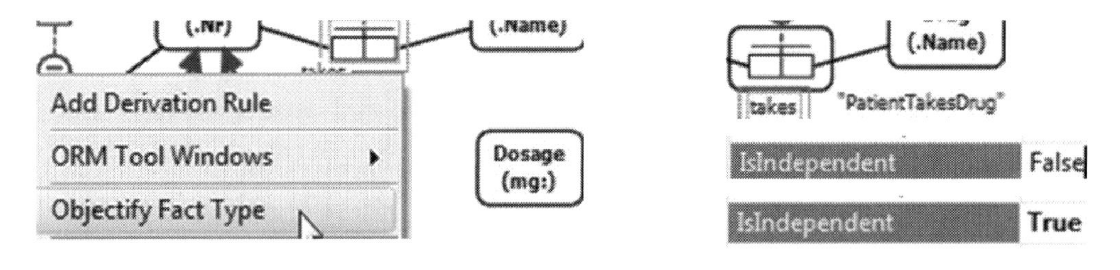

The label "Patient takes Drug !" now has an exclamation mark appended, indicating its independent status. Select this shape and edit its name to DrugTaking. You can do this *in situ* as shown below, or by editing its Name property. Now select the DrugTaking and Dosage shapes, open the Fact Editor, insert the predicate reading "uses", and press Ctrl+Enter to commit the new fact type.

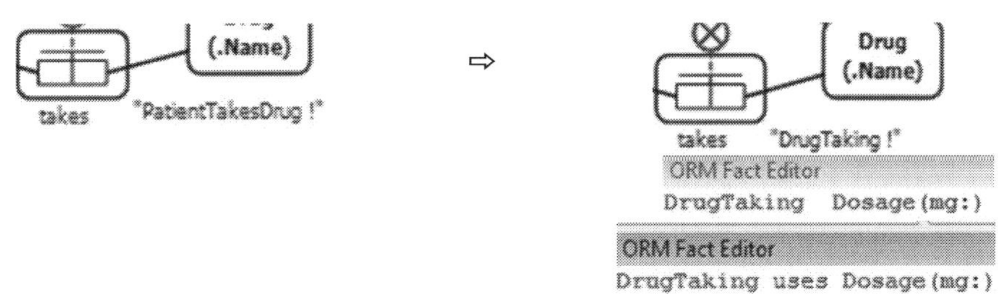

Now drag the uses predicate shape to the left of the Dosage shape, as shown below. Right-click the left role of the uses predicate and choose Add Uniqueness Constraint from its context menu, to obtain the final version of the ORM schema.

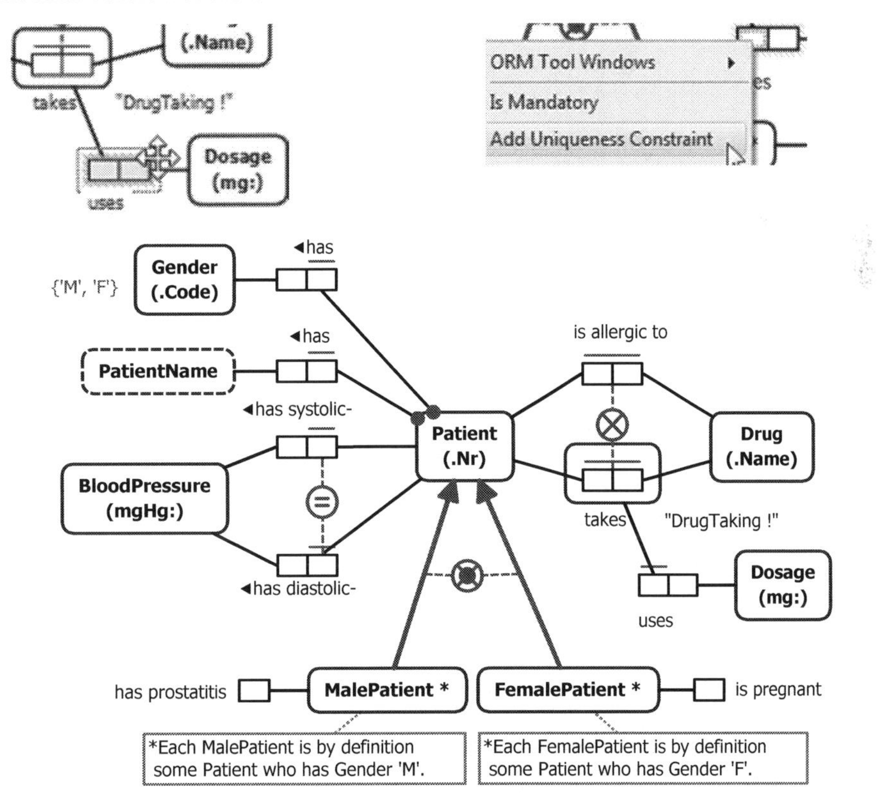

We are now ready for the relational mapping. Right-click an empty space in the Document Window, select Extension Manager ... > Relational View and press OK. Select the Relational View tab to view a diagram for the relational schema that is automatically generated from the ORM schema. Select the table shapes and drag them around to better align the foreign key relationship arrows, as shown below.

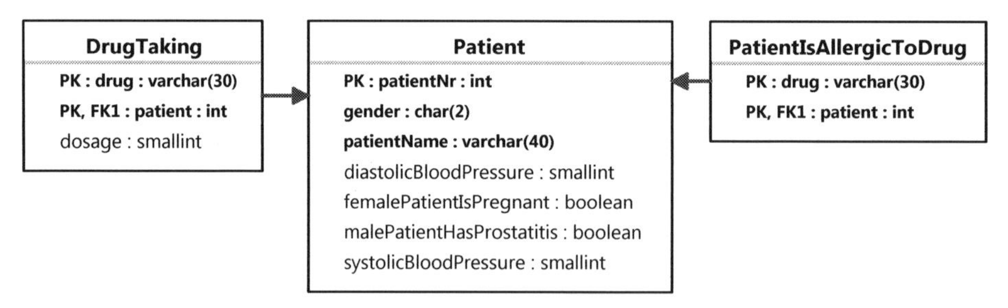

Primary and foreign key columns are annotated with "**PK**" or "**FK**" and non-nullable columns are displayed in **bold**. By default, NORMA's relational mapping procedure absorbs any functional fact types attached to the MalePatient and FemalePatient subtypes into the key table for their Patient supertype, thus resulting in the Boolean attributes shown.

Although the order of the columns in the relational tables has no bearing on the semantics, for presentation purposes it's often the case that some reordering of the generated columns is preferable. To move a column to a different position in its table, simply select the column and drag it to the desired position. For example, the following relational diagram has reordered columns in all three tables.

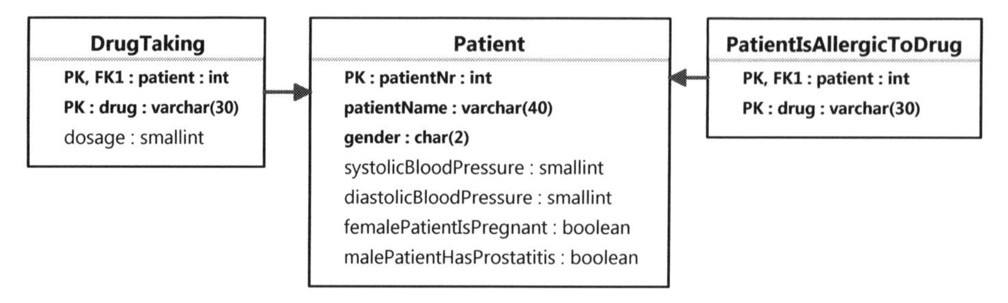

Value constraints, exclusive-or constraints, and set-comparison constraints are generally not displayed on the relational schema diagram. Code for value constraints is generated when using NORMA to generate SQL code for implementation. However, the current version of the public domain version of NORMA does not generate SQL code for more advanced ORM constraints such as the set-comparison constraints in this example.

Hence, while the ORM schema provides an excellent way to document the semantics of the business domain, in some cases you may need to do additional editing of the code generated by the current version of NORMA to ensure the completeness of the relational database implementation.

As discussed, for relational mapping NORMA by default absorbs functional details for subtypes into a supertype table. As an alternative mapping option, you can choose to map such subtype details into a separate table for the subtype. Let's try this now for the MalePatient and FemalePatient subtypes.

Select the subtyping connection from MalePatient to Patient, click the down-arrow in its AbsorptionChoice property, and change its setting from Absorbed to Not Absorbed.

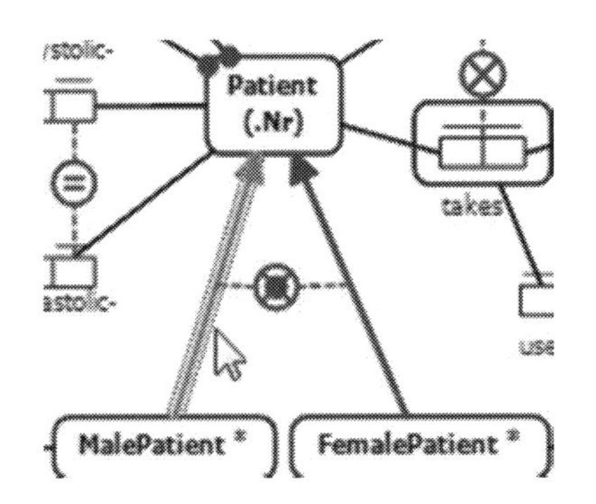

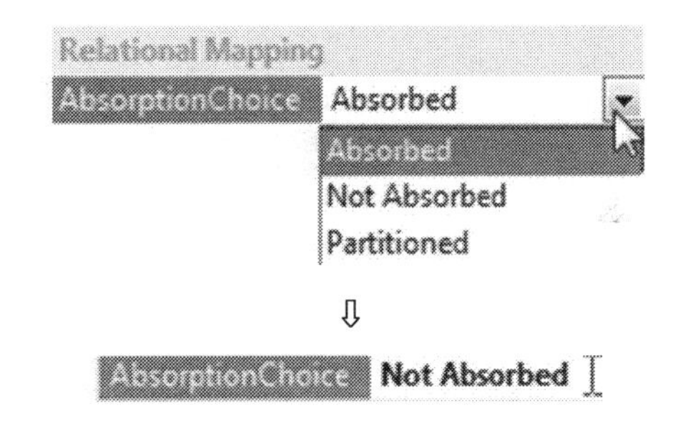

Another way to change the subtype mapping choice is to select the subtype shape and change its AbsorptionChoice setting from Absorbed (All Paths) to Separate. Try this now for the FemalePatient subtype, as shown below.

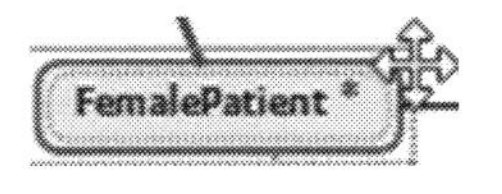

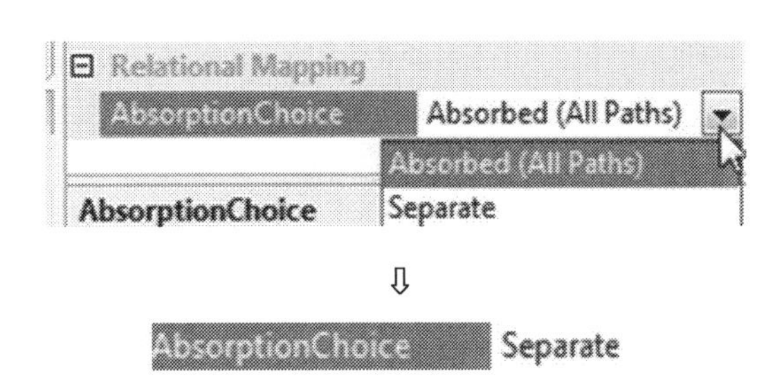

The relational schema diagram now displays with separate tables for MalePatient and FemalePatient. This five table relational schema is easier to understand than the previous version. However, the version based on subtype absorption, where the subtype details are mapped into the Patient table, is typically more efficient.

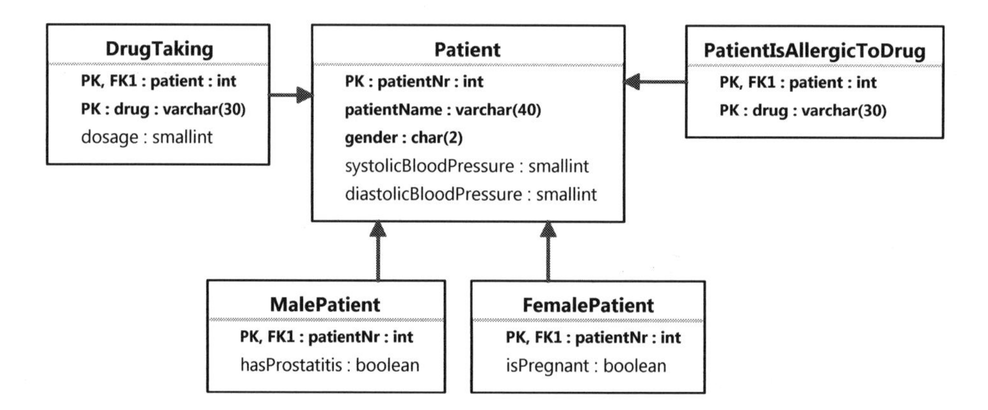

To complete this lab, save your work by pressing the Save icon in the main menu to open the Save File As dialog, then enter Lab3 as the FileName and press the Save button.

4 CSDP Step 7

The previous chapters covered the first six steps of the Conceptual Schema design Procedure (CSDP), in which we verbalized examples of the required information as atomic facts, drew the fact types, performed a population check, checked for object types that should be combined, noted any arithmetic derivation rules, added uniqueness (internal or external) and mandatory role (simple or disjunctive) constraints, noted any logical derivation rules, added any relevant value (object type value or role value) constraints, added any relevant set-comparison (subset, equality or exclusion) constraints, and added any relevant subtyping.

This chapter discusses *CSDP Step 7*, in which we perform the following tasks:

- Add frequency constraints
    - internal frequency constraints
    - external frequency constraints
- Add ring constraints
    - irreflexive constraints
    - asymmetric constraints
    - antisymmetric constraints
    - intransitive constraints
    - strongly intransitive constraints
    - acyclic constraints
    - locally reflexive constraints
    - symmetric constraints
    - transitive constraints
- Add value-comparison constraints
- Add cardinality constraints
    - Object cardinality constraints
    - Role cardinality constraints
- Add deontic constraints
- Add textual constraints
- Perform final checks

4.1 Frequency Constraints

Table 4.1 Roman triumvirates (incomplete member details)

Nr	*Start Year*	*Members*
1	60 BCE	Gaius Julius Caesar, Marcus Crassus, Gnaeus Pompeius Magnus
2	43 BCE	?

The report shown in Table 4.1 provides some details about the first and second triumvirates of ancient Rome, when it was jointly ruled by three of its citizens. For each included triumvirate, we must record the year it started, but it is optional whether we list its members. However, *if we do record any members of a triumvirate, we must record all three members.*

Figure 4.1 shows an ORM model for this report. Notice the number 3 attached by a dashed line to Triumvirate's role in the fact type Triumvirate includes FamousRoman. This is a *simple internal frequency constraint* to enforce the constraint highlighted in italics in the previous paragraph. This constraint verbalizes as follows:

Each Triumvirate **in the population of** "Triumvirate includes FamousRoman"

occurs there exactly 3 **times.**

Hence, if a triumvirate occurs in the fact table for Triumvirate includes FamousRoman it must occur there on three rows, as shown in Figure 4.1. This entails that a compound transaction must be used to populate the table (for each triumvirate, we either add all three members or we add none).

A frequency constraint is also called an *occurrence frequency constraint.* It constrains how many times an entry that occurs in any given population of the constrained role (or role sequence) occurs there. Like uniqueness constraints, frequency constraints are *local* constraints on the relevant role(s), not global constraints on the object type. In principle, we could treat a uniqueness constraint as a frequency constraint of frequency 1; but uniqueness constraints are so important that they deserve their own graphical notation (using a uniqueness bar). Note that a frequency constraint of zero doesn't make sense, because a frequency constraint applies only to an entry that already occurs at least once.

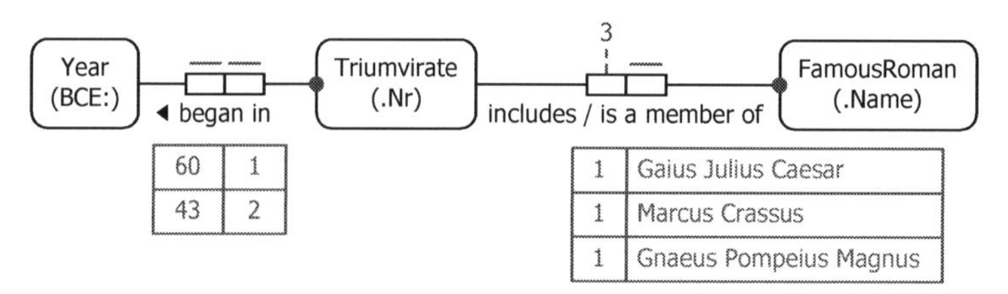

Figure 4.1 An ORM model for Table 4.1 including a simple frequency constraint

Table 4.2 Roman triumvirates (complete member details)

Nr	*Start Year*	*Members*
1	60 BCE	Gaius Julius Caesar, Marcus Crassus, Gnaeus Pompeius Magnus
2	43 BCE	Gaius Octavius, Marcus Antonius, Marcus Aemilius Lepidus

Now consider the report in Table 4.2. In this business domain, if a triumvirate is listed we must record all its members. To cater for this additional requirement, we add a mandatory role constraint to Triumvirate's role in the fact type Triumvirate includes FamousRoman, as shown in Figure 4.2. The combination of the mandatory role and frequency constraints on this role ensures that each recorded triumvirate includes exactly three members.

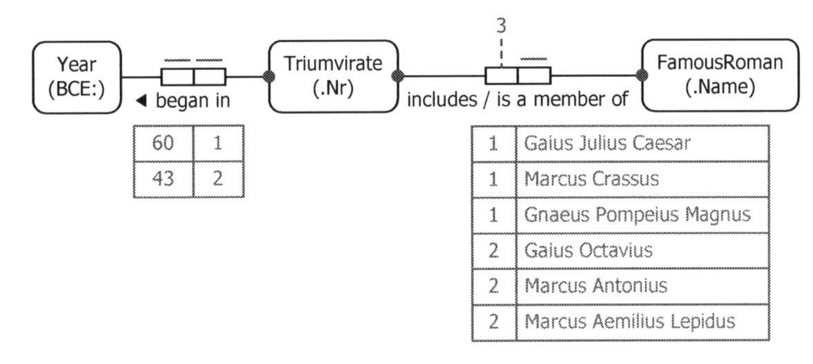

Figure 4.2 An ORM model for Table 4.2

A *compound internal frequency constraint* applies to multiple roles of the same fact type. If the constraint applies to two adjacent roles, the dashed line is connected to the junction of the roles. For example, the frequency constraint in Figure 4.3 verbalizes thus: **Each** Department, Year **combination in the population of** "Department in Year had staff of Gender in Quantity" **occurs there exactly** 2 **times.** Hence if we record the staff gender statistics for the sales department in a given year, we must include the staff numbers for both genders, as shown in the sample population.

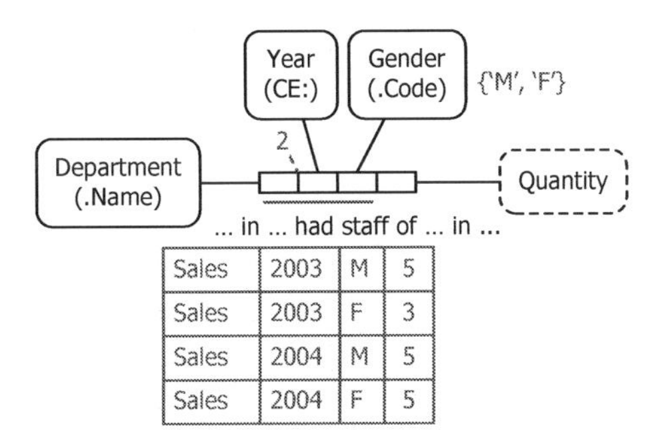

Figure 4.3 An ORM schema with a compound internal frequency constraint

Frequency constraints may also specify *frequency ranges* with a lower limit of at least 1 and/or an upper limit of at least 2. A lower limit of 1 is assumed by default. For display purposes, the following notations are used. Combinations of ranges are also allowed.

- $\leq n$ at most n, i.e. from 1 to n inclusive (where n is at least 2)
- $\geq n$ at least n, i.e. 1 or more (where n is at least 1)
- $n..m$ at least n and at most m (where $2 \leq n < m$)

For example, the ORM schema in Figure 4.4 includes three frequency range constraints. The frequency constraint displayed as "5..50" ensures that any department with employees recorded must have at least 5 and at most 50 members listed. The "≤ 3" frequency constraint ensures that each employee works on at most 3 current projects. The "≥ 4" frequency constraint ensures that each current project that has some employees recorded to work on it has at least 4 employees assigned to work on it.

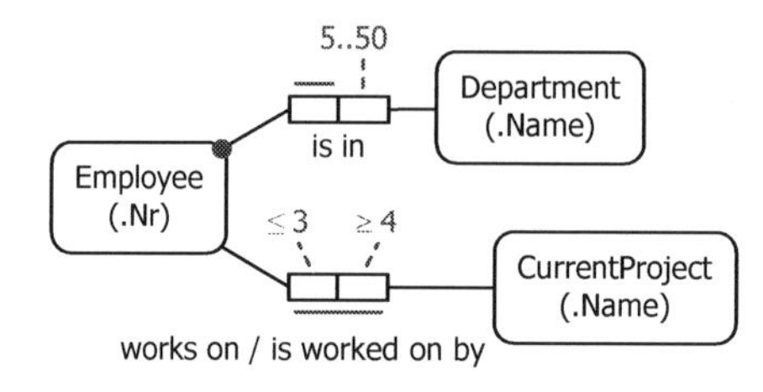

Figure 4.4 An ORM schema with some frequency range constraints

An *external frequency constraint* applies to roles from different predicates, and is displayed with an enclosing circle connected by dashed lines to the constrained roles. For example, many years ago I taught computer science at the University of Queensland in Australia, and we had a rule that no student could enroll in the same course more than twice. Students who failed a course on their first attempt were given only one more chance to pass the course on a subsequent enrolment. Figure 4.5 shows an ORM schema for this situation.

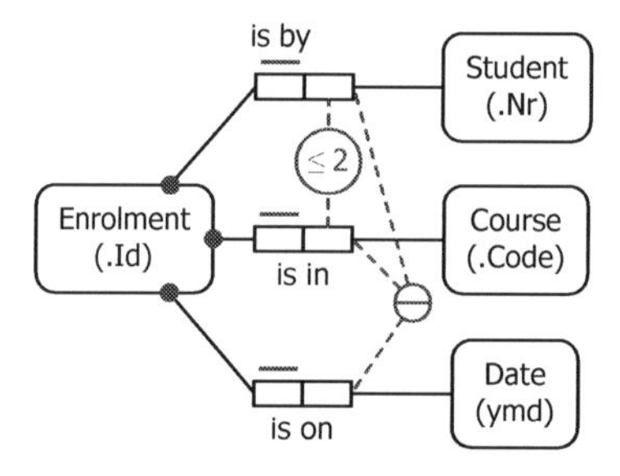

Figure 4.5 An ORM schema with an external frequency constraint

Here, the reference scheme Enrolment(.Id) indicates that enrolments are primarily identified by simple identifier. By default, NORMA assigns an auto-generated data type for Id reference modes. A natural but secondary reference scheme for enrolments is provided by the combination of the student, course and enrolment date. The external uniqueness constraint verbalizes as follows:

For each Student, Course, **and** Date
at most one Enrolment is by **that** Student
and is in **that** Course
and is on **that** Date.

The "≤ 2" external frequency constraint applied to the Student and Course roles shown ensures that no student can enroll more than twice in the same course. This constraint verbalizes as follows:

For each Student **and** Course,
there are at most 2 **instances of** Enrolment **such that**
that Enrolment is by **that** Student
and is in **that** Course.

4.2 Ring Constraints

Figure 4.6 shows an ORM schema and sample population to record brotherhood relationships among members of a family. In this small UoD, family members are identified simply by a given name. Both roles of the fact type FamilyMember is a brother of FamilyMember are hosted by the same object type. Fact types like this are called *ring fact types*, because the path from the object type through the predicate and back to the object type forms a ring. The sample data satisfies the uniqueness constraint on the fact type, but there is still something wrong with the data. See if you can spot the problem before reading on.

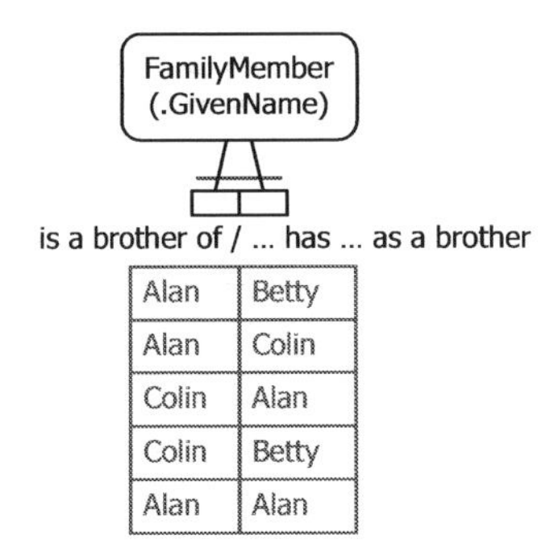

Figure 4.6 What's wrong with this model?

As you probably noted, the final row of data in the fact table should be rejected because nobody can be his own brother (see Figure 4.7(a)). A relationship *R* is *irreflexive* if and only if no object can bear the relationship *R* to itself. The top icon in Figure 4.7(b) intuitively visualizes an irreflexive relationship using a dot for an object and an arrow-tipped arc with a stroke through the arc to indicate the object cannot relate to itself. The simplified icon below it removes the arrow-tip[14], and is used in ORM to graphically depict an *irreflexive constraint.*

An irreflexive constraint is an example of a general class of constraints known as *ring constraints*. In ORM, a ring constraint may be applied only to a pair of roles that are compatible. Compatible roles are hosted by the same object type or by object types that are compatible (e.g. one type might be a subtype of the other, or both types may be overlapping subtypes). The pair of roles may come from a binary or longer fact type, or even from different fact types.

Graphically, the ring constraint shape is connected by a dashed line to the role pair that it constrains. If the roles are contiguous, the connector attaches to the junction of the roles, as shown in Figure 4.7(c). This irreflexive constraint may be verbalized as: **No** FamilyMember is a brother of **itself.** Currently, NORMA generates the following alternative verbalization:

No FamilyMember is a brother of **the same** FamilyMember.

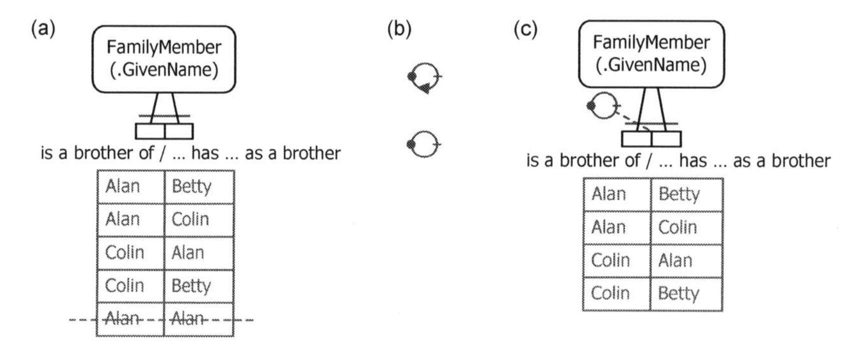

Figure 4.7 Adding an irreflexive ring constraint to the brotherhood relationship

Now consider the populated ORM schema in Figure 4.8. The sample data satisfies the uniqueness constraint and mandatory role constraints on the fact type, but there is still something wrong the data. See if you can spot the problem before reading on.

---

[14] Although removal of the arrow-tip makes the constraint icon somewhat less intuitive, it enables combinations of ring constraints to be depicted more clearly using a single icon.

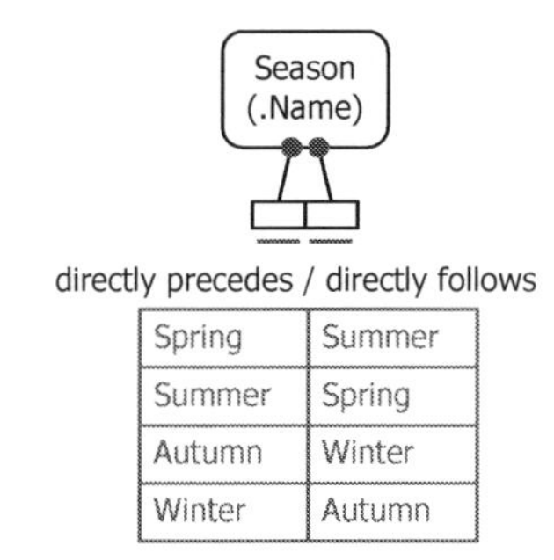

Spring	Summer
Summer	Spring
Autumn	Winter
Winter	Autumn

Figure 4.8 What's wrong here?

A season cannot directly precede the season that immediately precedes it (e.g. if spring directly precedes summer then summer can't directly precede spring). To enforce this restriction, we declare the direct precedence relationship to be *asymmetric*. A relationship *R* is asymmetric if and only if it satisfies the following condition: given any objects *a* and *b*, not necessarily distinct, if *a* bears the relationship *R* to *b* then *b* cannot bear the relationship *R* to *a*.

The top icon in Figure 4.9(a) intuitively visualizes an asymmetric ring constraint using a dot for each object, an arrow-tipped arc for the relationship in one direction, and a stroke through the other arrow-tipped arc to forbid the relationship in the other direction. The simplified icon just below it removes the arrow-tips, and is used in ORM to graphically depict an *asymmetric constraint.*

Graphically, the ring constraint shape is connected by a dashed line to the role pair that it constrains, as shown in Figure 4.9(b). The population of the fact type has now been adjusted to satisfy the asymmetric constraint, which verbalizes as follows.

If Season$_1$ precedes Season$_2$

then it is impossible that Season$_2$ precedes Season$_1$.

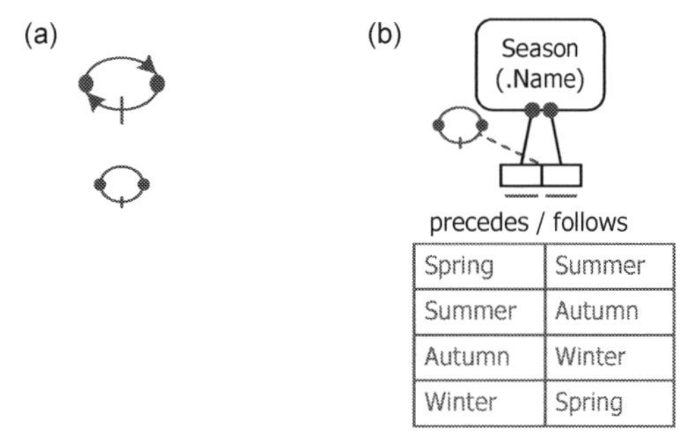

Spring	Summer
Summer	Autumn
Autumn	Winter
Winter	Spring

Figure 4.9 Adding an asymmetric ring constraint

The precedence relationship in Figure 4.9 is also irreflexive, since no season precedes itself. However, the definition of asymmetry includes the case where the objects *a* and *b* are the same, so asymmetry implies irreflexivity. Hence we do not add an irreflexive constraint to the schema in Figure 4.9, because that constraint is implied.

If we remove the irreflexive requirement from asymmetry we obtain the weaker notion of *antisymmetry*. A relationship *R* is antisymmetric if and only if it satisfies the following condition: given any *distinct* objects *a* and *b*, if *a* bears the relationship *R* to *b* then *b* cannot bear the relationship *R* to *a*.

For example, in Figure 4.10(a) the fact type FamilyMember is taller than FamilyMember is asymmetric, and hence both antisymmetric and irreflexive. In Figure 4.10(c), the fact type FamilyMember is at least as tall as FamilyMember is antisymmetric, and hence not irreflexive, since each person is at least as tall as himself/herself.

The top icon in Figure 4.10(b) intuitively visualizes an antisymmetric ring constraint using different kinds of dots to indicate distinct objects. The simplified icon just below it removes the arrow-tips, and is used in ORM to graphically depict an *antisymmetric constraint.*

Graphically, the ring constraint shape is connected by a dashed line to the role pair that it constrains, as shown in Figure 4.10(c). This antisymmetric constraint verbalizes as follows.

If FamilyMember$_1$ is at least as tall as FamilyMember$_2$ **and** FamilyMember$_1$ **is not** FamilyMember$_2$

then it is impossible that FamilyMember$_2$ is at least as tall as FamilyMember$_1$.

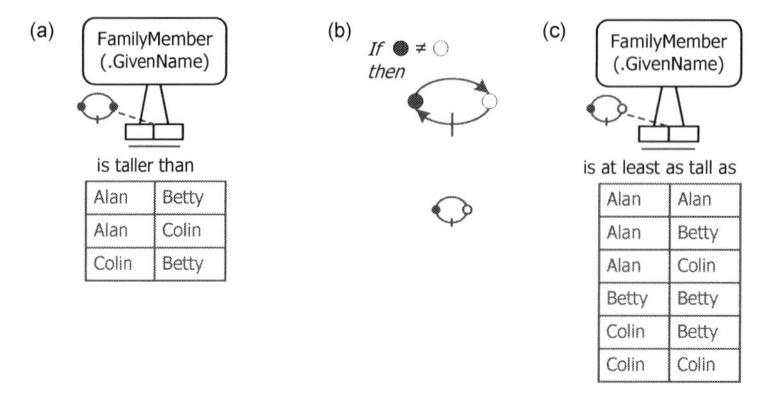

Figure 4.10 An antisymmetric ring constraint constrains only distinct objects

If two roles are mutually exclusive, an asymmetric constraint is implied between them, because no given object can populate both roles. For example, consider the sample population in Figure 4.11(a). Here, patient 157 is the husband of patient 158. If we now try to add the fact that patient 158 is the husband of patient 157 (and hence violate asymmetry), this will be rejected because the exclusion constraint forbids a patient from playing both the husband and wife roles. Thus, an asymmetric constraint is implied between the husband and wife roles in Figure 4.11(a), so we do not declare that ring constraint.

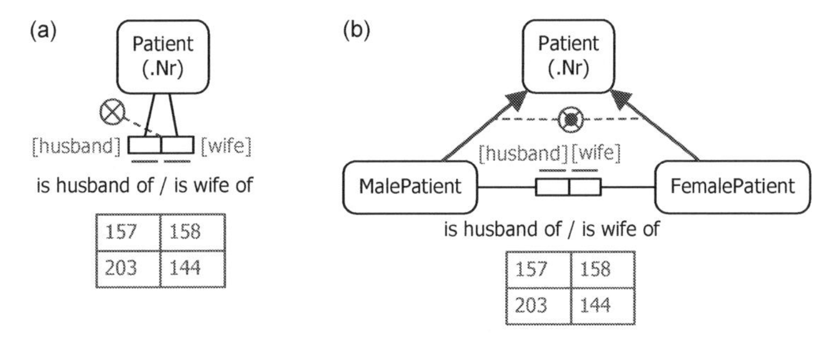

Figure 4.11 An exclusion constraint implies an asymmetric constraint

In Figure 4.11(b) the subtype partition constraint implies that the husband and wife roles are exclusive, which in turn implies an asymmetric constraint over these roles. Since asymmetry also implies irreflexivity and antisymmetry, the husband-wife role pair in each of the two schemas in Figure 4.11 has three implied ring constraints. To avoid useless clutter, these implied constraints are not displayed.

As background to our next ring constraint, we first provide some basic definitions. A binary relationship *R* is *transitive* if and only if it satisfies the following condition: given any objects *a*, *b*, and *c*, not necessarily distinct, if *a* bears the relationship *R* to *b*, and *b* bears the relationship *R* to *c* then *a* must bear the relationship *R* to *c*. For example, the ring fact type Person is older than Person is transitive. Transitive ring constraints are rarely used, because transitive relations are typically best dealt with by using a derive fact type, so we postpone their discussion till later. At this point we focus instead on intransitive ring constraints.

A binary relationship *R* is *intransitive*[15] (also called antitransitive or atransitive) if and only if it satisfies the following condition: given any objects *a*, *b*, and *c*, not necessarily distinct, if *a* bears the relationship *R* to *b* and *b* bears the relationship *R* to *c* then *a* cannot bear the relationship *R* to *c*. For example, the ring fact type Person is one year older than Person is intransitive.

---

[15] Some authors use "intransitive" in a weaker sense, to simply mean not transitive. To avoid confusion, this weaker notion is better named "nontransitive". A relation *R* is nontransitive if and only if there is at least one case where *a* bears the relationship *R* to *b* and *b* bears the relationship *R* to *c* but *a* does not bear the relationship *R* to *c*.

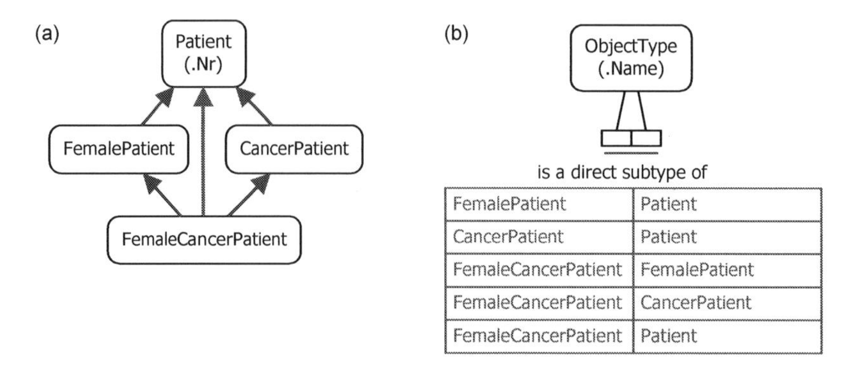

Figure 4.12 ORM does not allow indirect subtyping relationships to be asserted

As discussed in section 3.3, any asserted subtyping links must be direct rather than indirect, so the subtyping link from FemaleCancerPatient to Patient in Figure 4.12(a) is not allowed. Figure 4.12(b) shows a fragment of an ORM *metaschema* that can be used by a tool such as NORMA to store subtyping assertions in any given ORM model. Here the meta-fact type ObjectType is a direct subtype of ObjectType is populated with the subtyping details asserted in Figure 4.12(a). The final entry in the meta-table states that FemaleCancerPatient is a direct subtype of Patient. This is incorrect, because this subtyping link is indirect.

As an attempt to prevent such errors, we might constrain the meta-fact type ObjectType is a direct subtype of ObjectType to be intransitive by adding an *intransitive ring constraint*, as shown in Figure 4.13(b). The intuitive icon at the top of Figure 4.13(a) uses dots for objects and unadorned arrows for relationships between them. The arrow with a stroke indicates that this shortcut relationship is not allowed. The simplified icon below it removes the arrow-tips, and is used in ORM to depict an intransitive constraint. The intransitive ring constraint in Figure 4.13(b) verbalizes thus: **If** ObjectType$_1$ is a direct subtype of ObjectType$_2$ **and** ObjectType$_2$ is a direct subtype of ObjectType$_3$ **then it is impossible that** ObjectType$_1$ is a direct subtype of ObjectType$_3$.

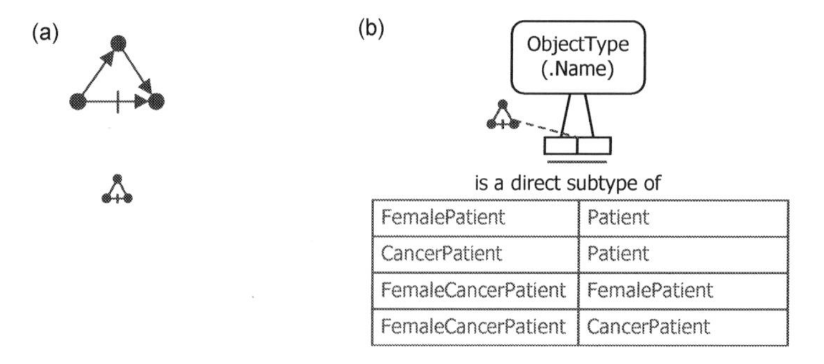

Figure 4.13 Adding an intransitive ring constraint

Now consider the expanded subtyping graph shown in Figure 4.14(a), which adds GirlCancerPatient as a further subtype. Figure 4.14(b) shows an ORM model for this graph. Here, the direct subtyping relationship is intransitive, but there's still a problem. Try to spot the problem before reading on.

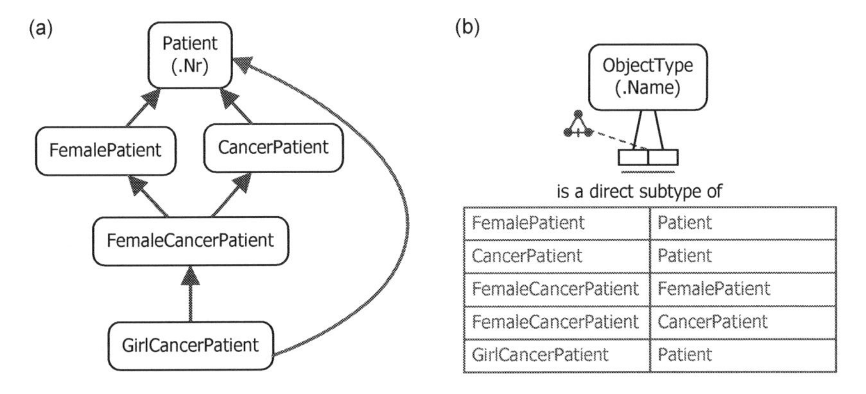

FemalePatient	Patient
CancerPatient	Patient
FemaleCancerPatient	FemalePatient
FemaleCancerPatient	CancerPatient
GirlCancerPatient	Patient

Figure 4.14 The subtyping relationship is intransitive but is still wrong

The subtyping link from GirlCancerPatient to Patient should not be asserted since it can be derived from the three subtyping links on the path from GirlCancerPatient through FemaleCancerPatient then CancerPatient to Patient. An intransitive constraint prevents shortcuts that jump over a single node in the graph, but it allows a shortcut to jump over more than one node, as in this case.

To block shortcuts that jump over any number of nodes (Figure 4.15 includes four such shortcuts), we declare the relationship to be *strongly intransitive*. A binary relationship *R* is *strongly intransitive* if and only if it satisfies the following condition: given any objects *a*, *b*, and *c*, not necessarily distinct, if *a* bears the relationship *R* to *b* and *b* has a *path* of one or more *R* relationships ending at *c* then *a* cannot bear the relationship *R* to *c*.

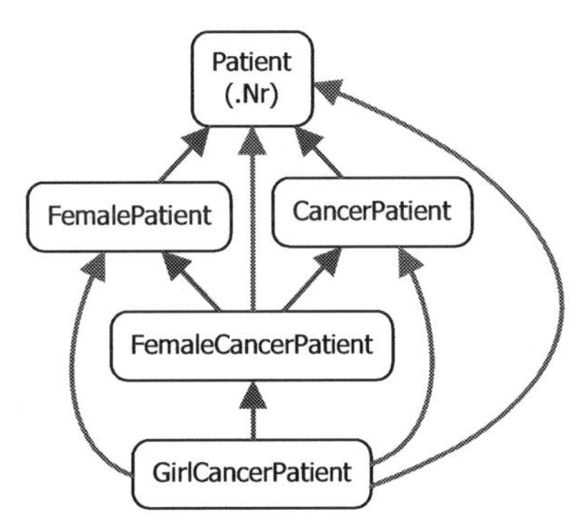

Figure 4.15 The four indirect subtyping links violate strong intransitivity

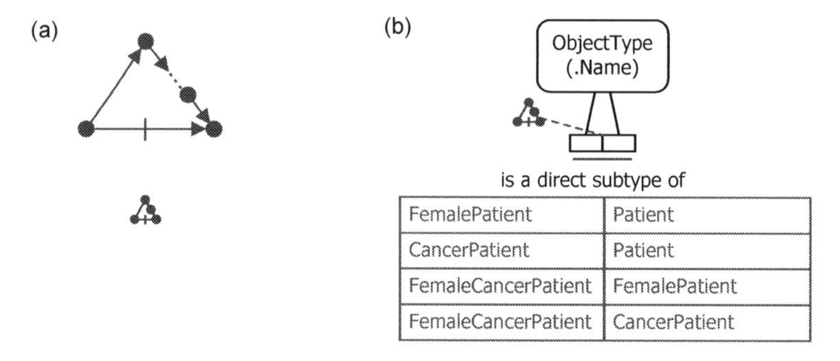

FemalePatient	Patient
CancerPatient	Patient
FemaleCancerPatient	FemalePatient
FemaleCancerPatient	CancerPatient

Figure 4.16 Declaring the subtyping relationship to be strongly intransitive

In practice, almost all intransitive relationships encountered in real situations are strongly intransitive. An intuitive icon for strong intransitivity is depicted at the top of Figure 4.16(a). The simplified icon below it is used in ORM to depict a *strongly intransitive constraint.* The strongly intransitive ring constraint in Figure 4.16(b) verbalizes as follows: **If** ObjectType$_1$ is a direct subtype of **some** ObjectType$_2$ **then it is not true that** ObjectType$_1$ **is indirectly related to** ObjectType$_2$ **by repeatedly applying this fact type**.

Strong intransitivity can be expensive to enforce because it involves recursion (a subtyping path from *a* to *b* is recursively defined as either a direct subtyping link from *a* to *b* or a direct subtyping link to some node *c* that has a subtyping path to *b*). Recursive constraints are most efficiently implemented in logical languages such as datalog or Prolog, but can be coded in SQL using its recursive union operator.

If a relation is both irreflexive and functional (i.e. it has at least one role with a simple uniqueness constraint), it is strongly intransitive by implication[16]. In that case a strongly intransitive constraint should not be declared. Figure 4.17 provides a simple example.

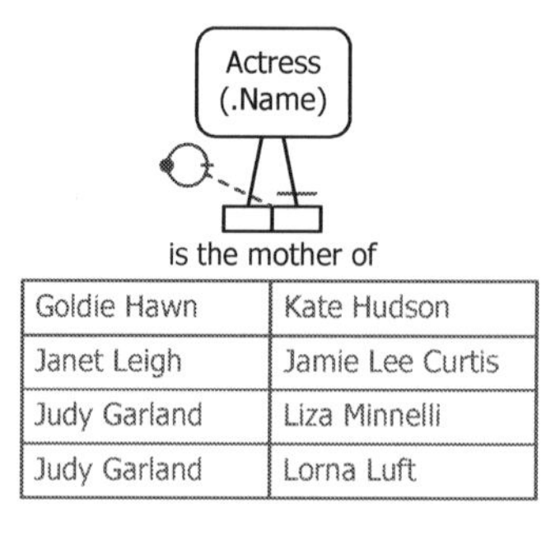

Goldie Hawn	Kate Hudson
Janet Leigh	Jamie Lee Curtis
Judy Garland	Liza Minnelli
Judy Garland	Lorna Luft

Figure 4.17 An irreflexive, functional relation is implied to be strongly intransitive

[16] For a proof of this implication, see p. 285 of Halpin & Morgan (2008).

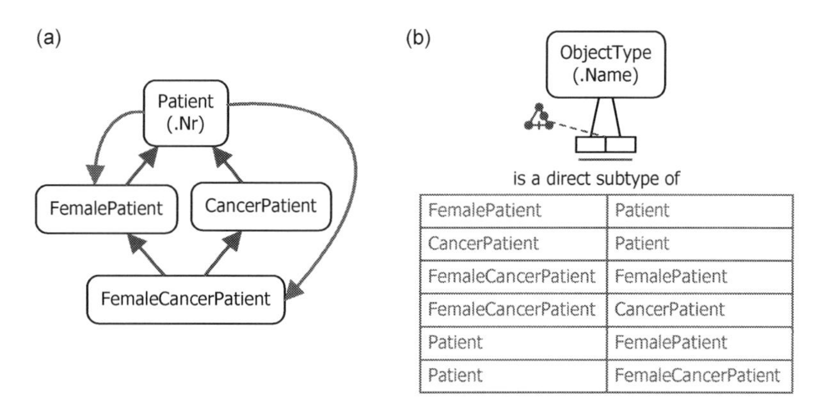

FemalePatient	Patient
CancerPatient	Patient
FemaleCancerPatient	FemalePatient
FemaleCancerPatient	CancerPatient
Patient	FemalePatient
Patient	FemaleCancerPatient

Figure 4.18 What's wrong here?

Now consider the subtyping graph shown in Figure 4.18(a), which adds subtyping links from Patient to FemalePatient and FemaleCancerPatient. Figure 4.18(b) shows an ORM model for this graph. Here, the direct subtyping relationship is strongly intransitive, but there's still a problem, as no supertype can be a proper subtype of one of its own subtypes.

If we added an asymmetric constraint to the Figure 4.18(b) model, this would forbid adding the subtyping link from Patient to FemalePatient, but it would not prevent adding the subtyping link from Patient to FemaleCancerPatient. In general, we need to constrain the subtyping graph so that no cycles of any length from one node back to itself can occur. To enforce this requirement, we add an *acyclic constraint*.

A binary relationship *R* is *acyclic* if and only if no object can cycle back to itself by applying one or more instances of the *R* relationship. The intuitive icon at the top of Figure 4.19(a) depicts acyclicity using dots for objects and arrows for relationships between them, with a dashed line allowing for more relationships in the cycle. The arrow with a stroke indicates that a relationship to complete the cycle is not allowed. The simplified icon below it removes the arrow-tips, and is used in ORM to depict an *acyclic ring constraint*. For compactness, ORM combines the shapes for acyclic and strongly intransitive constraints into a single shape as shown in Figure 4.19(b).

Figure 4.19 Constraint icons for (a) acyclic, and (b) acyclic + strongly intransitive

Figure 4.20(b) uses this combined constraint shape to declare the meta-fact type ObjectType is a direct subtype of ObjectType to be both acyclic and strongly intransitive. The acyclic constraint within this combination verbalizes as follows:

> **No** ObjectType **may cycle back to itself via one or more traversals through**
>
> ObjectType is a direct subtype of ObjectType.

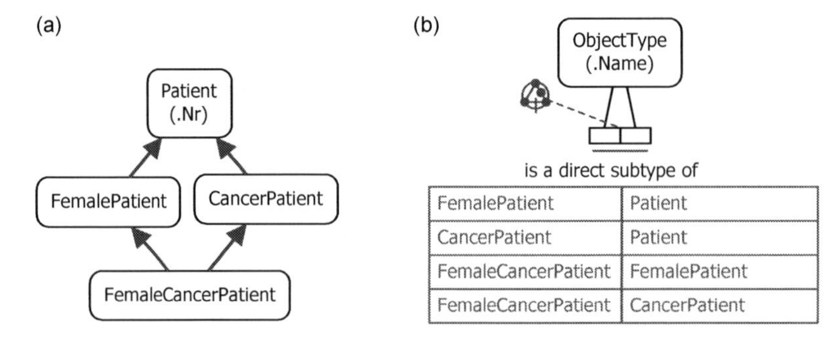

Figure 4.20 The subtyping relationship is acyclic and strongly intransitive

Since acyclicity includes the case where there is only one traversal through the relationship, an acyclic constraint implies an asymmetric constraint. Hence we do not complicate the shape any further by trying to add an implied asymmetric constraint.

Now consider the model in Figure 4.21(a), which recalls a schema considered earlier but this time uses a smaller population. The sample data satisfies the antisymmetric ring constraint, but is incomplete. Why? It omits the facts to record that each family member is at least as tall as himself/herself.

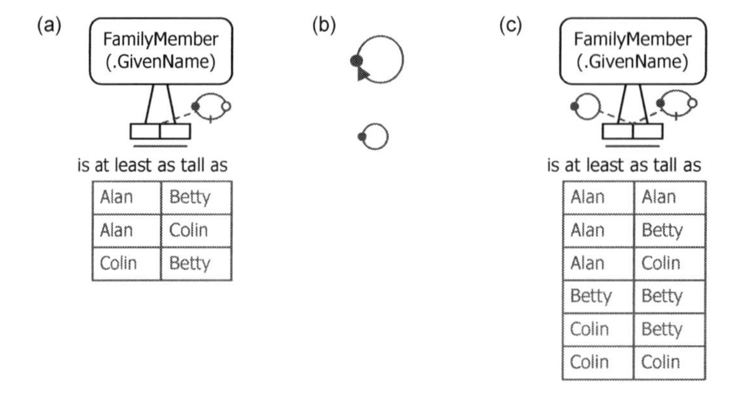

Figure 4.21 Adding a locally reflexive constraint

If we wish to ensure that the population of the fact type should be complete in this sense, we need to constrain the fact type to be *locally reflexive*. A binary relationship *R* is locally reflexive if and only if each object that bears relationship *R* to some object must bear relationship *R* to itself.

The intuitive icon at the top of Figure 4.21(b) uses a dot for an object and an arrow for the relationship. The simplified icon below it removes the arrow-tip, and is used in ORM to depict a *locally reflexive ring constraint*. The locally reflexive constraint in Figure 4.13(c) verbalizes as follows:

If $FamilyMember_1$ is at least as tall as **some** $FamilyMember_2$

then $FamilyMember_1$ is at least as tall as **itself**.

If we were to add a mandatory role constraint to the first role of the fact type FamilyMember is at least as tall as FamilyMember then the relationship would be reflexive over the population of FamilyMember.

In mathematics, the notion of reflexivity is often defined as global reflexivity. A relationship is *globally reflexive* if and only if every individual thing bears that relationship to itself. For example the identity relationship depicted by the equals sign "=" is globally reflexive since each thing is identical to itself. However, globally reflexive relations are typically never stored in data models, so ORM does not include any graphical shape for a globally reflexive constraint. Note that the NORMA tool uses "reflexive" to mean locally reflexive, not globally reflexive.

The NORMA tool also supports *purely reflexive* ring constraints. A relationship is purely reflexive if and only if any given object can bear that relationship only to itself. However any schema with a purely reflexive constraint can be replaced by an equivalent schema that does not use a purely reflexive constraint. Hence purely reflexive constraints are never needed, and their use is deprecated.

Now suppose we wish to record which US states neighbor which US states. Figure 4.22(a) shows some sample data, and Figure 4.22(b) shows an attempt to model this. Can you spot any potential problem with this model?

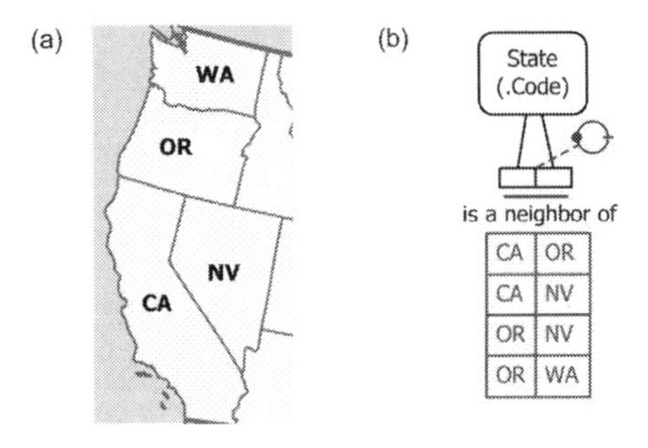

Figure 4.22 A model fragment to record neighboring states of the US

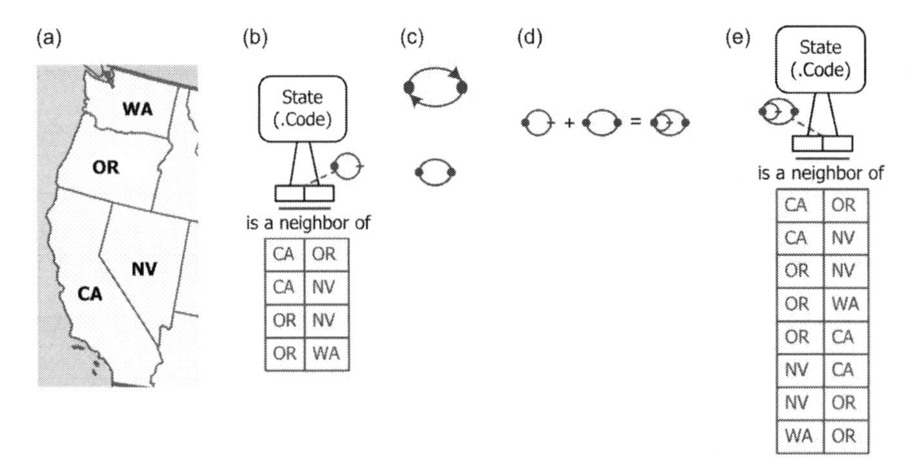

Figure 4.23 Adding a symmetric constraint

To save page turning, the sample data and model are redisplayed in Figure 4.23(a) and Figure 4.23(b), which correctly applies an irreflexive constraint since no state can be its own neighbor. However, the fact table in Figure 4.23(b) records neighborhood facts in one direction only. For example, the row with tuple (CA, OR) records that California is a neighbor of Oregon, but there is no row with the tuple (OR, CA). So to find all the neighbors of Oregon you need to find every row with "OR" in the left-hand column and see what state it is paired with, and then find every row with "OR" in the right-hand column and see what state it is paired with. Note that, to save space, I've omitted Oregon's neighbor Idaho (statecode = ID) from the data.

It's easier for a human to find all the neighbors of a state if we list the neighborhood facts in both directions, as shown in the fact table of Figure 4.23(e). You then simply find the state in the left-hand column and look at its right-hand neighbors. To ensure that the neighborhood facts are stored in both directions, we declare the fact type State is a neighbor of State to be *symmetric*.

A binary relationship *R* is symmetric if and only if given any objects *a* and *b*, not necessarily distinct, if *a* bears the relationship *R* to *b* then *b* bears the relationship *R* to *a*. The top icon in Figure 4.23(c) intuitively depicts a symmetric relation. ORM uses the simplified shape below to depict a *symmetric ring constraint.*

To save space, ORM uses a single shape to combine an irreflexive constraint with a symmetric constraint, as shown in Figure 4.23(d). The symmetric constraint within the combined constraint applied in Figure 4.23(e) verbalizes thus:

If $State_1$ is a neighbor of $State_2$

then $State_2$ is a neighbor of $State_1$.

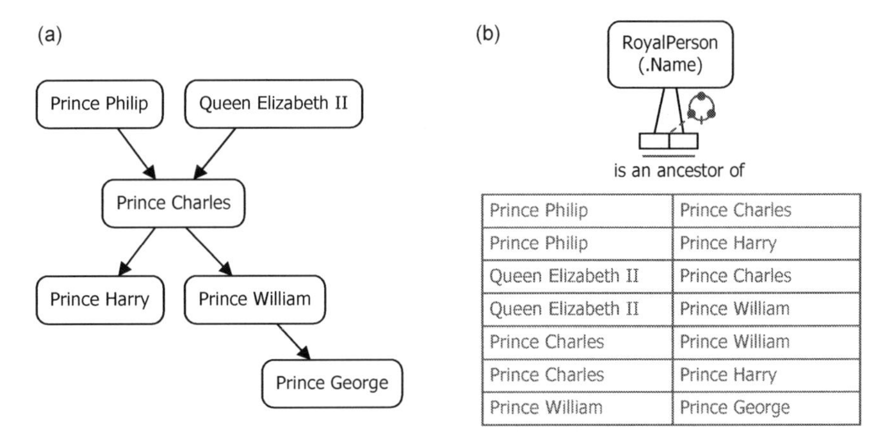

Prince Philip	Prince Charles
Prince Philip	Prince Harry
Queen Elizabeth II	Prince Charles
Queen Elizabeth II	Prince William
Prince Charles	Prince William
Prince Charles	Prince Harry
Prince William	Prince George

Figure 4.24 A model fragment to record ancestor relations in the British royalty

Now consider the fragment of a genealogy graph for the British royalty shown in Figure 4.24(a). Suppose we need to model who is an ancestor of whom based on this graph. Figure 4.24(b) shows an ORM model that attempts to do this, by using an ancestry relationship that is acyclic. The fact table shown satisfies the constraints, but is incomplete, as it omits some of the ancestry facts (e.g. Prince Philip is also an ancestor of Prince William and Prince George).

If we really wish to ensure that all the ancestorhood facts are asserted, we need to constrain the fact type RoyalPerson is an ancestor of RoyalPerson to be *transitive*. A binary relationship *R* is transitive if and only if, given any objects *a*, *b* and *c*, not necessarily distinct, if *a* bears the relationship *R* to *b* and *b* bears the relationship *R* to c, then *a* must bear the relationship *R* to *c*. Figure 4.25(b) shows an intuitive icon for a *transitive ring constraint* as well as the simplified shape used in ORM. Figure 4.25(c) shows the shape for combined acyclic and transitive constraints.

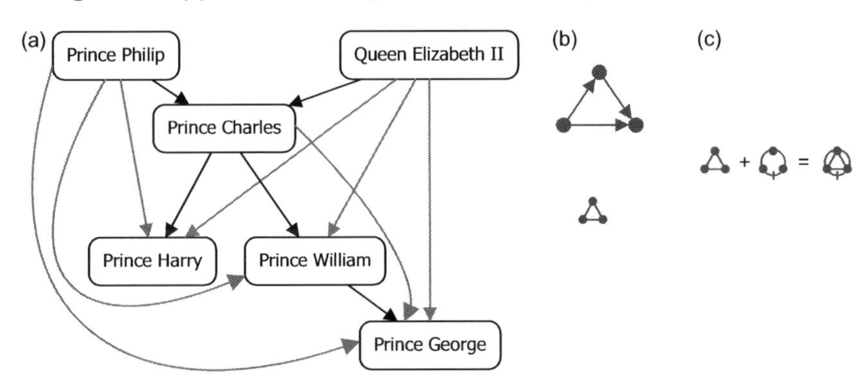

Figure 4.25 Here, the ancestorhood relationship is both acyclic and transitive

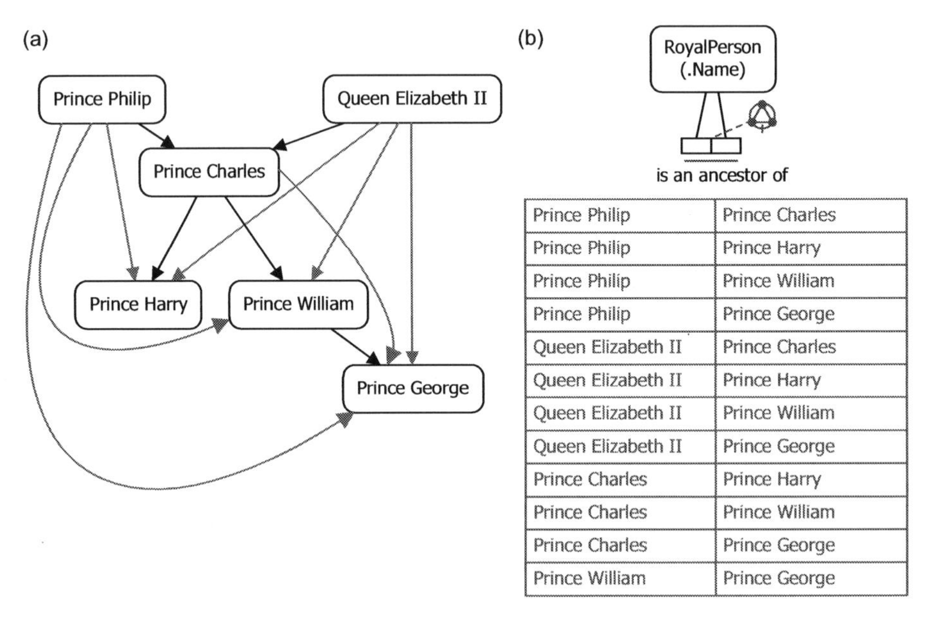

Prince Philip	Prince Charles
Prince Philip	Prince Harry
Prince Philip	Prince William
Prince Philip	Prince George
Queen Elizabeth II	Prince Charles
Queen Elizabeth II	Prince Harry
Queen Elizabeth II	Prince William
Queen Elizabeth II	Prince George
Prince Charles	Prince Harry
Prince Charles	Prince William
Prince Charles	Prince George
Prince William	Prince George

Figure 4.26 Constraining ancestorhood to be transitive as well as acyclic

Figure 4.26(b) shows the populated ancestorhood fact type constrained to be both acyclic and transitive. The transitive constraint verbalizes as follows:

If RoyalPerson$_1$ is an ancestor of RoyalPerson$_2$ **and** RoyalPerson$_2$ is an ancestor of RoyalPerson$_3$

then RoyalPerson$_1$ is an ancestor of RoyalPerson$_3$.

Unlike the other ring constraints, the locally reflexive, symmetric and transitive ring constraints are "positive" in the sense that they require certain facts to be included in the population. The other ring constraints are "negative", in the sense that they prevent certain facts from being included. As you will have noticed, the three negative ring constraints lead to larger populations than would be required in their absence. This is especially the case for transitive relations.

For example, Figure 4.26(a) has only five direct ancestry links but also includes seven indirect ancestry links because of the transitivity constraint. As the number of direct links grows, the number of indirect links required by transitivity can become very large indeed. Apart from increasing the data storage requirements, this makes the data entry task of asserting all those links quite onerous. To avoid this onerous task, it's typically better to assert the direct links, and then use a derivation rule to derive the indirect links. Figure 4.27 shows how to do this for our royal ancestorhood example. In this case, a direct link corresponds to a parenthood relationship. The derivation rule is recursive because the ancestorhood predicate is used in both the head and the body of the rule.

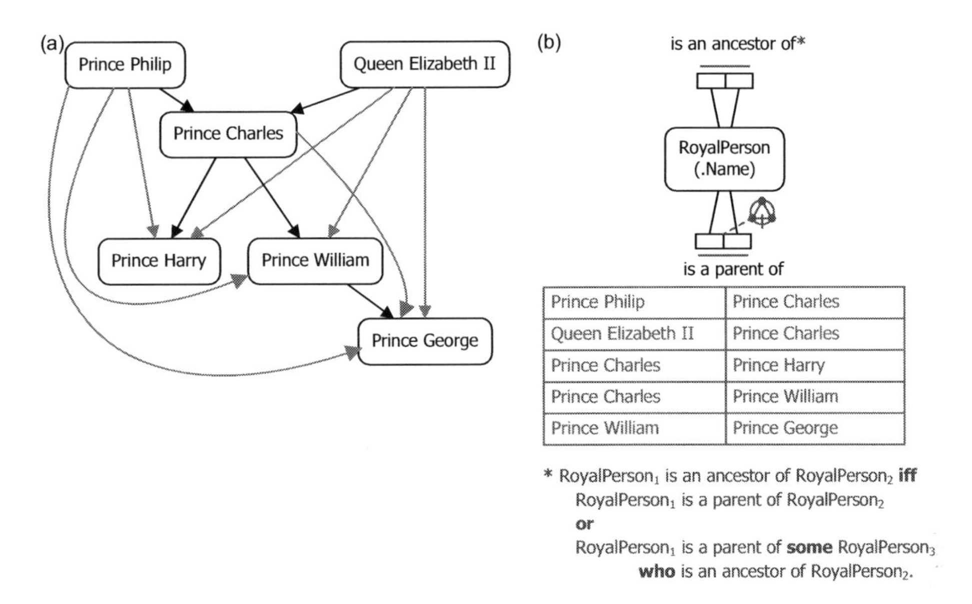

Figure 4.27 Deriving ancestorhood facts from parenthood facts

There is no need to declare acyclic and transitive constraints on the ancestorhood fact type because these are implied by the derivation rule in conjunction with the acyclic constraint on the parenthood fact type. Even if you decide to store the derived fact type (derived and stored fact types display with a double asterisk "**"), you've still saved a lot of work for the data entry.

For locally reflexive fact types you can choose to remodel by deriving the reflexive part of the population, but this is a small saving. For symmetric fact types, you can choose to remodel using an asymmetric fact type to store the data in one direction only (saving half the data entry) and derive the facts for the other direction.

For example, the state neighborhood model in Figure 4.23 can be remodeled using the fact type State is a pre-neighbor of State, where "pre-neighbor" means a neighbor whose name comes alphabetically before the other. In this case, the prior name ordering constraint (implemented in SQL with a lexical "<" operator) implies acyclicity and hence asymmetry. The full neighborhood fact type can then be derived using the following rule:

State$_1$ is a neighbor of State$_2$ **iff**

State$_1$ is a pre-neighbor of State$_2$

or State$_2$ is a pre-neighbor of State$_1$.

We have now covered all the individual ring constraints supported in ORM, as well as a number of their combinations. Ignoring the deprecated purely-reflexive constraint, here is a list of the allowed ring constraint combinations in ORM:

Reflexive + symmetric
Reflexive + antisymmetric
Reflexive + transitive
Reflexive + transitive + antisymmetric
Symmetric + transitive
Symmetric + irreflexive
Symmetric + intransitive
Symmetric + strongly intransitive
Asymmetric + intransitive
Asymmetric + strongly intransitive
Transitive + irreflexive
Transitive + antisymmetric
Transitive + asymmetric
Acyclic + transitive
Acyclic + intransitive
Acyclic + strongly intransitive

If you enter a ring constraint in the NORMA tool, it automatically displays which other ring constraints may be combined with it, and it also prevents you from choosing illegal combinations of ring constraints.

4.3 Value-Comparison Constraints

Two object types are said to be *comparable* if it is meaningful to compare their instances. Compatible object types are comparable, because they may share instances (e.g. Person and MalePerson). Some object types that do not overlap are still comparable. For example, PersonHeight(m:) and BuildingHeight(m:) are comparable because their values are based on the same measurement unit.

Roles are comparable if they are hosted by the same object type or by comparable object types. A *value-comparison constraint* may be applied over a pair of comparable roles to restrict how a value for one role compares with a value for the other, using one of six comparison operators: <, ≤, >, ≥, =, ≠.

The operators = and ≠ should rarely be used in this context, since in typical cases, where the constrained roles are hosted by compatible types, value-equality and value inequality constraints are best replaced by pair equality and pair exclusion constraints respectively.

Table 4.3 Extract of a report about famous scientists

Name	*Born*	*Died*
Galileo Galilei	1564	1642
Isaac Newton	1643	1727
Albert Einstein	1879	1955
Stephen Hawking	1942	?

As a simple example where a value-constraint should be applied, consider the report extract about famous scientists shown in Table 4.3. Some people who allow the possibility of reincarnation find it interesting that Newton was born the year after Galileo died. At any rate, you might wish to try modeling this report in ORM before reading on.

Figure 4.28 shows two equivalent ways to model this example using a value-comparison constraint. Graphically, a value-comparison constraint is depicted by a circled operator, connected by dashed lines to the two roles it constrains. If the operator is ordered (i.e. one of <, ≤, >, ≥) an arrow-tip is added to one of these lines to show the direction in which the operator is applied. Two dots are added to the circle to represent the value instances being compared, indicating that the constraint compares individual values, not sets of values.

The value-comparison constraint in Figure 4.28(a) verbalizes as shown below, using "**is less than**" for the < operator. The value-comparison constraint in Figure 4.28(b) has a similar verbalization, using "**is greater than**" for the > operator.

For each Scientist,
if that Scientist was born in **some** Year_1
and died in **some** Year_2
then Year_1 **is less than** Year_2.

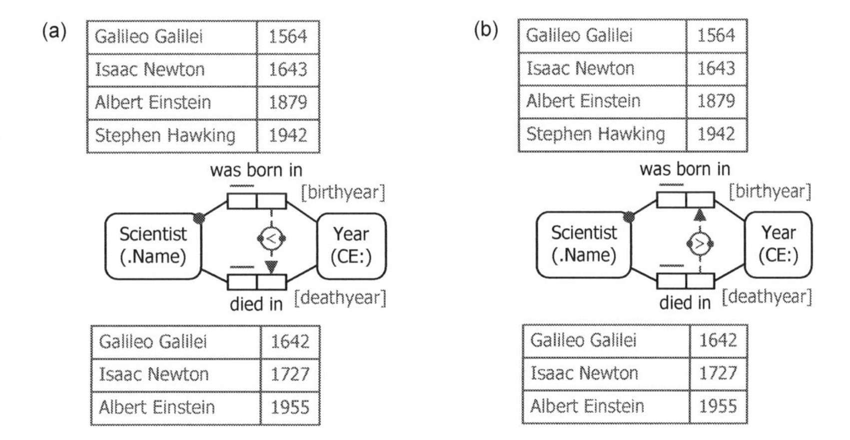

Figure 4.28 Two ORM models for Table 4.3 using a value-comparison constraint

Typically, the roles constrained by a value-comparison constraint both occur in many-to-one (*n*:1) binary fact types, as in the previous example. Sometimes however, one or both of the constrained roles may appear in an *m:n* fact type. Figure 4.29 provides two examples. The model in Figure 4.29(a) allows that an employee may be hired more than once. Here we interpret the constraint to mean that for each employee, his/her birthdate occurs before *every* date on which he/she is hired. This constraint verbalizes as follows: **For each** Employee, **if that** Employee was born on **some** Date$_1$ **and** was hired on **some** Date$_2$ **then** Date$_1$ **is less than** Date$_2$.

The model in Figure 4.29(b) stores synonym relationships between English verbs in one direction only. Pre-synonyms are alphabetically earlier than their post-synonyms. The < value constraint provides an efficient way to ensure the pre-synonym relationship is acyclic. While the sample data might suggest that the relationship is transitive, in general this is not the case, so transitivity is not added as a constraint or as part of the derivation rule for synonymy.

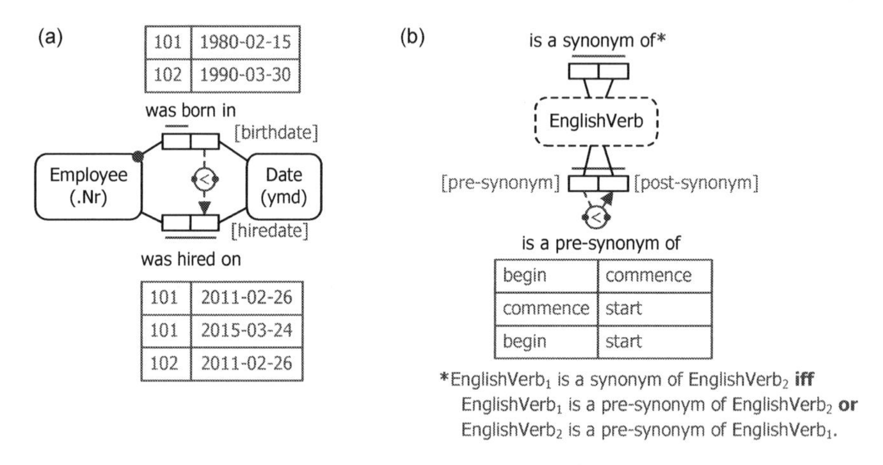

Figure 4.29 Value-comparison constraints involving an *m:n* fact type

The schemas in Figure 4.30 provide some examples of value-comparison constraints where the constrained roles are hosted by different but comparable object types. The ≤ operator verbalizes as "**is less than or equal to**".

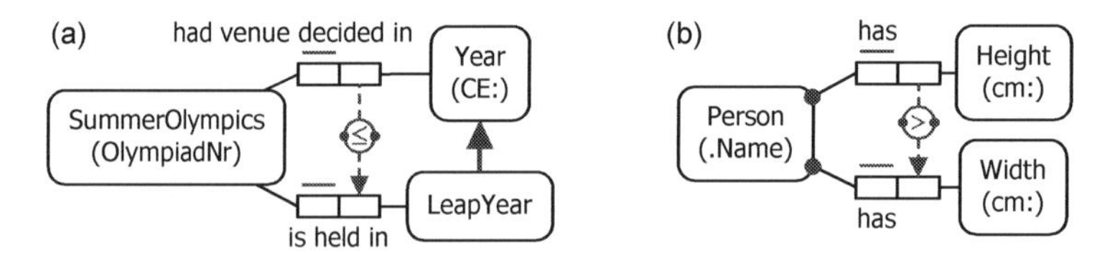

Figure 4.30 Value-comparison constraints over roles hosted by different types

4.4 Other Constraints and Final Checks

The *cardinality* of a set is the number of members in the set. For example, the cardinality of {Phobos, Deimos}, the set of Martian moons, is two. Using "#" for the cardinality function this may be written #{Phobos, Deimos} = 2. In ORM, an *object cardinality constraint* restricts the cardinality of the population of an object type for each state of the database. A *role cardinality constraint* restricts the cardinality of the population a specified role for each state of the database[17].

A *simple cardinality constraint* restricts the cardinality to a whole number (0, 1, 2, etc.) or to a range of whole numbers, and is depicted graphically by prepending "#" to the cardinality specification next to the constrained object type or role. Table 4.4 summarizes the graphical notations and cardinality verbalizations used. The final column shows how to specify the cardinality when entering the constraint in a properties sheet in NORMA. Although allowed, a cardinality constraint of 0 is typically pointless as it means the population is always empty.

Table 4.4 Displaying, verbalizing, and entering simple cardinality constraints

Graphical notation	*Cardinality Verbalization*	*Cardinality entry in NORMA*
# ≤ *n*	**at most** *n*	0..*n*
# = *n*	**exactly** *n*	*n*
# ≥ *n*	**at least** *n*	*n*.. (where *n* > 0)
# *n*..*m*	**at least** *n* **and at most** *m*	*n*..*m* (where *n* > 0 and *m* > *n*)

Of the four cases shown in Table 4.4, the first case (# ≤ *n*) is typically the only one used as a simple cardinality constraint, because when *n* is a positive number the other constraints exclude the possibility of an empty database, which is typically the initial state of any database. However, all four cases may be used as a component of a *disjunctive cardinality constraint.*

A disjunctive cardinality constraint restricts the cardinality to conform to at least one of multiple, simple cardinality constraint specifications, which are listed as entries in a set, with the set enclosed in braces "{ }" and the entries separated by commas. Graphically, a disjunctive

---

[17] Some entity relationship modeling approaches use the term "cardinality constraint" to indicate whether a relationship end is single-valued or multi-valued, which is a very different sense from the way this term is used in ORM.

cardinality constraint is depicted by prepending "#" to the set of possible cardinalities. For example, #{0, 2} indicates the cardinality must be 0 or 2, and #{≤3, 7, 9..10} indicates the cardinality must be 0, 1, 2, 3, 7, 9 or 10.

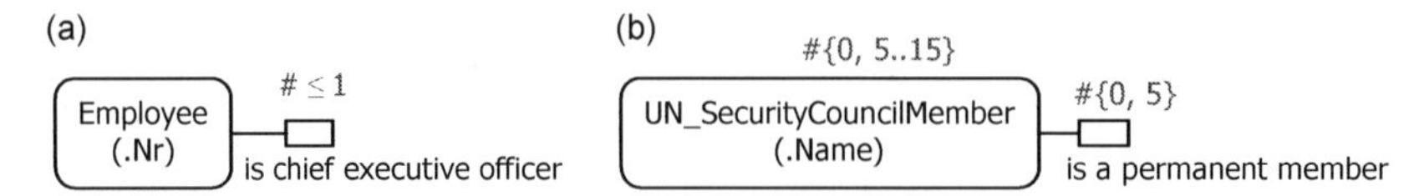

Figure 4.31 Cardinality constraints on (a) a role, and (b) an object type and role

Figure 4.31(a) shows an example of a simple role cardinality constraint to ensure that, at any given time, at most one employee is recorded as chief executive officer. This constraint has the following verbalization.

For each population of "Employee is chief executive officer",

the number of Employee instances **is at most** 1.

In practice, the United Nations Security Council should have 15 members of whom 5 are permanent members. The disjunctive cardinality constraints in Figure 4.31(b) require that if we record any UN security council members at all, we must record who are the five permanent members, and we may record zero or more of the ten non-permanent members. These cardinality constraints verbalize as follows.

Each population of UN_SecurityCouncilMember **contains**

exactly 0 **or at least** 5 **and at most** 15 **instances**.

For each population of "UN_SecurityCouncilMember is a permanent member",

the number of UN_SecurityCouncilMember **instances is exactly** 0 **or exactly** 5.

Role cardinality constraints may be applied only to roles in unary fact types. In practice, object cardinality constraints are rarely used, and should not be declared if they are implied by existing value constraints, as is the case for the examples shown in Figure 4.32. Note that in these examples, the comparator is "≤", rather than "=".

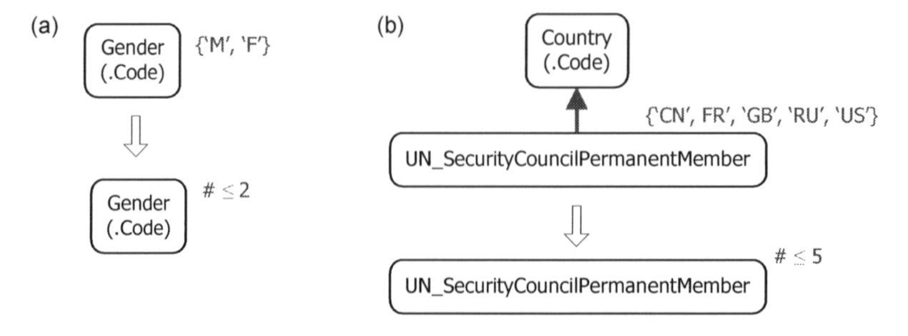

Figure 4.32 Here the cardinality constraints are implied so should not be declared

All of the constraints discussed so far have alethic *modality*. An *alethic constraint* is a condition that *must* be satisfied by each state of the fact base. Any attempted update that violates an alethic constraint will be simply rejected by the information system. For example, given the uniqueness constraint that each person was born on at most one date, if we try to add a second birthdate for a person this will be rejected.

ORM also allows you to declare constraints of deontic modality. A *deontic constraint is* a condition that *ought* to be satisfied, but may in practice be violated. An update that violates a deontic constraint will be accepted by the information system. Recorded violations of a deontic constraint should be communicated either automatically or on request to a relevant authority so that actions can be taken if needed to minimize such violations in future.

As a classic example of deontic constraints, consider an information system that records marriages in a culture where monogamy is the only legal option. Ignoring same-sex unions, Figure 4.33(a) models this situation using the fact type Person is a husband of Person. The exclusion constraint and the spanning uniqueness constraint are both alethic. The spanning uniqueness constraint allows the marriage relationship to be many-to-many (polygamy). However, the two simple uniqueness constraints (depicted with an "o" on the uniqueness bar, and colored blue) declare that the marriage relationship ought to be one-to-one (monogamy). These deontic uniqueness constraints verbalize as follows.

It is obligatory that each Person is a husband of **at most one** Person.

It is obligatory that each Person is a wife of **at most one** Person.

The schema in Figure 4.33(b) includes alethic constraints to ensure that the parenthood relationship is acyclic, and that each person has at most two parents. The other ring constraint, displayed with dotted lines and colored blue, is a strongly intransitive constraint of deontic modality. This allows for the possibility of incest, while declaring that such an abhorrent practice ought not to happen. This deontic constraint has the following verbalization:

It is obligatory that if $Person_1$ is a parent of **some** $Person_2$

then it is not true that $Person_1$ **is indirectly related to** $Person_2$

by repeatedly applying this fact type.

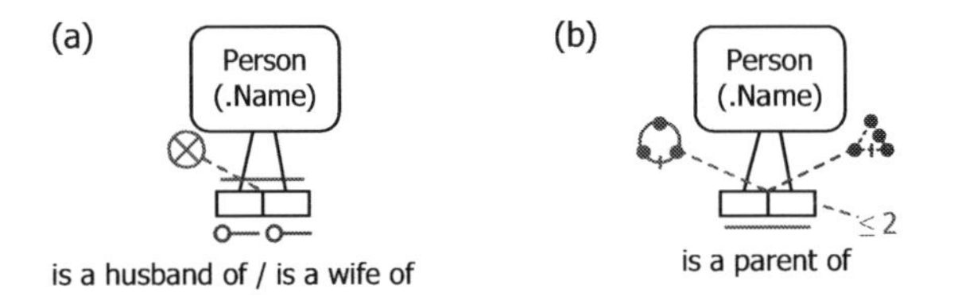

Figure 4.33 These ORM schemas have both alethic and deontic constraints

Table 4.5 Main graphical constraint icons used in ORM

Constraint Kind	*Alethic Constraint Icon*	*Deontic Constraint Icon*
Internal Uniqueness		
External Uniqueness		
Simple Mandatory		
Inclusive-Or		
Subset		
Equality		
Exclusion		
Exclusive-Or		
Frequency examples	2 (<2)	°2 (<2)
Irreflexive		
Asymmetric		
Antisymmetric		
Intransitive		
Strongly Intransitive		
Acyclic		
Reflexive		
Symmetric		
Transitive		
Value-Comparison example		
Cardinality examples	# ≤ 2 #{0, 5..15}	°# ≤ 2 °#{0, 5..15}

Table 4.5 summarizes the icons used for the main kinds of graphical constraints used in ORM. Alethic constraints are colored violet, whereas deontic constraints are colored blue. Most deontic constraint icons also include a small "o", based on the *O* (**It is obligatory that**) operator of modal logic. Deontic versions of ring and value-comparison constraints use dotted lines instead of solid lines. Combined shapes for combinations of ring constraints are not shown in this table.

If an alethic constraint is declared, its deontic version can never be violated and hence should not be declared. For example, if each person is constrained to have only one birthdate it's pointless to add an obligation in this regard.

We have now covered all of the ORM graphical constraint kinds currently supported in the NORMA tool. Although these enable us to graphically depict almost all the constraints likely to be met in a typical business domain, sometimes we might encounter a constraint for which no ORM graphical notation exists. In this case, we should specify the constraint *textually*, preferably in some formal but readable language.

For example, the ORM schema fragment in Figure 4.34 concerns a business domain in which employees in general may be assigned to many projects, but newly hired employees may be assigned to at most one project. The fact type Employee is assigned to Project is many-to-many, so has a spanning uniqueness constraint. The *textual constraint* depicted here as a footnote to that fact type strengthens the uniqueness constraint to a simple uniqueness constraint for newly hired employees, so for them the project assignment relationship is many-to-one. This is an example of a restricted uniqueness constraint.

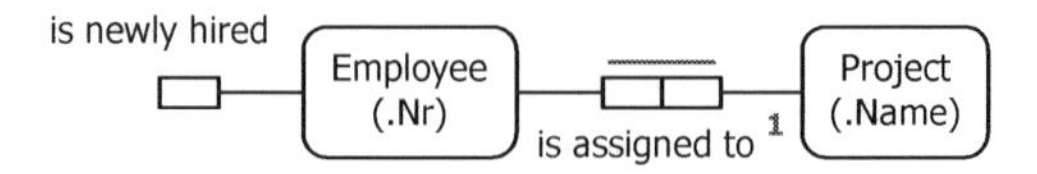

[1] **Each** Employee **who** is newly hired is assigned to **at most one** Project.

Figure 4.34 A restricted uniqueness constraint specified as a textual constraint

Step 7 of the CSDP concludes with some basics checks to help ensure that the schema is correct and complete. First we check to see whether the schema is *internally consistent*. Basically, a schema is internally consistent if its constraints do not contradict one another when we populate it with examples. The NORMA tool carries out many constraint consistency checks for you automatically, but it doesn't yet cater for every possibility. For example, the constraint pattern in Figure 4.35 is inconsistent because populating the fluency fact type results in a contradiction (can you see why?), but this error is not yet detected by NORMA.

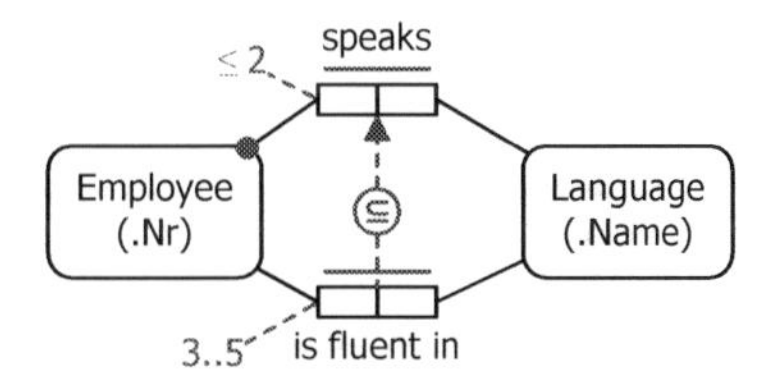

Figure 4.35 This faulty schema is not internally consistent

A schema is *externally consistent* if it agrees with the original requirements and examples used to develop the schema. One check for external consistency is to populate fact types with examples (as in CSDP Step 2), and see whether they satisfy all the constraints. If not, either some constraints are wrong, or the sample data is wrong, or the original requirements were wrongly specified. As part of the overall checking procedure, a domain expert should indicate whether the verbalizations of all the constraints and derivation rules are correct.

While the above checking process can help detect incorrect constraints, it does not guarantee that there are no *missing* constraints. For that we need the relevant background knowledge, or a set of examples that is known to be significant in all respects (which is not always attainable).

In a correct ORM schema, all fact types are atomic and distinct. Hence, there is no *asserted redundancy* (i.e. no fact is asserted twice). Checks for atomicity of fact types were built-in earlier in the CSDP. Although the conceptual schema should be redundancy-free in this sense, it's often acceptable to have redundancy in the external schema (e.g. different screen forms may have some facts in common).

By default, any relational schema generated by NORMA from a correct ORM schema is fully normalized, and hence redundancy-free. If a database stores the same fact in more than one place, and the fact is updated in one place without also updating its other occurrences, the database becomes inconsistent and the redundancy is *unsafe*. However, if constraints or rules on the physical database are enforced to ensure that all occurrences of the same fact entry are updated together, the redundancy is safe. For performance reasons, such *controlled denormalization* is sometimes worthwhile.

As a check for *derived redundancy*, we determine whether an asserted fact can also be derived by applying derivation rules to other facts. If so, we should include a fact type that is either (fully) derived or semiderived to avoid needless fact assertions. For example, if we assert the mass and volume of a planet we can simply derive the density of the planet using a simple derivation rule. Checks for arithmetic and logical derivation rules are built-in earlier in the CSDP, but a final pass over the schema in this regard might find some cases missed earlier.

Derived redundancy can sometimes be harmless. Recall that ORM allows you to require derived and semiderived fact types to derive then store their results. Storing the derivation results and having them automatically recomputed on update of their source fact types can significantly speed up the execution of queries. This is an example of using materialized views to boost performance.

As final check, we should try to ensure that the schema is *complete* with respect to the original requirements. To do this systematically, go through each requirement individually, and identify which aspects of the schema cater for it. If some requirements are not met, extend the schema to address them.

4.5 NORMA Lab 4

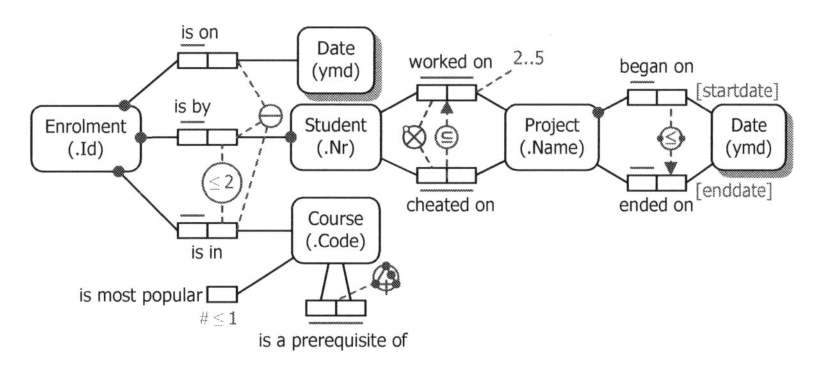

Figure 4.36 A Visio diagram of an ORM schema to be entered in NORMA

Figure 4.36 shows an ORM schema that illustrates most aspects of the ORM graphical notation introduced in this chapter. The fact type Course is a prerequisite of Course stores only direct prerequisites, so is acyclic and strongly intransitive. The external frequency constraint was discussed earlier. The 2..5 frequency range constraint ensures that if we record any workers for a given project we must record at least 2 and at most 5 students for this work. The value-comparison constraint ensures that a project cannot end before it starts. The role cardinality constraint ensures that at most one course is recorded to be the most popular course. The deontic exclusion constraint obliges students not to cheat on any projects they work on. This diagram was drawn using Microsoft Visio, but for this lab we'll enter the schema in the NORMA tool.

If needed, please review NORMA Labs 1, 2 and 3. Now open Visual Studio, press File > New > File to open the New File dialog. Then select General > Object-Role Modeling File and press Open. In the Fact Editor, enter the following fact types in the usual way:

Enrolment(.Id) is on Date(ymd)
Enrolment is by Student(.Nr)
Enrolment is in Course(.Code)
Course is a prerequisite of Course
Student worked on Project(.Name)
Student cheated on Project
Project began on Date
Project ended on Date.

Select the Date shape and drag it to the right of the project predicates, so that it appears duplicated with a shadow. Then move and align the various shapes and predicate readings to lay them out roughly as shown in Figure 4.36.

Now add the mandatory role, internal uniqueness, external uniqueness, and subset constraints depicted in Figure 4.36, in the usual way, as described in previous labs. At this stage, your schema diagram should appear as shown below.

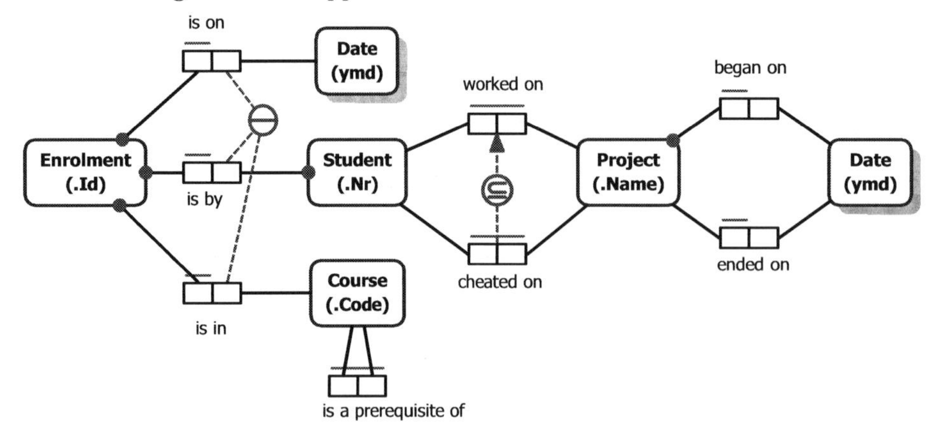

Now expand the Object Types list in the ORM Model Browser, select each *value type* in the list, and in the Properties sheet set its datatype properties as shown below:

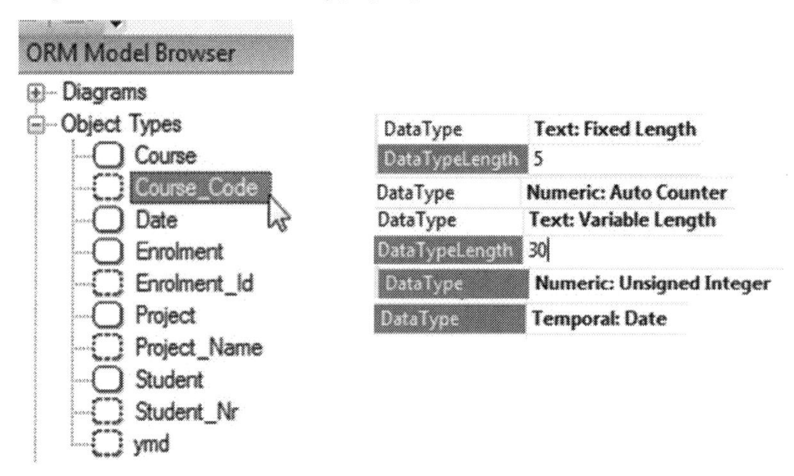

Select Date's role in the fact type Project began on Date, and enter the *role name* "startdate" in its Name property in the Properties sheet. The role name now appears inside square brackets near the role. Drag this name to the right of the predicate as shown below.

Similarly, add the rolename "enddate" to Date's role in the fact type Project ended on Date. The "startdate" and "enddate" role names will be used by NORMA for column names when mapping the fact types to a relational schema.

Now drag the *Value Comparison Constraint* shape from the ORM Toolbox to a position between the startdate and enddate roles, then click the down-arrow in its Operator property to open a drop-down list of comparison operators, and select the "≤" operator.

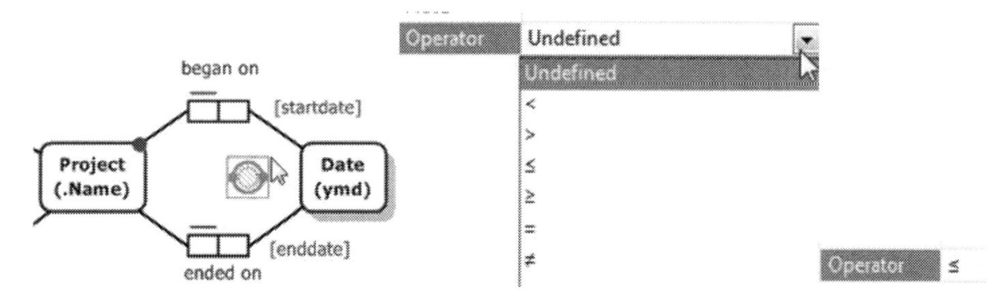

The chosen operator is now displayed inside the constraint shape. Double-click the constraint shape and slowly select the startdate role then the enddate role. The numbers 1 and 2 appear temporarily in the role boxes to indicate the order in which you selected the roles. Now double-click to commit the constraint, which should now appear as shown below.

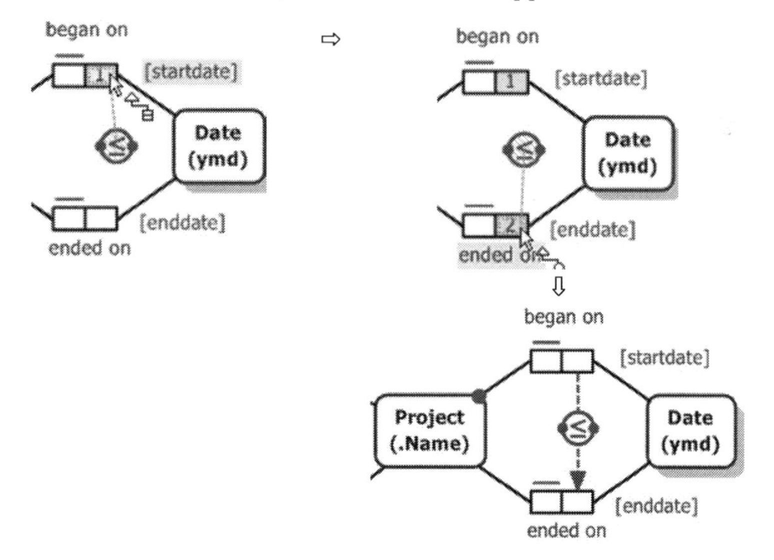

Now select the value-comparison constraint shape, and view its verbalization in the ORM verbalization Browser.

For each Project,
if that Project began on **some** $Date_1$
and ended on **some** $Date_2$
then $Date_1$ **is less than or equal to** $Date_2$.

Now drag a *Frequency Constraint* shape from the Toolbox to a position on the right of the fact type Student worked on Project. By default the frequency constraint displays as "≤ 2". Now edit the constraint's MaxFrequency and MinFrequency properties in the Properties sheet, changing them to 5 and 2 respectively.

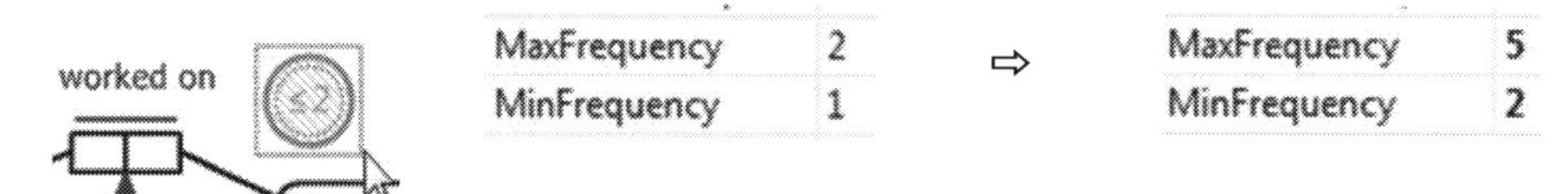

Double-click the constraint shape, then click Project's role in the fact type. The role box is temporarily numbered 1. Now double-click to commit the constraint.

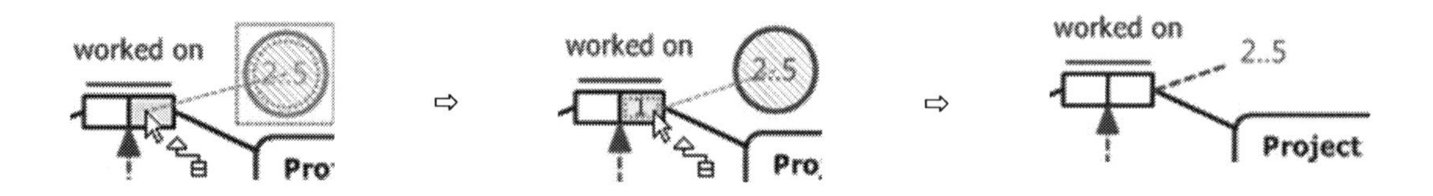

Select the constraint shape, and view its verbalization in the ORM Verbalization Browser.

Each Project **in the population of** "Student worked on Project"

occurs there at least 2 **and at most** 5 **times.**

Now drag a Frequency Constraint shape from the Toolbox to a position near the Student and Course roles in the fact types Enrolment is by Student and Enrolment is in Course. The default frequency of "≤ 2" is what we want so there is no need to change it. Now double-click the constraint shape, and slowly select the Student role then the Course role, and double-click to commit the constraint.

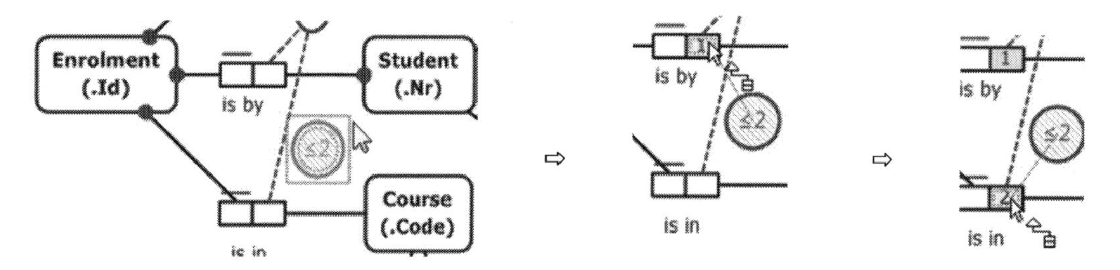

That completes the entry of the external frequency constraint, which now displays as shown opposite. Now view its verbalization.

For each Student **and** Course,
there are at most 2 **instances of** Enrolment **such that**
that Enrolment is by **that** Student
and is in **that** Course.

Now drag a *Ring Constraint* shape from the Toolbox to the right of the fact type Course is a prerequisite of Course, then in the Properties sheet click the down-arrow in its RingType property to display a drop-down list of ring constraint options with a check box for each. Now select the Acyclic check-box. NORMA now highlights in bold the other ring constraints which may be used in conjunction to the acyclic constraint.

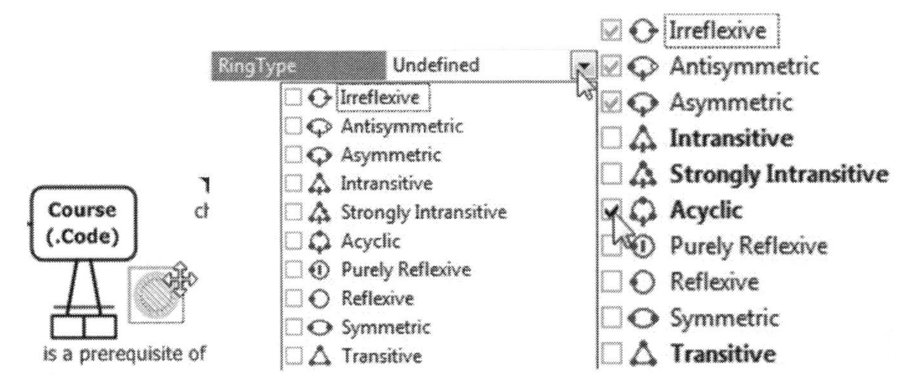

Now select the Strongly Intransitive check-box. NORMA unbolds all the options other than Acyclic, indicating that these cannot be used in conjunction with the two ring constraints you have already selected. The combined ring constraint shape is now displayed. Double-click the constraint shape, slowly click each role of the fact type, then double-click to commit the constraint, which now displays as shown below.

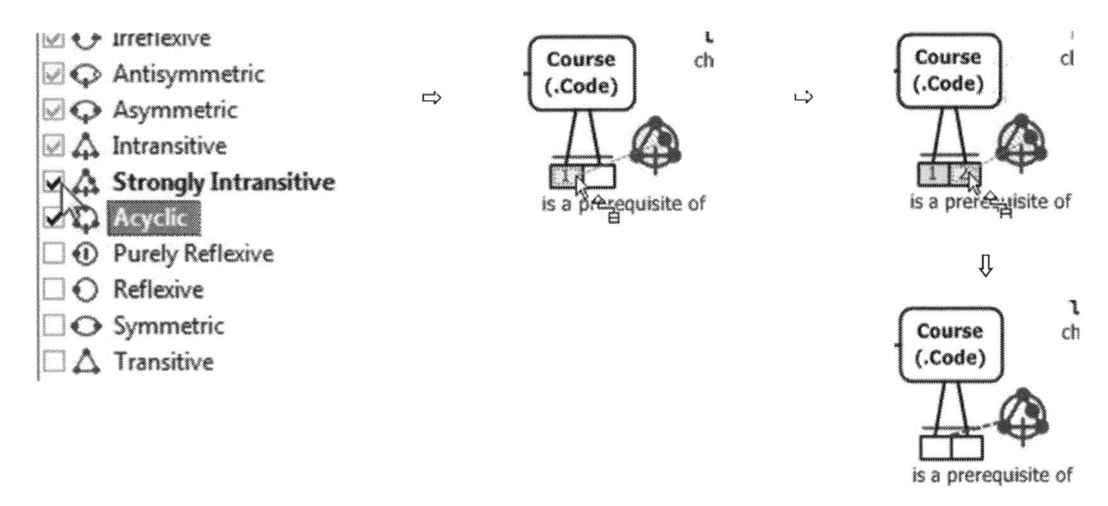

That completes the entry of the two ring constraints. Now select the constraint shape and view the verbalization.

No Course **may cycle back to itself via one or more traversals through**
Course is a prerequisite of Course.

If $Course_1$ is a prerequisite of **some** $Course_2$
then it is not true that $Course_1$ **is indirectly related to** $Course_2$
by repeatedly applying this fact type.

Now use the Fact Editor to enter the unary fact type Course is most popular, then select its role and in the Properties sheet edit its CardinalityConstraint property entry to 0..1, then press Enter to commit the constraint, which now displays as "# ≤ 1". Now drag the constraint shape to position it below the role as shown below.

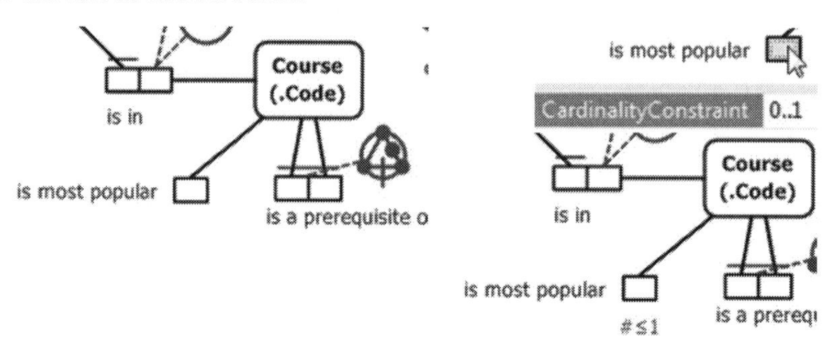

Now select the constraint shape and view the verbalization.

For each population of "Course is most popular",
the number of Course **instances is at most** 1.

Now, in the usual way, add an *exclusion constraint* between the Student roles in the fact types Student worked on Project and Student cheated on Project. By default, NORMA assumes constraints are of alethic modality, so the exclusion constraint contradicts the subset constraint. NORMA detects this problem and issues an error message which you can view in the Verbalization Browser.

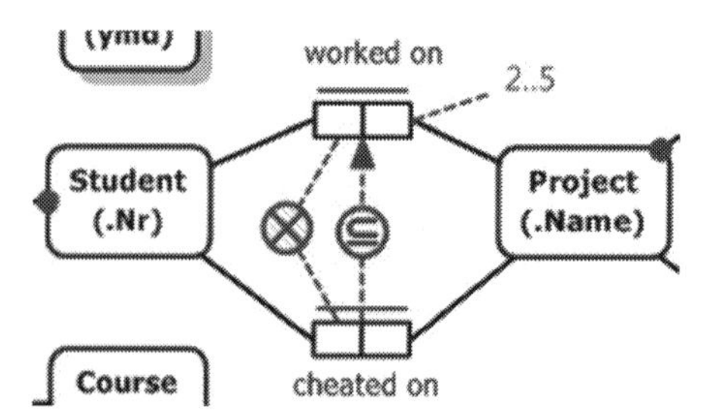

Model Error: Constraints 'ExclusionConstraint1' in model 'ORMModel1' are in a state of contradiction.

Select the exclusion constraint shape, and in the Properties sheet double-click the Modality property to toggle its value from Alethic to Deontic.

The full schema now displays as shown below.

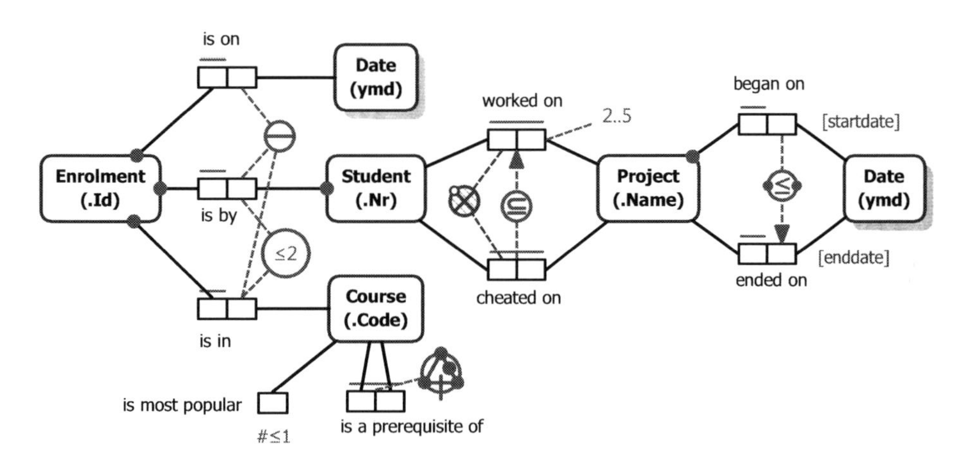

The deontic exclusion constraint still displays in an error state, because currently NORMA has not yet implemented an algorithm to detect when constraint patterns involving deontic constraints are permitted. If you wish, you can turn off the error display as follows. Right-click the constraint shape, and select Validation Errors > Disable Error Display > Overlapping exclusion and subset constraints are contradictory from its context menu.

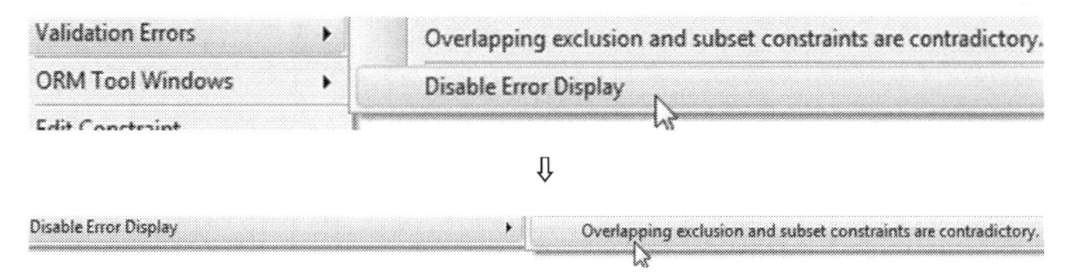

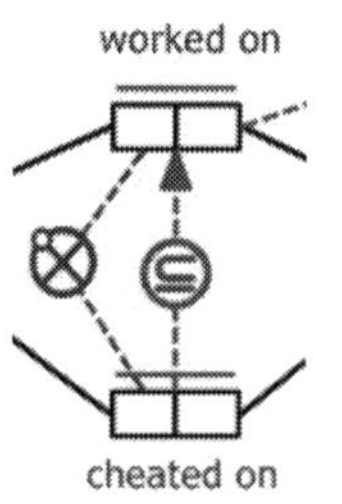

The deontic exclusion constraint now displays without red error fill, as shown opposite, and the error message is removed from the Error List display. Note that this turns off display of *all* errors resulting from conflicting subset and exclusion constraints. With our example, there is only once such error; but if you later apply an alethic subset and exclusion constraint combination that is contradictory, this will not be flagged as an error.

Hence it's a good idea to turn on error display for all error categories when doing a final pass over the model.

Although sample data are useful for validating models, it can be annoying to see the model in an error state simply because you haven't supplied sufficient data to satisfy all the constraints. Similarly, you might know the model is in an incomplete state (e.g. you just introduced an entity type with no reference scheme, but you plan to add that later) and don't want NORMA to display this as an error state. For situations like these it can be very handy to suppress display of unwanted error messages.

To see all the error categories for which NORMA performs automated error checking, click any empty space on the Document Window, then in the Properties Window click the ellipsis "..." button at the right of the ErrorDisplay field. The *Error Filter dialog* is now displayed. If you have not turned off any error display, all the categories are checked as shown opposite. Sample population errors can be turned off from this dialog, or by disabling Sample Population Errors in the relevant shape's context menu Validation Errors option.

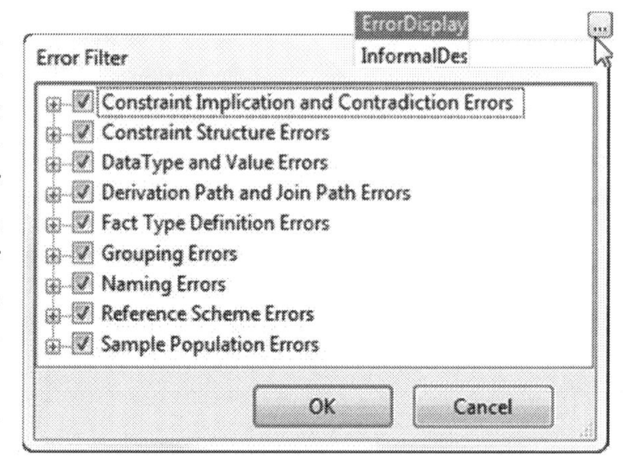

If instead you disabled error display for the contradicting exclusion and subset constraints as discussed previously, the check-box for the Constraint Implication and Contradiction Errors option will have blue fill. Expand the "+" button for this option to see the detailed list of subcategories for this kind of error.

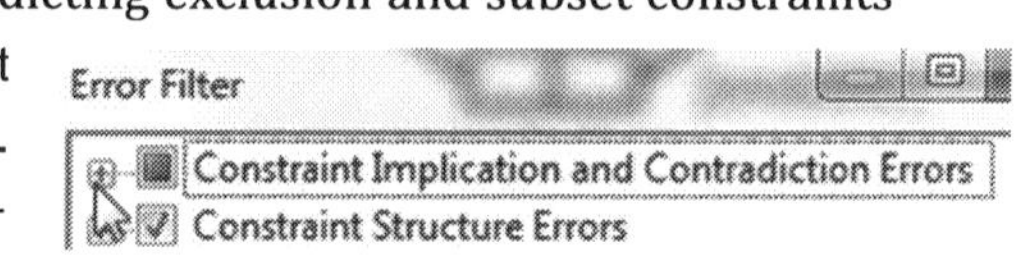

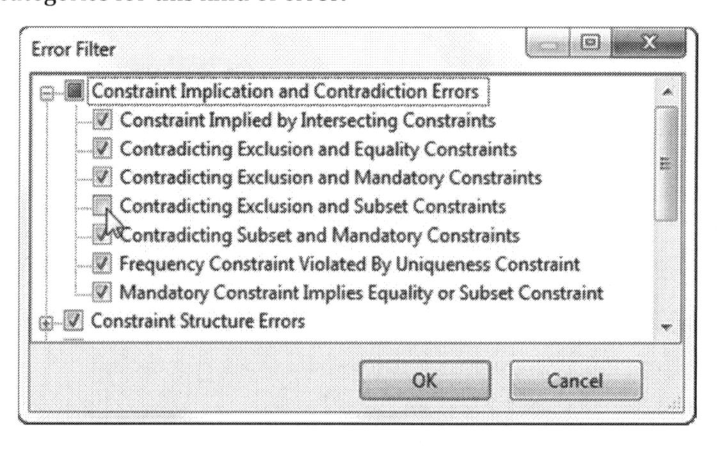

We are now ready for the relational mapping. Right-click an empty space in the Document Window, select Extension Manager ... > Relational View and press OK. Select the Relational View tab to view a diagram for the relational schema that is automatically generated from the ORM schema. Select the table shapes and drag them around to better align the foreign key relationship arrows, as shown below. As usual, the relational diagram does not display the relational equivalent of some of the ORM constraints.

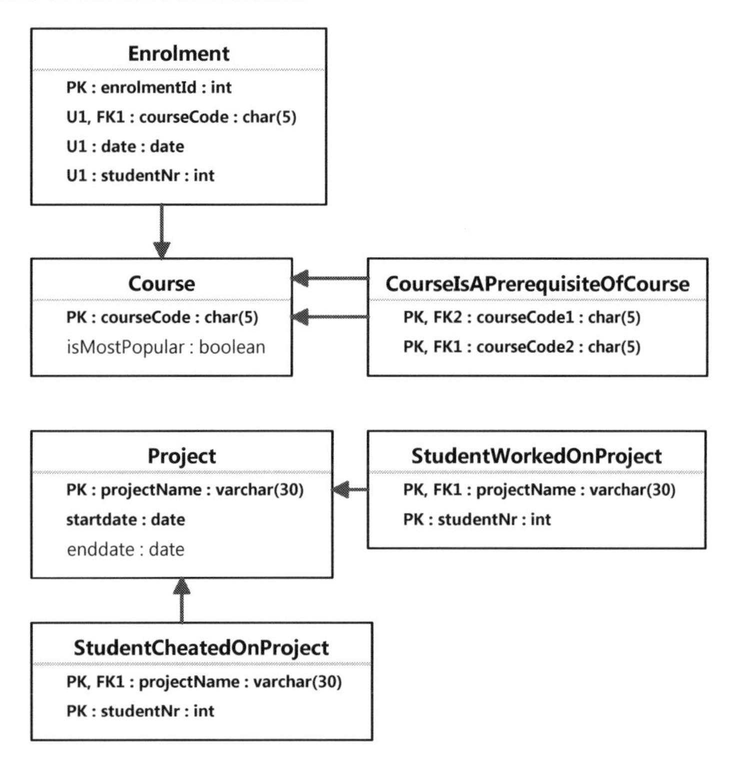

Currently, NORMA's relational mapping procedure provides only limited support for external constraints such as the subset constraint from the fact type Student cheated on Project to Student worked on Project. In this case, the ORM subset constraint should really map to a composite foreign key relationship from the table StudentCheatedOnProject to the table StudentWorkedOnProject, but this is not captured in the above relational schema. The designers of NORMA are aware of this issue, and plan to address this problem in the future.

Now save your model as Lab4.orm.

Appendix A: Generating SQL Code

As discussed, ORM allows you to visualize and verbalize in rich detail the semantics underlying the information requirements for a business domain. Using appropriate transformation procedures, an ORM model may also be used to facilitate the design of high quality models in other approaches such as ER and UML, even though many of the ORM constraints and rules might need to be represented only in textual form in such systems. Basic procedures for mapping ORM to ER and UML are discussed in sections 8.5 and 9.8 respectively of Halpin & Morgan (2008).

For implementation, ORM models may at least in principle also be mapped to a variety of target systems such as relational database systems, deductive databases, semantic web systems, NoSQL database systems, third generation programming languages (3GLs) such as C# and Java, and the extensible markup language (XML). Currently, the NORMA tool provides basic support for mapping ORM schemas to relational databases, 3GLs and XML. The Further Resources section indicates where to find some discussion on mapping ORM to semantic web languages and a deductive database system.

In this book, the lab sessions at the end of each chapter gave examples of mapping ORM schemas to relational database schemas using the NORMA tool. The relational mapping procedure used by NORMA is based on ORM's Rmap (Relational Mapping) procedure, which groups fact types into table schemes using mapping rules such as the following:

- Map each fact type with a composite uniqueness constraint to a separate table.
- Map fact types with functional roles hosted by the same object type into the same table, keyed on the object type's identifier. Map 1:1 fact types to a single table, generally favouring fewer nulls.
- Map each independent object type with no functional roles to a separate table.

A detailed discussion of ORM's Rmap procedure, including many worked examples, can be found in chapter 11 of Halpin & Morgan (2008).

Once you have a relational view generated by NORMA, you may choose to map this schema to SQL code in a relational database system using the NORMA tool. Alternatively, you could copy the relational view to another relational modeling tool and use that to generate the SQL code.

The rest of this appendix discusses the basic procedure for using NORMA to map a relational schema to SQL code, using the relational view generated in NORMA Lab 2 as an example.

The diagram shown below summarizes the ORM to relational mapping, this time annotating the relational schema with the following footnote constraint on the Athlete table: phoneNr **is not null or** emailAddress **is not null**.

This additional constraint captures the inclusive-or constraint on the ORM schema. In general, it's helpful to annotate the relational view with a relational equivalent of each ORM constraint that is not visually depicted in NORMA relational view diagram. As discussed in Lab2, there is no need with this example to generate a relational version of the derivation rule, as it would be implicitly understood.

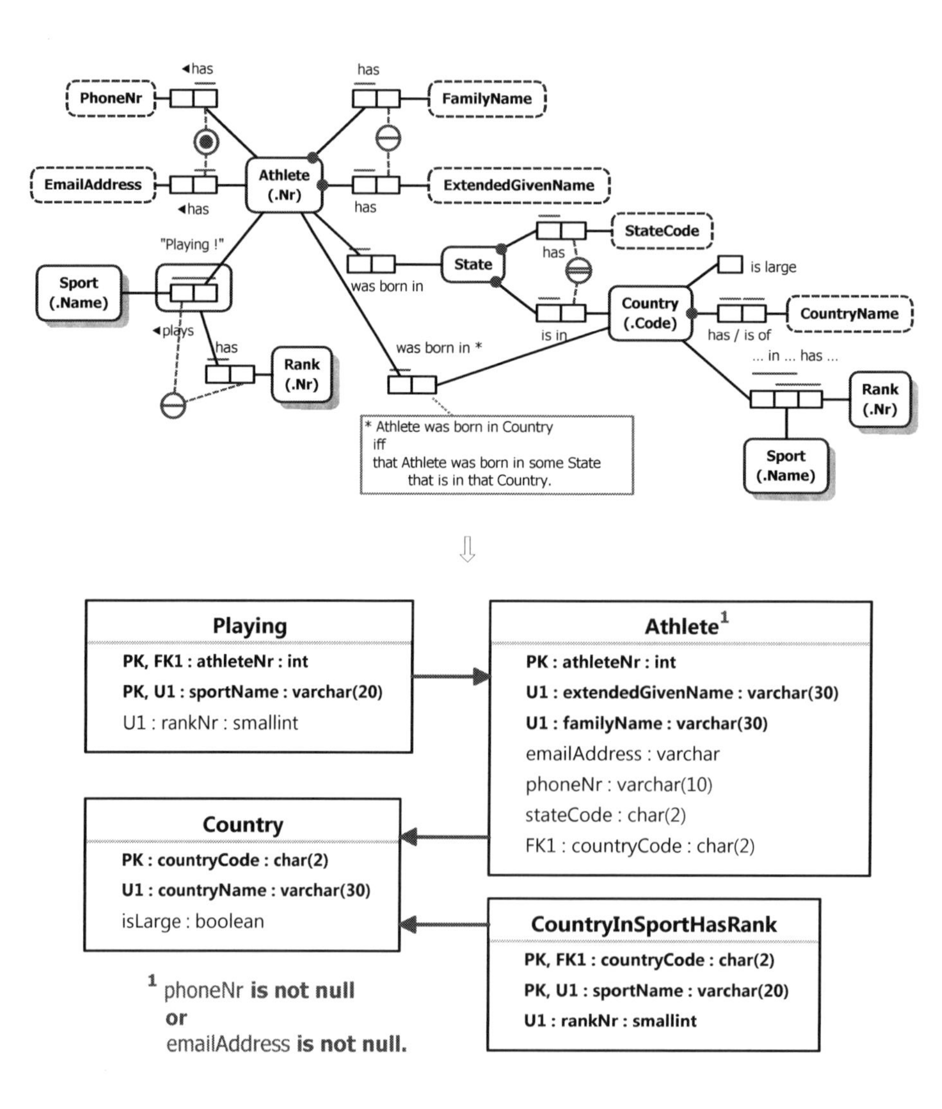

To generate code (SQL code or other code) from an ORM schema, you need to first create a new *project* in Visual Studio. Open Visual Studio and choose File > New > Project from the main menu. In the New Project dialog choose a Project type and Template. You could choose many options here, but for this lab let's choose Visual C# and Windows Forms Application. Edit the Name of the project to "Lab2Project" and press OK.

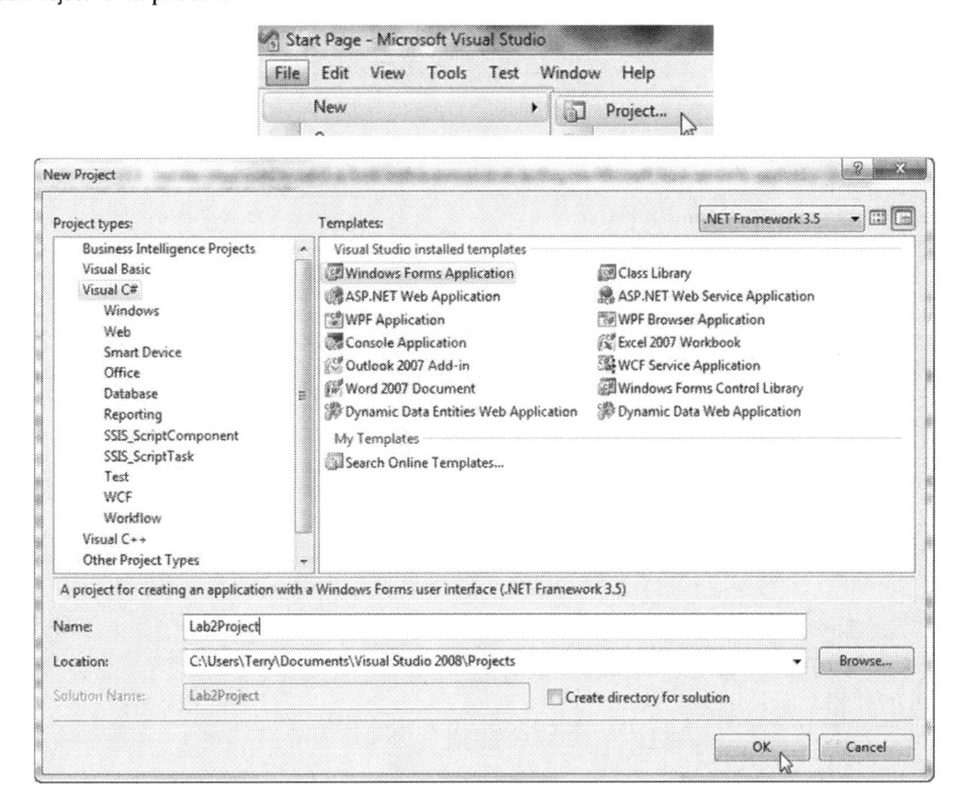

From the main menu, choose Project > Add Existing Item... . In the Add Existing Item dialog, press the down-arrow at the right of the file type list on the right of the File name field, and select All Files (*.*).

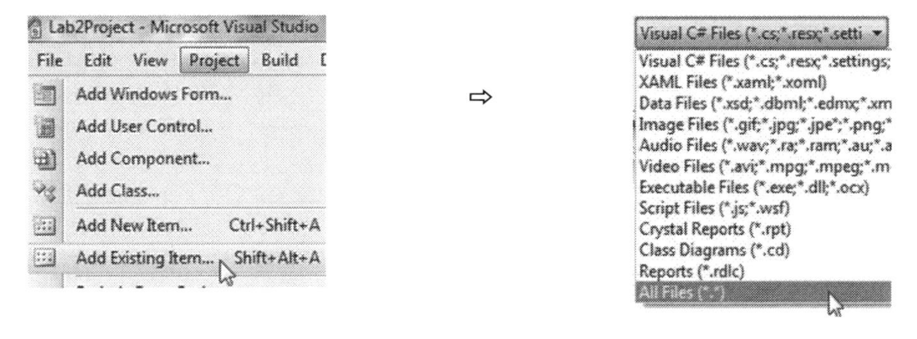

Expand the Libraries explorer within the dialog to locate your Lab2.orm file that you previously saved at the end of NORMA Lab 2, then select that file and press Add to add a copy of that file to the project. If you later want to make changes to the ORM file inside the project, do it to that copy.

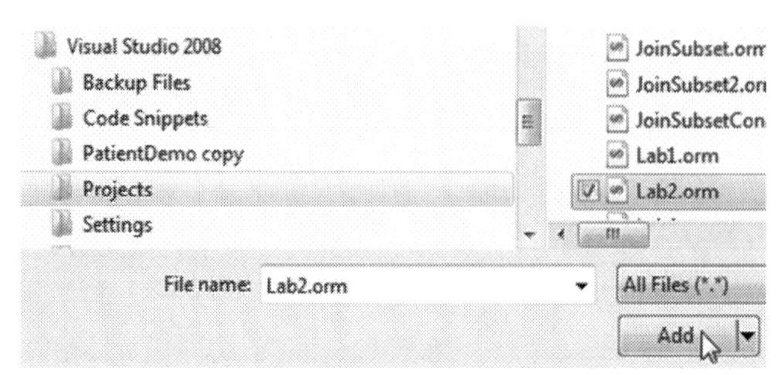

From the main menu, choose View > Solution Explorer to open the *Solution Explorer* Window, and then inside that window select the Lab2.orm file.

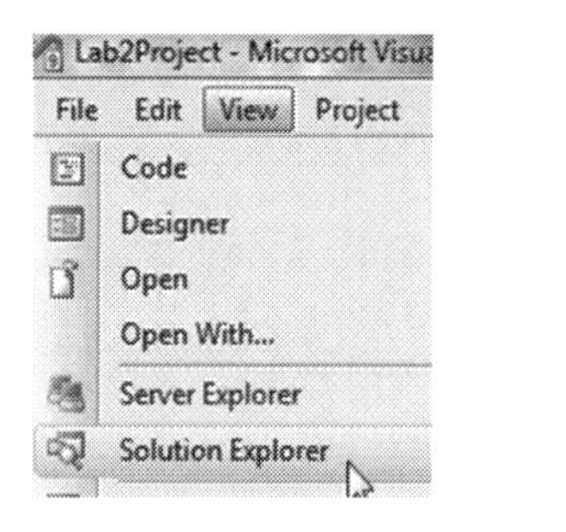

⇨

In the *Properties Window,* check that “ORM CustomTooL” is the value for the Custom Tool property (this should be there by default).

The ORMGeneratorSettings property should be visible below it (if not, click a different item in Solution Explorer and reselect your ORM file).

Now click the ellipsis “...” button at the right of the ORMGeneratorSettings field.

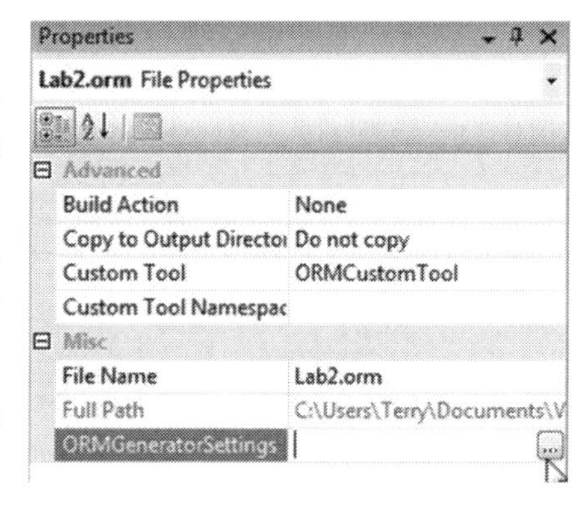

The ORM Generator Selection dialog now appears, so you can select the target(s) for code generation. For this lab, let's choose SQL Server by selecting the check-box for that option. Then press the Save Changes button.

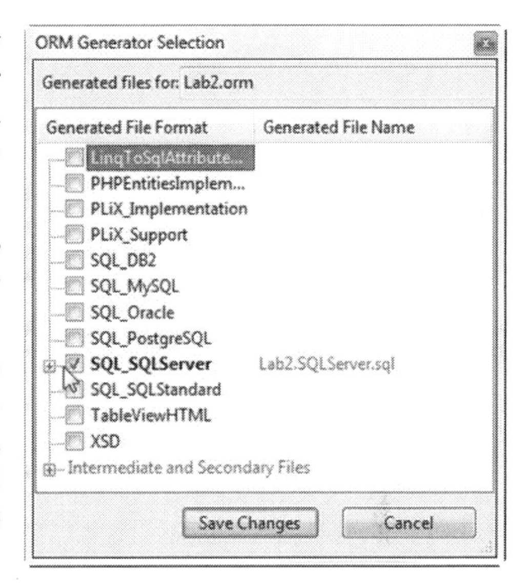

After the changes are saved and the SQL code has been generated, the dialog disappears.

In Solution Explorer, press the expand button "+" for Lab2.orm to see the list of generated files. To see the SQL code generated, double-click the SQL file Lab2.SQLServer.sql (or right-click the file and choose Open from its context menu).

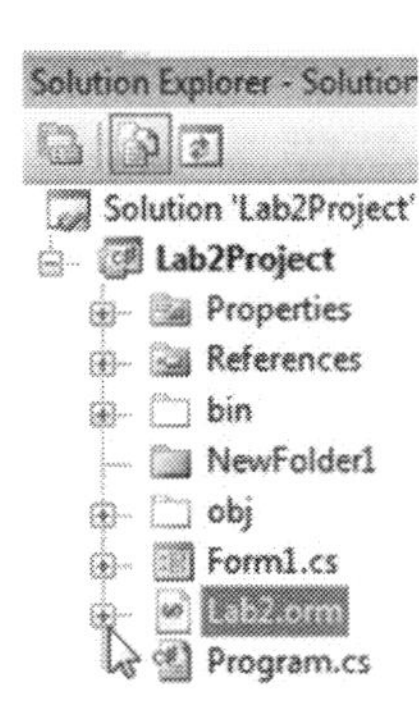

⇨

The code generated for SQL Server is now shown in a separate window. Some of the lines of code may be too long to fit on the screen. To fix this problem, ensure that the code is word-wrapped in the window by setting this option in Visual Studio as follows. From the main menu, choose Tools > Options to open the Options dialog. Then choose Text Editor > All Languages > General, check the Word wrap option, and press OK.

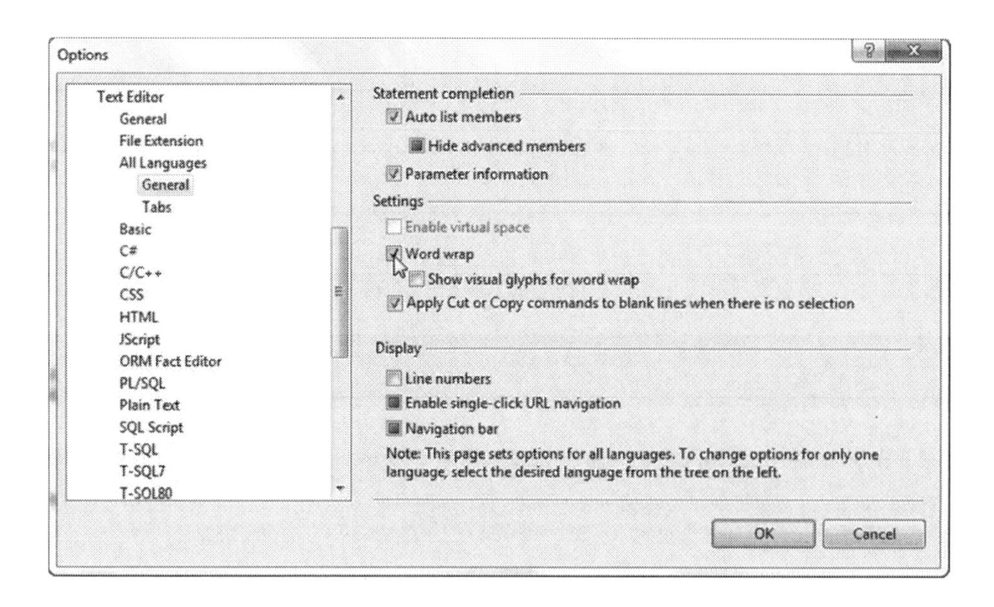

The SQL code generated is shown below. By default, NORMA maps character strings to Unicode character strings (e.g. nvarchar and nchar are used instead of varchar and char).

```
CREATE SCHEMA ORMModel1

GO

GO

CREATE TABLE ORMModel1.Athlete

(

  athleteNr int NOT NULL,

  extendedGivenName nvarchar(30) NOT NULL,

  familyName nvarchar(30) NOT NULL,

  emailAddress nvarchar(max),

  phoneNr nvarchar(10),

  stateCode nchar(2),

  countryCode nchar(2),

  CONSTRAINT Athlete_PK PRIMARY KEY(athleteNr),

  CONSTRAINT Athlete_UC UNIQUE(familyName, extendedGivenName)

)

GO

CREATE TABLE ORMModel1.Country

(

  countryCode nchar(2) NOT NULL,
```

```
    countryName nvarchar(30) NOT NULL,
    isLarge bit,
    CONSTRAINT Country_PK PRIMARY KEY(countryCode),
    CONSTRAINT Country_UC UNIQUE(countryName)
)
GO
CREATE TABLE ORMModel1.CountryInSportHasRank
(
    countryCode nchar(2) NOT NULL,
    sportName nvarchar(20) NOT NULL,
    rankNr smallint CHECK (rankNr >= 0) NOT NULL,
    CONSTRAINT CountryInSportHasRank_PK PRIMARY KEY(countryCode, sportName),
    CONSTRAINT CountryInSportHasRank_UC UNIQUE(sportName, rankNr)
)
GO
CREATE TABLE ORMModel1.Playing
(
    athleteNr int NOT NULL,
    sportName nvarchar(20) NOT NULL,
    rankNr smallint CHECK (rankNr >= 0),
    CONSTRAINT Playing_PK PRIMARY KEY(athleteNr, sportName)
)
GO
CREATE VIEW ORMModel1.Playing_UC (sportName, rankNr)
WITH SCHEMABINDING
AS
    SELECT sportName, rankNr
    FROM
        ORMModel1.Playing
    WHERE rankNr IS NOT NULL
GO
CREATE UNIQUE CLUSTERED INDEX Playing_UCIndex ON ORMModel1.Playing_UC(sportName,
rankNr)
GO
ALTER TABLE ORMModel1.Athlete ADD CONSTRAINT Athlete_FK FOREIGN KEY (countryCode)
REFERENCES ORMModel1.Country (countryCode) ON DELETE NO ACTION ON UPDATE NO ACTION
GO
```

```
ALTER TABLE ORMModel1.CountryInSportHasRank ADD CONSTRAINT CountryInSportHasRank_FK
FOREIGN KEY (countryCode) REFERENCES ORMModel1.Country (countryCode) ON DELETE NO
ACTION ON UPDATE NO ACTION

GO

ALTER TABLE ORMModel1.Playing ADD CONSTRAINT Playing_FK FOREIGN KEY (athleteNr)
REFERENCES ORMModel1.Athlete (athleteNr) ON DELETE NO ACTION ON UPDATE NO ACTION

GO

GO
```

As discussed earlier, when generating a relational view or SQL code, the current version of NORMA does not provide complete coverage of the rich array of ORM constraints. Simple mandatory role constraints, internal and external uniqueness constraints, and basic value constraints are catered for, but mapping of many other constraint categories is yet to be supported. Until such support is added, you may need to edit the generated SQL code manually.

For example, the footnoted constraint annotation on the relational schema that corresponds to the inclusive-or constraint in the ORM schema is not captured in the SQL code. You should add this manually by including the following code in the create table statement for the Athlete table

```
CHECK (phoneNr IS NOT NULL OR emailAddress IS NOT NULL)
```

Further details on SQL and mapping of ORM constraints and derivation rules can be found in Halpin & Morgan (2008).

To see code generation for other targets, repeat the procedure discussed above for the ORMGeneratorSettings, press the ellipsis button, select the desired options, save changes, and open the relevant files to see the code generated. For example, to see the C# code generated, select the ORM file in Solution Explorer, expand the abstract PLIX xml entry and double-click the .cs file under it. Note that C# was generated because we initially set up the project as a C# project. If instead we had created a Visual Basic project then VB code would have been generated.

Do not delete generated files from Solution Explorer. If you wish to remove any generated files, open the ORMGeneratorSettings property of the ORM file, deselect the generator types that you don't want, and then choose Save Changes. The unwanted generated files will then be removed.

If you wish to save your work before exiting Visual Studio, press the Save option in the main menu.

Appendix B: ORM Symbol Glossary

This summary of the ORM graphical notation is based directly on my standard ORM symbol glossary, and is used here with my permission.

Construct and Examples	*Explanatory Comments*
Entity type Country or Country or Country	Named soft rectangle, named hard rectangle, or named ellipse. The soft rectangle shape is the default.
Value type CountryCode or CountryCode or CountryCode	Named, dashed, soft rectangle (or hard rectangle or ellipse).
Entity type with popular reference mode Country (.code) Course (.code) Company (.name) Building (.nr)	Abbreviation for injective reference relationship to value type, e.g. Country has / is of CountryCode
Entity type with unit-based reference mode Height (cm:) Mass (kg:) Salary (USD:) Price (EUR:) Height (cm: Length) Salary (USD: Money) Price (EUR: Money)	Abbreviation for reference fact type, e.g. Height has / is of cmValue Optionally, the unit type may be displayed (as shown opposite).
Entity type with general reference mode Website (URL) Weblink (URL)	Abbreviation for reference fact types, e.g. Website is identified by URL Weblink is identified by URL
Independent object type Country ! CountryCode !	Instances of the type may exist, without playing any elementary fact roles.
External object type Address^	Object type is defined in another model. This notation is tentative (yet to be finalized).

Construct and Examples	*Explanatory Comments*

Predicate (unary, binary, ternary, etc.)

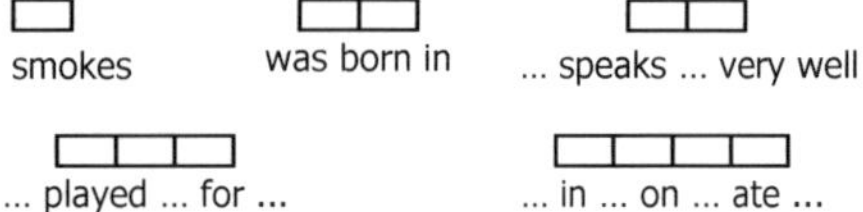

Ordered set of role boxes with at least one predicate reading in mixfix notation. If shown, object placeholders are denoted by "...". If placeholders are not shown, unaries are in prefix and binaries are in infix notation.

Duplicate type or predicate shape

If an object type or predicate shape is displayed more than once (on the same page or different pages) it is shadowed.

Unary fact type

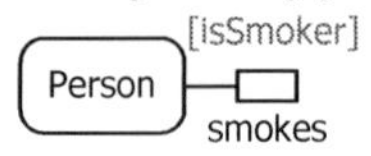

Attaching a role box to an object type shape means that only instances of that object type may play that role (e.g. here, the smokes role may be played only by instances of the Person object type). A role name may be added in square brackets.

Binary fact type

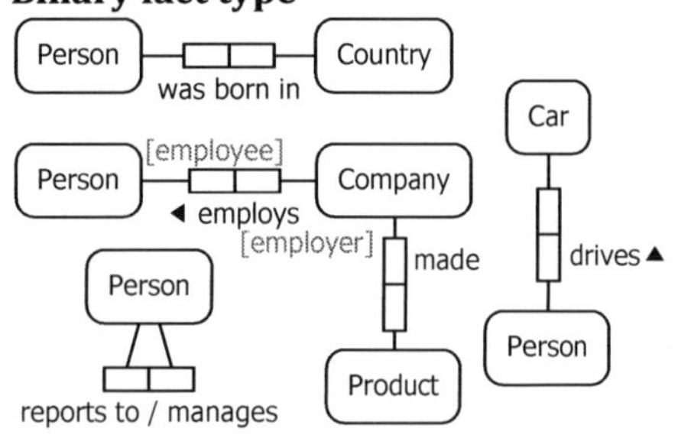

By default, predicate readings (binary or longer) are read left-to-right or top-to-bottom. An arrow-tip is used to display a different reading direction. Role names may be displayed in square brackets beside their role. Forward and inverse readings for binaries may be shown together, separated by "/".

Ternary fact type

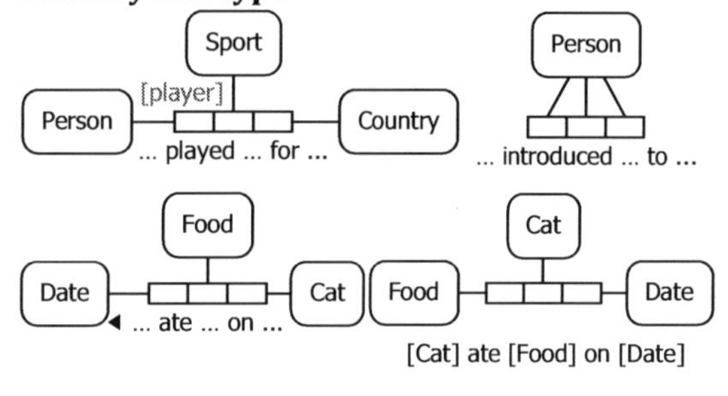

Role names may be added in square brackets. Arrow-tips are used to reverse the default left-right or top-down reading order. Reading orders other than forward and reverse are shown using named placeholders.

Quaternary fact type

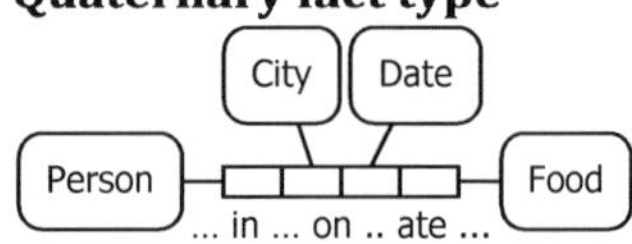

The above notes for the ternary case apply here also. Fact types of higher arity (number of roles) are also permitted.

Construct and Examples	*Explanatory Comments*

Objectification

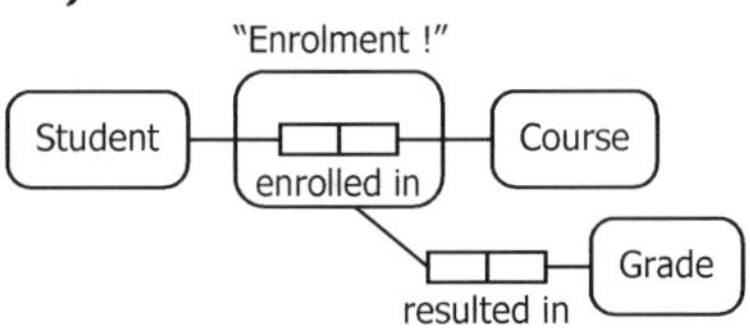

The enrolment fact type is objectified as an entity type whose instances can play roles. In this example, the objectification type is independent, so we can know about an enrolment before the grade is obtained.

Internal uniqueness constraint (UC) on unary

These examples are equivalent. By default, fact types are assumed to be populated with sets of facts (not bags of facts), so no whole fact may be duplicated.

Internal UCs on a binary fact type

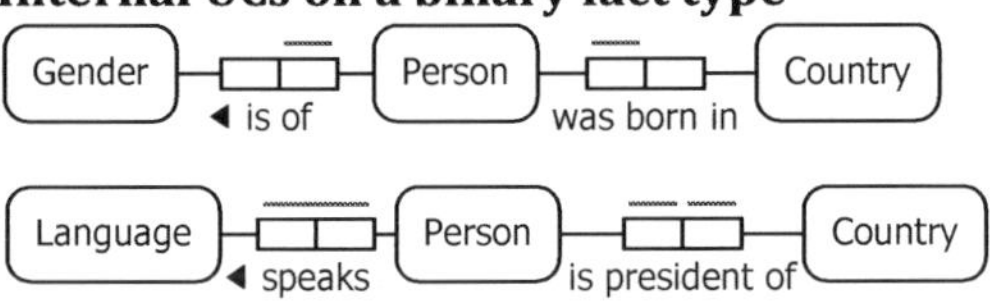

The examples show the 4 possible patterns: 1:*n* (one-to-many); *n*:1 (many-to-one); *m*:*n* (many-to-many); 1:1 (one-to-one).

Internal UCs on ternaries

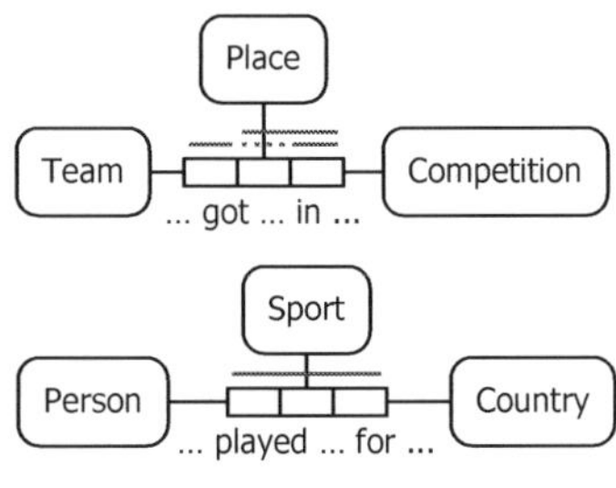

The first example has two, 2-role UCs: the top UC forbids ties; the other UC ensures that each team gets only place per competition (a dotted line excludes its role from the UC). The second example has a spanning UC (many-to-many-to-many). For an *n*-ary (*n* > 2) fact type to be atomic, each UC on it must span at least n–1 roles.

Simple mandatory role constraint

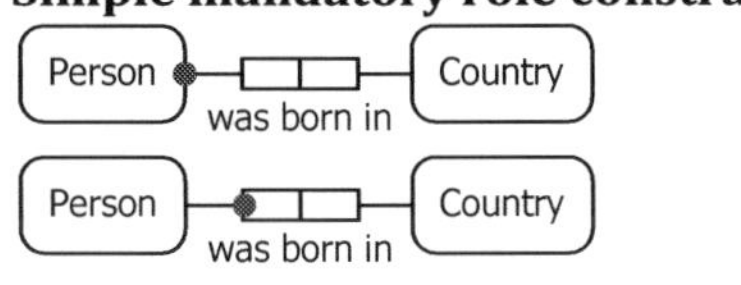

The example constraint means that each person was born in some country. The mandatory role dot may be placed at either end of the role connector.

Inclusive-or constraint

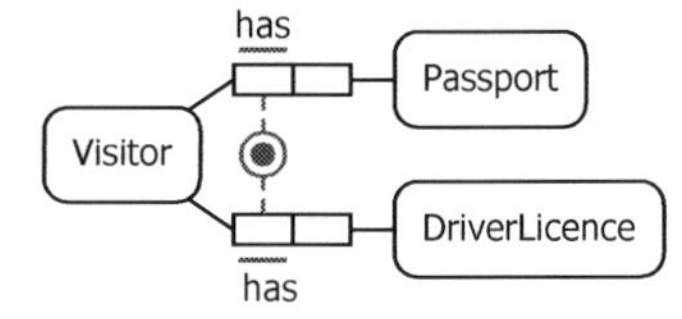

An inclusive-or constraint is also called a disjunctive mandatory role constraint. The constraint is displayed as a circled dot connected to the constrained roles. The example constraint means that each visitor referenced in the model must have a passport or a driver licence (or both).

Construct and Examples	***Explanatory Comments***

Preferred internal UC

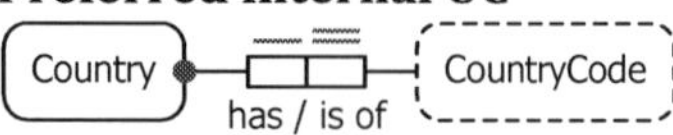

A double bar on a UC indicates it underlies the preferred reference scheme.

External UC

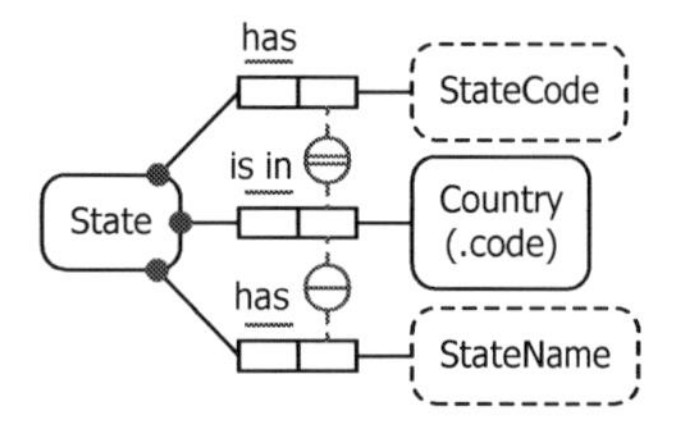

A double-bar indicates that the constrained roles provide the preferred reference for the object type at the other end. Here, each state is primarily identified by combining its country and state code. Each combination of country and state name also applies to only one state.

Object type value constraint

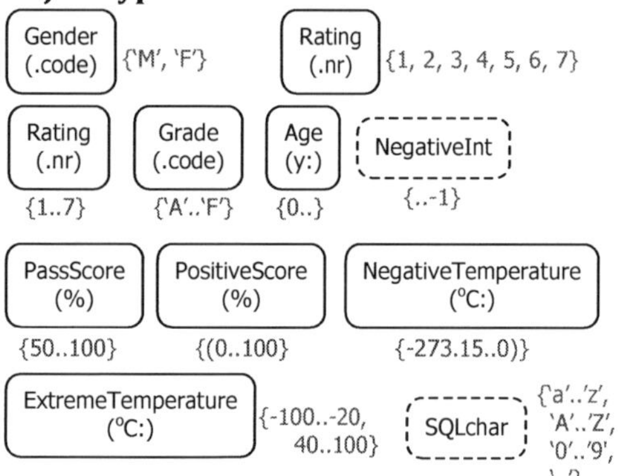

The allowed values may be specified as a list of discrete values and/or value ranges. The two examples shown opposite specify an enumerated list of values.
Ranges are inclusive of end values by default. Round brackets exclude an end value. Square brackets explicitly declare inclusion, e.g. the constraint on PositiveScore may also be specified as {(0..100]}.
Multiple combinations may also be specified.

Role value constraint

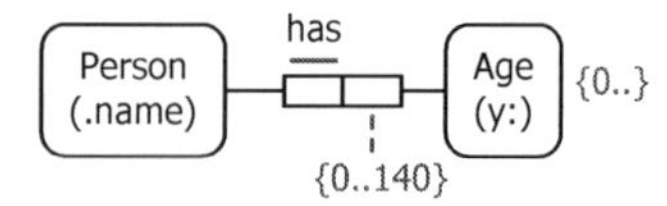

As for object type value constraints, but connected to the constrained role. Here, an age of a person must be at most 140 years.

Subset constraint

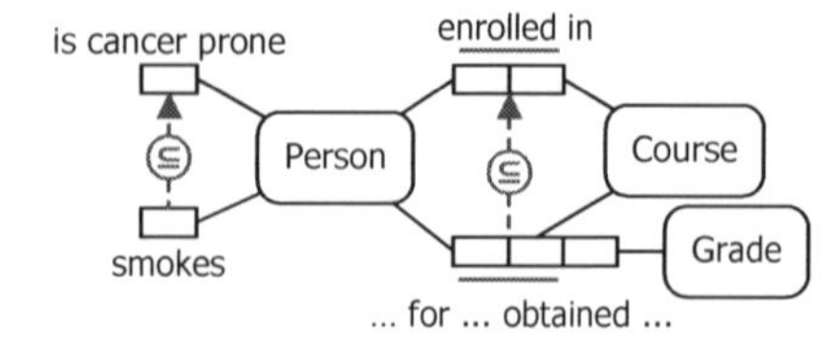

The arrow points from the subset end to the superset end (e.g. **if a** Person smokes **then that** Person is cancer prone). The role sequences at both ends must be compatible. A connection to the junction of 2 roles constrains that role pair.

Construct and Examples	*Explanatory Comments*
Join subset constraint 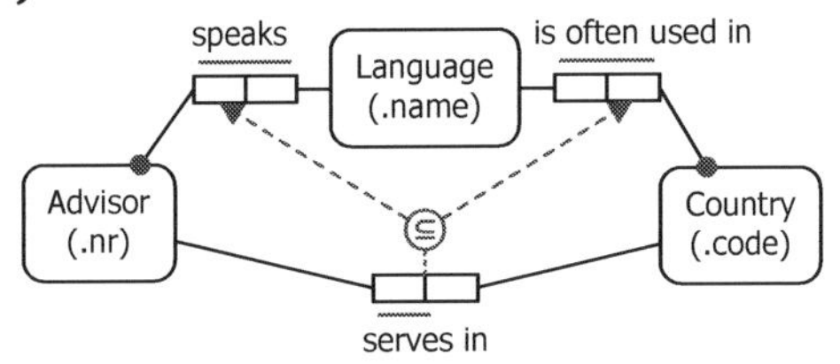	The constrained role pair at the superset end is projected from a role path that involves a conceptual join on Language. The constraint declares that if an advisor serves in a country then that advisor must speak a language that is often used in that country.
Exclusion constraint 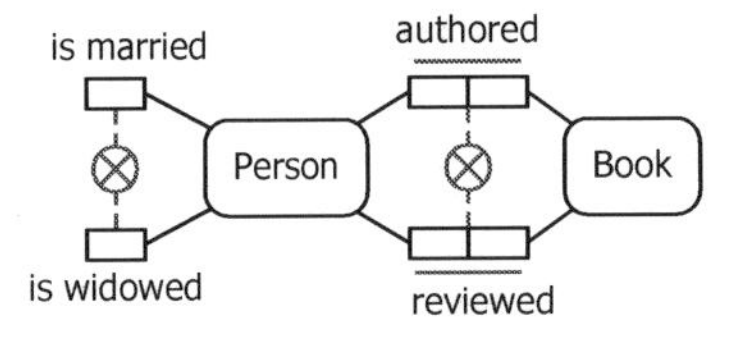	These exclusion constraints mean that no person is both married and widowed, and no person reviewed and authored the same book. Exclusion may apply between 2 or more compatible role sequences, possibly involving joins.
Exclusive-or constraint 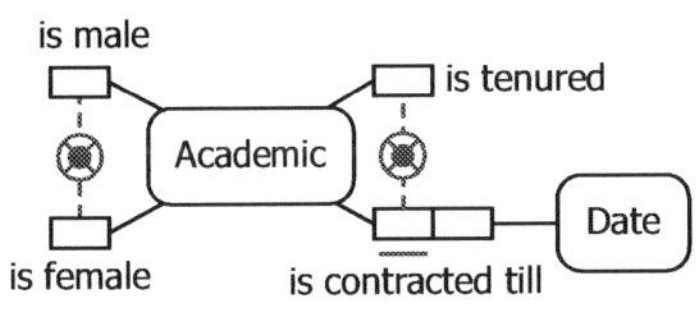	An exclusive-or constraint is simply the conjunction of an inclusive-or constraint and an exclusion constraint. Also known as an xor constraint.
Equality constraint 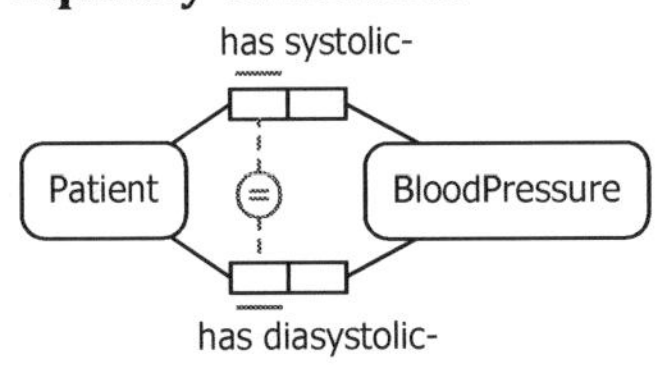	This equality constraint means that a patient's systolic BP is recorded if and only if his/her diastolic BP is recorded. An equality constraint may apply between 2 or more compatible role sequences, possibly involving joins.
Derived fact type, and derivation rule 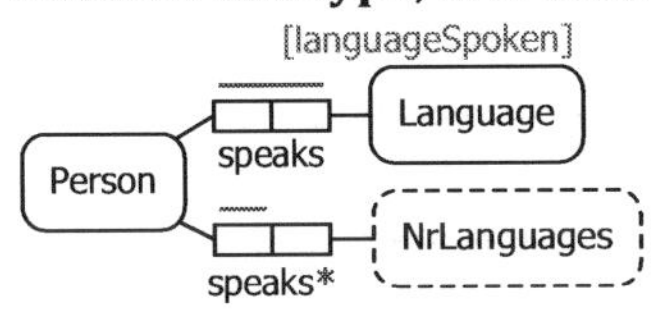	A fact type is either asserted, derived, or semiderived. A derived fact type is marked with an asterisk "*". A derivation rule is supplied. A double asterisk "**" indicates derived and stored (eager evaluation).

Construct and Examples	*Explanatory Comments*

Semiderived fact type, and derivation rule

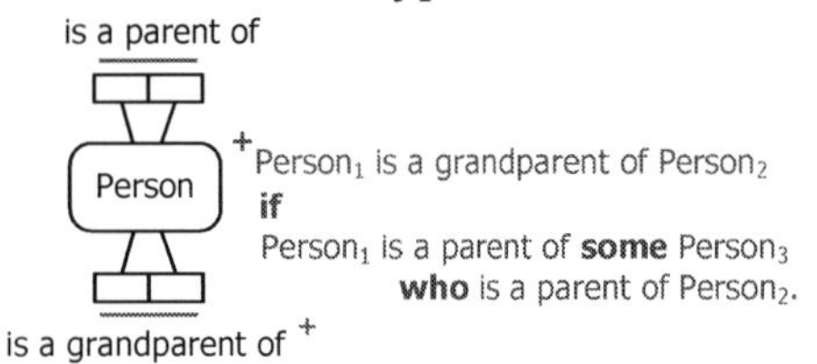

A fact type is semiderived if some of its instances may be derived, and some of its instances may be simply asserted. It is marked by "⁺" (half an asterisk). "⁺⁺"indicates semiderived and stored (eager evaluation for derived instances).

Subtyping

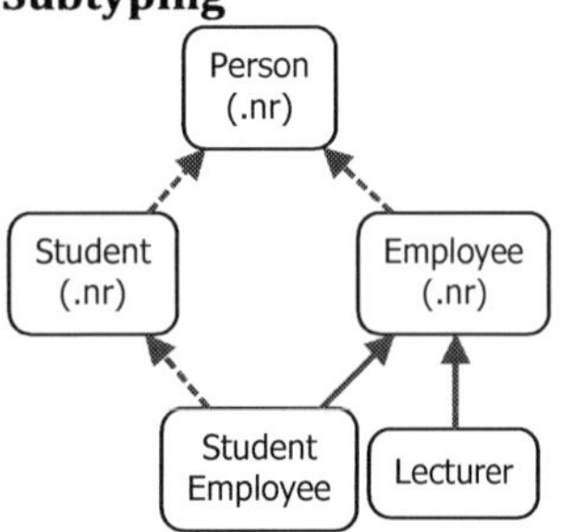

All subtypes are proper subtypes. An arrow runs from subtype to supertype. A solid arrow indicates a path to the subtype's preferred identifier (e.g. here, student employees are primarily identified by their employee number). A dashed arrow indicates the supertype has a different preferred identifier.

Subtyping constraints

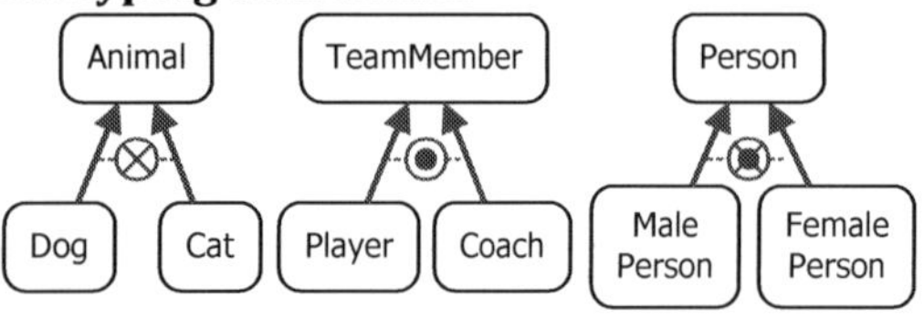

A circled "X" indicates the subtypes are mutually exclusive. A circled dot indicates the supertype equals the union of the subtypes. The combination (xor constraint) indicates the subtypes partition the supertype (exclusive and exhaustive).

Subtype derivation status

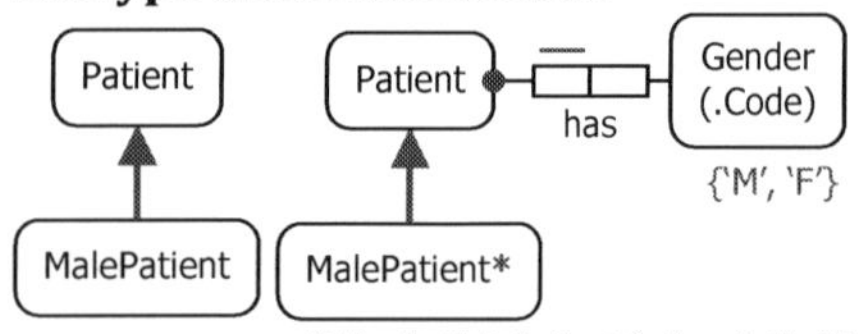

* **Each** MalePatient **is by definition**
some Patient **who** has Gender 'M'.

is a parent of

Person

Grandparent⁺

⁺**Each derived** Grandparent **is by definition**
some Person **who** is a parent of **some** Person
who is a parent of **some** Person.

A subtype may be asserted, derived (denoted by "*"), or semiderived (denoted by "⁺"). If the subtype is asserted, it has no mark appended and has no derivation rule. If the subtype derived or semiderived, a derivation rule is supplied.

Construct and Examples	*Explanatory Comments*

Internal frequency constraint

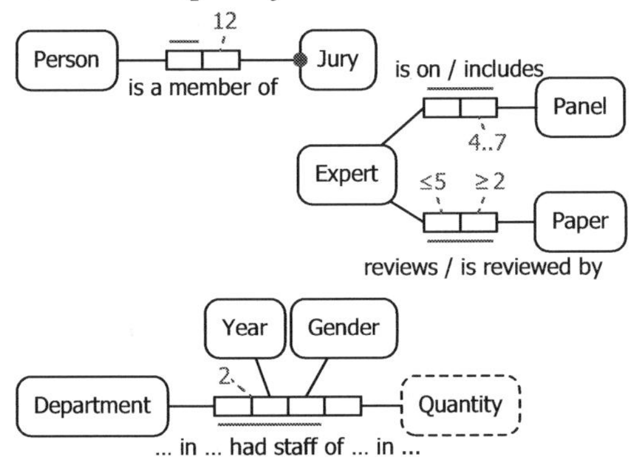

This constrains the number of times an occurring instance of a role or role sequence may appear in each population. Here: each jury has exactly 12 members; each panel that includes an expert includes at least 4 and at most 7 experts; each expert reviews at most 5 papers; each paper that is reviewed is reviewed by at least 2 experts; and each department and year that has staff numbers recorded in the quaternary appears there twice (once for each gender).

External frequency constraint

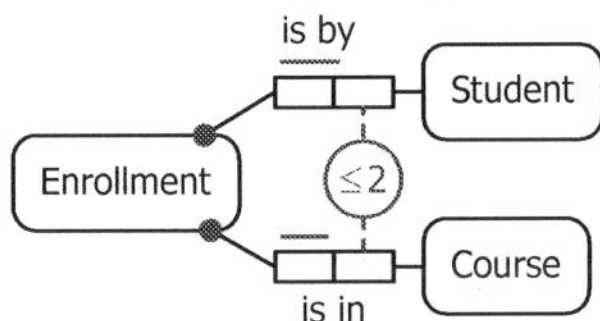

The example external frequency constraint has the following meaning. In this context, each combination of student and course relates to at most two enrolments (i.e. a student may enroll at most twice in the same course).

Value-comparison constraint

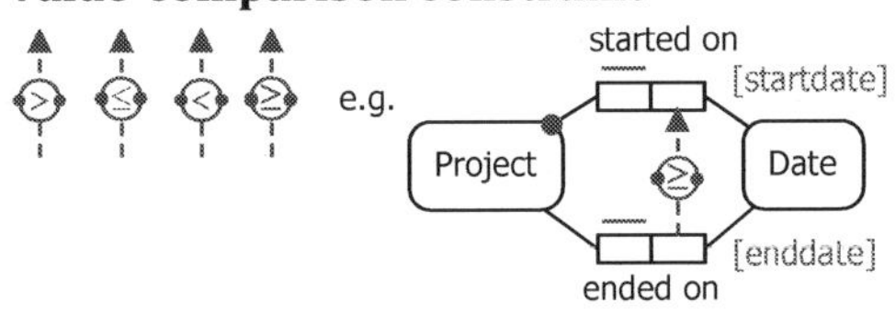

The example value-comparison constraint verbalizes as follows: **For each** Project, **if that** Project started on **some** Date$_1$ **and** ended on **some** Date$_2$ **then** Date$_2$ **is greater than or equal to** Date$_1$.

Object cardinality constraint

The example constraints ensure that at any given time there is at most one president and either 0 or at least 5 and at most 15 members of the UN Security Council.

Role cardinality constraint

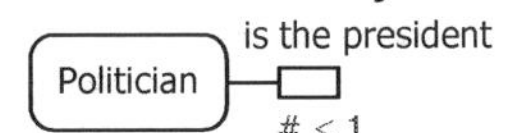

The example constraint ensures that at most one politician is the president (at any given time).

Construct and Examples	Explanatory Comments
Ring constraints A Irreflexive — Reflexive (locally) Asymmetric — Symmetric Antisymmetric Intransitive — Transitive Strongly Intransitive Acyclic Asymmetric + Intransitive Acyclic + Intransitive Acyclic + Strongly Intransitive Symmetric + Irreflexive etc. ObjectType is a direct subtype of	A ring predicate *R* is locally reflexive if and only if, for all *x* and *y*, *xRy* implies *xRx*. E.g. “knows” is locally but not globally reflexive. Reflexive, symmetric and transitive properties may also be enforced using semiderivation rather than by constraining asserted fact types. The example constrains the subtyping relationship in ORM to be both acyclic (no cycles can be formed by a chain of subtyping connections) and strongly intransitive (no object type *A* can be both a direct subtype of another type *B* and an indirect subtype of *B*, where indirect subtyping means there is a chain of two or more subtyping relationships that lead from *A* to *B*). Ring constraints may be combined only if they are compatible, and one is not implied by the other. ORM tools ensure that only legal combinations are allowed.
Deontic constraints Uniqueness o— Mandatory o Subset, Equality, Exclusion Frequency ^{o}f Irreflexive — Acyclic Asymmetric — Asym-Intrans Intransitive — Acyclic-Intrans Antisymmetric — Symmetric Strongly Intransitive — etc. E.g. Person ≤2 is a parent of	Unlike alethic constraints, deontic constraint shapes are colored blue rather than violet. Most include “o” for “obligatory”. Deontic ring constraints instead use dashed lines. In the parenthood example, the alethic frequency constraint ensures that each person has at most two parents, the alethic ring constraint ensures that parenthood is acyclic, and the deontic ring constraint makes it obligatory for parenthood to be strongly intransitive.

Construct and Examples	Explanatory Comments

Textual constraints

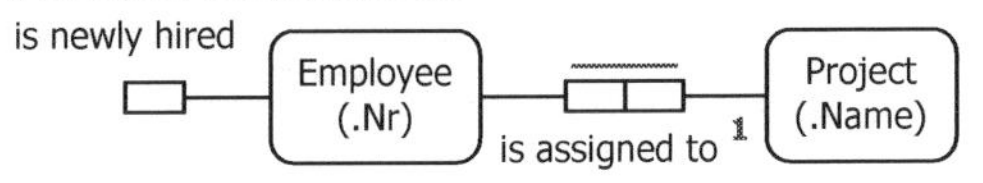

[1] **Each** Employee **who** is newly hired
is assigned to **at most one** Project.

First-order constraints with no graphic notation may be expressed textually in the FORML 2 language. This example uses footnoting to capture a restricted uniqueness constraint.

Objectification display options

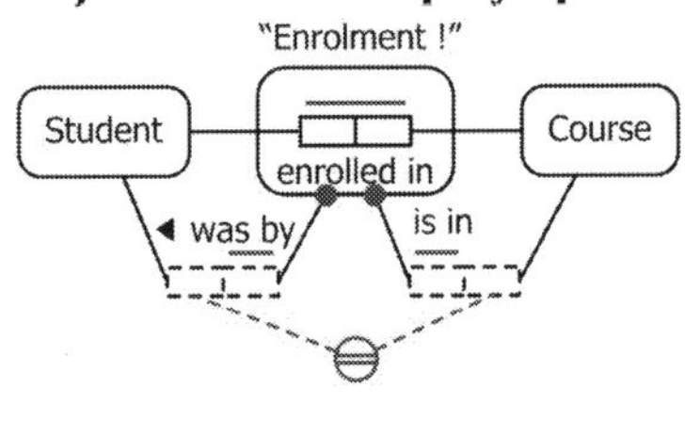

Enrolment !

Internally, link fact types connect objectified associations to their component object types. By default, display of link fact types is suppressed. If displayed, link predicate shapes use dashed lines. Objectification types may also be displayed without their defining components, using an object type shape containing a small predicate shape, as in this Enrolment example.

Appendix C: Further Resources

Some Relevant References:

The following book provides an in-depth coverage of ORM including a more formal treatment of its underlying theory including schema equivalence and schema transformation theorems. For further practice with ORM, it includes hundreds of exercise questions with answers provided for all odd-numbered questions. It also discusses other information modeling approaches such as ER, and UML, and how they relate to ORM. Additionally, it provides a solid introduction to relational database theory and SQL, and both forward and reverse engineering between ORM and SQL. It also briefly discusses other database-related topics such as deductive databases and the semantic web.

Halpin, T. & Morgan T. 2008, *Information Modeling and Relational Databases, 2nd edition*, Morgan Kaufmann.

The following book provides a detailed introduction to a deductive database system based on the LogiQL language.

Halpin, T. & Rugaber, S. 2014, *LogiQL: A Query Language for Smart Databases*, CRC Press, Boca Raton.

http://www.crcpress.com/product/isbn/9781482244939#.

The following journal articles provide brief overviews of ORM.

Halpin, T. 2010, 'Object-Role Modeling: Principles and Benefits', *International Journal of Information Systems Modeling and Design*, Vol. 1, No. 1, IGI Global, pp. 32-54.

Halpin, T. 2011, 'Fact-Orientation and Conceptual Logic', *Proc. 15th International EDOC Conference*, IEEE Computer Society, Helsinki, pp. 14-19.

Some Relevant Websites:

My website www.orm.net includes recent news about ORM as well as many other articles on ORM and related topics, and links to other relevant websites. The Resources page of this website also contains links to my articles that have been published in the online *Business Rules Journal* (http://www.brcommunity.com/). These include articles on ORM verbalization of business rules, modeling temporal aspects of information systems, data modeling for the semantic web using languages such as the Web Ontology Language (OWL), and logical data modeling for deductive databases using LogiQL.

The ORM Foundation website www.ORMFoundation.org includes a library with many ORM resources, including the Visio ORM2 stencil, as well an online forum for discussing ORM-related topics.

The Fact-Based Modeling Working Group (www.factbasedmodeling.org) is working on an exchange metamodel for fact-based modeling approaches such as ORM, with an aim to have it officially adopted by an industry or standards group.

The NORMA tool is available as a free plug-in to Microsoft Visual Studio (2005 or later edition). A Community Edition of Visual Studio 2013 is accessible at http://www.visualstudio.com/products/visual-studio-community-vs. The text on the license agreement for this edition includes the following conditions:

"Here's how Visual Studio Community can be used in organizations:

- An unlimited number of users within an organization can use Visual Studio Community for the following scenarios: in a classroom learning environment, for academic research, or for contributing to open source projects.
- For all other usage scenarios: In non-enterprise organizations, up to 5 users can use Visual Studio Community. In enterprise organizations (meaning those with 250 PCs or $1 Million US Dollars in annual revenue), no use is permitted beyond the open source, academic research, and classroom learning environment scenarios described above."

The NORMA plug-in itself can be downloaded as a zip file from SourceForge at http://sourceforge.net/projects/orm/. To download NORMA for an earlier version of Visual Studio (e.g. 2008), click the "NORMA for VisualStudio" folder to show its subfolders, then click the top subfolder (e.g. 2015-01-CTP) to show its subfolders, and then select the relevant zip file. Alternatively, you can download the relevant NORMA zip file from the ORM Foundation website at http://www.ormfoundation.org/.

The NORMA tool itself is under development at ORM Solutions LLC, whose website (http://ormsolutions.com/) includes access to a web-based viewer for viewing ORM models online.

In addition to NORMA, various other ORM-related tools are available, some free and some commercial. For example, the ActiveFacts tool supports conceptual queries over ORM models using the Constellation Query Language. For further details on this tool, see http://dataconstellation.com/ActiveFacts/index.shtml.

Index

F

G

H

I

J

L

M

T

U

V

X

Printed in Great Britain
by Amazon